Wyndham Lewis

Wyndham Lewis
A Critical Guide

Edited by Andrzej Gąsiorek
and Nathan Waddell

EDINBURGH
University Press

© editorial matter and organisation Andrzej Gąsiorek and
    Nathan Waddell, 2015
© the chapters their several authors, 2015

Edinburgh University Press Ltd
The Tun – Holyrood Road
12(2f) Jackson's Entry
Edinburgh EH8 8PJ

www.euppublishing.com

Typeset in 10.5/13 Adobe Sabon by
Servis Filmsetting Ltd, Stockport, Cheshire,
and printed and bound in Great Britain by
CPI Group (UK) Ltd, Croydon CR0 4YY

A CIP record for this book is available from the British Library

ISBN 978 0 7486 8567 7 (hardback)
ISBN 978 0 7486 8569 1 (webready PDF)
ISBN 978 0 7486 8568 4 (paperback)
ISBN 978 0 7486 8570 7 (epub)

Contents

Notes on Contributors

Faith Binckes is Senior Lecturer in Modern and Contemporary Literature in the Department of English, Bath Spa University.

David Bradshaw is Professor of English Literature at Oxford University and a Fellow of Worcester College.

Paul Edwards is the author of *Wyndham Lewis: Painter and Writer* (2000) and General Editor of the forthcoming *Collected Works of Wyndham Lewis*, to be published by Oxford University Press.

Ann-Marie Einhaus is a Lecturer in Modern and Contemporary Literature in the Department of Humanities at Northumbria University in Newcastle-upon-Tyne.

Andrzej Gąsiorek is Professor of Twentieth-Century Literature and Head of the English Literature Department at the University of Birmingham.

Julian Hanna is Assistant Professor of English at the University of Madeira, Portugal.

Miranda Hickman is Associate Professor of English at McGill University in Montréal, Canada.

Louise Kane is an Associate Lecturer at the University of Birmingham.

Scott W. Klein is Professor and Chair of English at Wake Forest University.

Alan Munton is an Honorary Research Fellow in the Department of English at the University of Exeter.

Michael Nath is Senior Lecturer in English Literature and Creative Writing at the University of Westminster. http://michaelnath.wordpress. com

Ian Patterson is Director of Studies in English and Librarian and Keeper of the Old Library at Queens' College, Cambridge.

Ivan Phillips is Associate Dean of School (Learning and Teaching) in the School of Creative Arts at the University of Hertfordshire.

Nathan Waddell is an Assistant Professor of Literary Modernism in the School of English at the University of Nottingham.

Jamie Wood is a Partner at Odey Asset Management LLP and an independent scholar currently completing a post-doctoral study of modernism and the grotesque.

List of Abbreviations

Texts by Lewis

ABR   *The Art of Being Ruled*, ed. Reed Way Dasenbrock (Santa Rosa: Black Sparrow Press, [1926] 1989).

ACM   *America and Cosmic Man* (London and Brussels: Nicholson & Watson, 1948).

AG   *The Apes of God*, ed. Paul Edwards (Santa Barbara: Black Sparrow Press, [1930] 1981).

ALW   *Anglosaxony: A League that Works* (Toronto: Ryerson, 1941).

AIP   *America, I Presume* (New York: Howell, Soskin, 1940).

B1   *BLAST 1*, ed. Wyndham Lewis (Santa Barbara: Black Sparrow Press, [1914] 1981).

B2   *BLAST 2*, ed. Wyndham Lewis (Santa Barbara: Black Sparrow Press, [1915] 1981).

BB   *Blasting and Bombardiering: An Autobiography (1914–1926)* (London: John Calder, [1937] 1982).

C   *The Childermass: Section I* (London: Chatto and Windus, 1928).

CD   *The Caliph's Design: Architects! Where is your Vortex?*, ed. Paul Edwards (Santa Barbara: Black Sparrow Press, [1919] 1996).

CHC   *Creatures of Habit, Creatures of Change: Essays on Art, Literature and Society, 1914–1956*, ed. Paul Edwards (Santa Barbara: Black Sparrow Press, 1989).

CPP   *Collected Poems and Plays*, ed. Alan Munton (Manchester: Carcanet, 1979).

CWB   *The Complete Wild Body*, ed. Bernard Lafourcade (Santa Barbara: Black Sparrow Press, 1982).

CYD   *Count Your Dead: They Are Alive! Or, A New War in the Making* (London: Lovat Dickson, 1937).

DPA   *The Demon of Progress in the Arts* (London: Methuen, 1954).

DY   *Doom of Youth* (London: Chatto & Windus, 1932).

E1   *The Enemy 1*, ed. Wyndham Lewis (Santa Rosa: Black Sparrow Press, [1927] 1994).

E3   *The Enemy 3*, ed. Wyndham Lewis (Santa Rosa: Black Sparrow Press, [1929] 1994).

H   *Hitler* (London: Chatto and Windus, 1931).

HA   *The Human Age – Book Two: Monstre Gai, Book Three: Malign Fiesta* (London: Methuen, 1955).

HC   *The Hitler Cult* (London: Dent, 1939).

JAH   *The Jews: Are they Human?* (London: George Allen and Unwin, 1939).

L   *The Letters of Wyndham Lewis*, ed. W. K. Rose (London: Methuen, 1963).

LWE   *Left Wings over Europe: Or, How to Make a War About Nothing* (London: Jonathan Cape, 1936).

MMB   *The Mysterious Mr Bull* (London: Robert Hale, 1938).

MWA   *Men without Art*, ed. Seamus Cooney (Santa Rosa: Black Sparrow Press, [1934] 1987).

P   *Paleface: The Philosophy of the 'Melting Pot'* (London: Chatto and Windus, 1929).

P/L   *Pound/Lewis: The Letters of Ezra Pound and Wyndham Lewis*, ed. Timothy Materer (New York: New Directions Books, 1985).

RA   *Rude Assignment: An Intellectual Autobiography*, ed. Toby Foshay (Santa Barbara: Black Sparrow Press, [1950] 1984).

RL   *The Revenge for Love*, ed. Reed Way Dasenbrock (Santa Rosa: Black Sparrow Press, [1937] 2000).

SC   *Self Condemned*, ed. Rowland Smith (Santa Barbara: Black Sparrow Press, [1954] 1983).

SF   *Satire & Fiction, Preceded by the History of a Rejected Review* (London: The Arthur Press, 1930).

T1   *Tarr*, ed. Paul O'Keeffe (Santa Rosa: Black Sparrow Press, [1918] 1990).

T2   *Tarr*, ed. Scott W. Klein (Oxford: Oxford University Press, [1928] 2010).

TWM   *Time and Western Man*, ed. Paul Edwards (Santa Rosa: Black Sparrow Press, [1927] 1993).

UP   *Unlucky for Pringle: Unpublished and Other Stories*, ed. C. J. Fox and Robert T. Chapman (London: Vision, 1973).

WA   *The Writer and the Absolute* (London: Methuen, 1952).

WLA   *Wyndham Lewis on Art: Collected Writings, 1913–1956*, ed.

Walter Michel and C. J. Fox (London: Thames and Hudson, 1969).

Texts by Others

CVA   Richard Cork, *Vorticism and Abstract Art in the First Machine Age – Volume 1: Origins and Development* (London: Gordon Fraser, 1976).

EWL   Paul Edwards, *Wyndham Lewis: Painter and Writer* (New Haven, CT and London: Yale University Press, 2000).

GWL   Andrzej Gąsiorek, *Wyndham Lewis and Modernism* (Tavistock: Northcote House, 2004).

JFA   Fredric Jameson, *Fables of Aggression: Wyndham Lewis, the Modernist as Fascist* (Berkeley, Los Angeles and London: University of California Press, 1979).

KWL   Hugh Kenner, *Wyndham Lewis* (London: Methuen, 1954).

MTE   Jeffrey Meyers, *The Enemy: A Biography of Wyndham Lewis* (London and Henley: Routledge and Kegan Paul, 1980).

MWL   Jeffrey Meyers (ed.), *Wyndham Lewis: A Revaluation* (Montreal: McGill-Queen's University Press, 1980).

SSG   Paul O'Keeffe, *Some Sort of Genius: A Life of Wyndham Lewis* (London: Jonathan Cape, 2000).

VEA   William C. Wees, *Vorticism and the English Avant-Garde* (Manchester: Manchester University Press, 1972).

VNP   Mark Antliff and Scott W. Klein (eds), *Vorticism: New Perspectives* (Oxford: Oxford University Press, 2013).

WLC   Andrzej Gąsiorek, Alice Reeve-Tucker, and Nathan Waddell (eds), *Wyndham Lewis and the Cultures of Modernity* (Farnham: Ashgate, 2011).

Introduction

Andrzej Gąsiorek and Nathan Waddell

Wyndham Lewis (1882–1957) was one of the twentieth century's most important artistic and intellectual figures. Painter, novelist, poet, dramatist, short-story writer, cultural critic, political commentator, walking encyclopaedia, and raconteur, Lewis was, and continues to be, inimitable as a man and as a modernist. The uncompromising experimentalism of his literary and critical prose bears the influence of such contemporaries as T. S. Eliot, William Faulkner, Ernest Hemingway, Aldous Huxley, James Joyce, George Orwell, Ezra Pound, Gertrude Stein, and Virginia Woolf, all of whom Lewis attacked in his work even though he respected them as major writers who should not be ignored. Likewise, the strange, often visionary qualities of his paintings are the products of a lifelong, highly learned engagement with European life and culture. Lewis is also without equal as a critic of visual, literary, architectural, balletic, and musical modernisms. Books like *Time and Western Man* (1927), *Men without Art* (1934), *The Writer and the Absolute* (1952), and *The Demon of Progress in the Arts* (1954) attest the lasting significance of his critical powers, his 'extraordinary versatility' amounting, in Fredric Jameson's view, to 'genius'.[1]

Lewis was at the heart of artistic developments in the second decade of the twentieth century in particular. A man of great energy, he emerged in these years as a writer of powerful short stories, the influential novel *Tarr* (1918), the path-breaking Expressionist play *Enemy of the Stars* (1914), and the important essay 'Inferior Religions' (1917). Lewis was also an experimental painter, a theorist of the new arts, and an editor of three modernist 'little magazines': *BLAST* (1914–15), *The Tyro* (1921–2), and *The Enemy* (1927–9). He was linked with emerging art tendencies and movements, most notably Cubism, Expressionism, Italian Futurism, and Kandinskyan abstraction. He worked in the Omega Workshops run by Roger Fry, which he left in 1913 after a quarrel over a commission for the Ideal Home Exhibition of that year, and he helped to run the Rebel Art Centre financed by Kate Lechmere before another falling out (with Lechmere) brought that enterprise to an end. He participated in the organisation of several pre-war exhibitions, and, with Pound, he presided over the birth of Vorticism, the movement that evolved out of Cubo-Futurism as an 'English' response, and significant contribution, to modern European painting.

In the 1920s and 1930s Lewis embarked on a series of critical books about the state of contemporary civilisation. Having experienced the First World War at first hand, Lewis was initially keen to re-convene the Vorticists and to continue with the pre-war avant-gardist project. But he gradually came to believe that post-war English society had altered decisively and that the avant-gardism he favoured could only play a minimal role in helping to effect the social and cultural transformation he desired. Lewis thus gradually moved to a detailed exploration and critique of post-war life. His critical project was eventually split into several individually published works, among them such key critical texts as *The Art of Being Ruled* (1926), *Time and Western Man*, and *The Lion and the Fox* (1927), on the one hand, and remarkable novels like *The Childermass* (1928) and *The Apes of God* (1930), on the other. In the broadest sense, these books were collectively devoted, as Lewis put it, 'to the work of radical analysis of the ideas by which our society has been taught to live' (*E3* p. 49). It was during this phase (and in these books) that Lewis became an oppositional figure and an important early exponent of cultural criticism.

This was also the period in which Lewis rewrote and republished such earlier works as the novel *Tarr* (1928), which had been serialised in *The Egoist* between 1916 and 1917 (and then published as a book in 1918), and the 'wild body' stories, which he revised and collected together in *The Wild Body* (1927); demonstrated his externalist conception of satire in *The Apes of God*, writing *Satire and Fiction* (also 1930) and *Men without Art* in defence of it; and produced some hastily written and deeply objectionable books about the rise of National Socialism in Germany and the politics of appeasement. It is these books that have caused Lewis to be judged harshly by posterity. There can be no question that Lewis during the thirties adopted political positions that deserve our opprobrium and that need to be criticised. But they also need to be related to the cultural politics of the period, and understood as a disastrous attempt on his part to ward off an impending world war. Leaving England in the late 1930s, Lewis was in Canada for the bulk of the Second World War, returning to England in 1945. For the last twelve years of his life he continued to write and to paint; worked as the art correspondent for *The Listener* between the years 1946 and 1951;

completed the second and third volumes of *The Human Age* trilogy that he had begun with *The Childermass* (which, along with the novels *Tarr* and *The Revenge for Love* (1937), were broadcast on the radio by the BBC); and witnessed the staging of the controversial Tate exhibition *Wyndham Lewis and Vorticism* in 1956.

Given the provocations for which he has become famous, it is not surprising that Lewis's detractors have not been in short supply. It is undeniable that during the first two decades of his career Lewis was attracted to far-right political positions, to intellectual hierarchies, and to deterministic models of human agency. However, Lewis's 'commitments' are rarely as clear-cut as many commentators would have them be. Moreover, his politics changed over time, his early pro-authoritarian stance intensifying during the late 1920s and early 1930s, before switching in the late 1930s to a pro-democratic posture that his decriers often ignore. Lewis's authoritarian propensities were inseparable from a parallel drive to educate his readers about, and to free them from, ideological deceptions. He was vexed by what he saw as the torpor of the general social mass, yet at certain points in his work he was also convinced that ordinary citizens could, if they were willing to make the necessary effort, bring about significant political change. As he put it in *Rude Assignment*: 'The best variety of intellectuals ... are by no means enamoured of the Ivory Tower. They do not want to speak to the stars, but to men' (*RA* p. 15). In addition, his critical approach, even in his most disquieting moments of political analysis, reads more like a dialogic, in-process, and experimental staging of arguments. His almost Žižekian mixing of multiple ideas from high and low culture in a clash of voices and possible positions gives rise to a modernism of style and structure in his writing, one that goes a long way towards explaining the changeability of his opinions over time. 'To think', Lewis declared, 'is to be split up' (*RA* p. 70).

This present volume of essays seeks to introduce Lewis's brand of modernism – and his criticisms of the very modernism he had helped to inaugurate – to first-time readers of his work, to provide a critical guide to the controversial elements of his output, and to offer new readings of Lewis's literary and critical writings against a backdrop of relevant social and cultural histories. Essays on Lewis's major novels – *Tarr*, *The Apes of God*, *The Revenge for Love*, *The Human Age*, and *Self Condemned* – explore his achievement as one of modernism's least-understood stylistic and thematic innovators. Likewise, essays on Lewis's pre-war writing, his satirical aesthetic, his involvement in Vorticism and avant-gardism, his modernism, his views on war, culture, race, gender, politics, and technology, and on his legacy present him as a figure central to artistic modernism and to early twentieth-century culture in Britain and Europe more generally. Readers of this book may or may not find Lewis a congenial figure, but our goal as editors has been to help students, scholars, and interested general readers alike see that he was at the heart of British modernism, making important contributions to it as a writer, painter, and critic, and that his role in the growth of twentieth-century British culture was a significant one. His work stands as a reminder of the need for writers to be free 'to speculate, to criticize, to create: such is the ultimate desideratum of the writer, as man-of-letters. To speculate, among other things, about social questions; to criticize . . . the conduct of public affairs' (*WA* p. 29). And although Lewis, with an irony missed by his detractors, styled himself 'the Enemy', he was not a 'partisan of *outsideness*' but a vociferous supporter of enlightened debate. 'Criticism', he maintained, 'is merely the introduction of the outside light into a dark place' (*RA* p. 71).

Note

1. Fredric Jameson, 'Wyndham Lewis's *Timon*: The War of Forms', in *VNP* pp. 15–30: p. 25.

Chapter 1

Pre-War Writing

Louise Kane

When Wyndham Lewis published his first piece of writing – a short story titled 'The "Pole"' in the May 1909 issue of Ford Madox Hueffer's *English Review* – he was a young man of twenty-six. Between this first publication and the outbreak of the First World War in July 1914, he went on to publish another twenty-two pieces of writing, all of which appeared in periodicals and newspapers, along with, of course, his very own magazine, the equally iconic and iconoclastic *BLAST*. Having obtained his first literary agent, J. B. Pinker, in 1910, he was also writing the drafts for what would become *Tarr* (1918) and *Mrs. Dukes' Million* (written in 1908–9, but not published until 1977) during this period. While the rejection of *Tarr* by potential publishers as 'not marketable' (*L* p. 44) may have been a bitter disappointment to Lewis, this rejection forced him to concentrate on his periodical publications – a collection of writings that constitutes one of the most fascinating yet overlooked parts of his *oeuvre*.

Of the 300 or so periodical publications Lewis produced between 1909 and his death in 1957, it is the work he produced between 1909 and 1914 that provided the bedrock for his literary (and artistic) career and that form the basis of this chapter. The first part of this chapter explores the ten publications Lewis produced between 1909 and 1911, several of which were later reworked as *The Wild Body* (1927).[1] The second part examines how, after a self-imposed break during which Lewis sought to focus more on his painting, he returned triumphantly to his 'writing' role in 1914, contributing articles to various magazines before establishing *BLAST*. This chapter defines and describes the content, style, and perspectives that characterised Lewis's pre-war writing, but it remains essential, especially at a point in scholarship at which Lewis and his works have still not received some of the recognition conferred upon the more famous 'Men of 1914', to trace Lewis's work with reference to the wider context of an emerging, nascent aesthetics of pre-war modernist magazines, as well as the important biographical events that formed and shaped his early work.

The Brittany Sketches: 1909–11

Lewis first ventured to Brittany, France, with Henry Lamb in July 1907. Lamb would go on to become a founding member of the Camden Town Group, the anti-Academy but somewhat exclusive band of Post-Impressionist artists with whom Lewis would experience a fractious relationship in June 1911, but in the summer of 1907 the two young men were both inexperienced artists exploring the North-Western French coast (*SSG* pp. 81–8). This trip was not Lewis's first sojourn abroad. Between 1902 and 1907 he spent much of his time on the Continent, residing in Paris for several months at a time and holiday-ing in various parts of Europe, including Spain, Germany, and the Netherlands. However, it was the primitive Breton environment, with its peasants, their *pardons* (essentially religious ceremonies which often turned into rowdy festivals), and eclectic *pensions* that left the biggest impression on Lewis. A year after his first visit, he returned to Brittany, travelling for the most part alone this time, save for a brief visit with his mother. Having travelled through Northern Spain in May, Lewis arrived by boat at Cherbourg and made the journey to the Breton villages of Moëlan, Quimperlé, and Le Pouldu in July 1908, before moving on to Plouhinec and La Faouët through August to October.

Between May 1909 and February 1911, Lewis would produce no fewer than ten publications based on these Breton trips. For Lewis, 'these papers' were an attempt to 'deal with some of [his] experiences in Brittany' (*CWB* p. 222), and they appeared in *The English Review* and two other modernist British little magazines: Douglas Goldring's *The Tramp* (1910–11) and A. R. Orage's *New Age* (1907–22). Brittany had had a profound effect on Lewis, informing some of the recurring themes and traits that would crystallise into a recognisable Lewisian style. One of these traits was Lewis's use of a close, observational style through which his characters were constructed almost as portrait figures. He had first honed this technique at the Slade School of Art, winning a Certificate in Figure Drawing in 1900. 'The "Pole"', together with the two other pieces Lewis published in *The English Review* in 1909, 'Some Innkeepers and Bestre' and 'Les Saltimbanques', saw Lewis translate this particular artistic gift into writing, 'drawing' out his figures and care-fully delineating their appearance and characteristics.

'The "Pole"' appeared in the May 1909 issue of *The English Review*.

At this point, Ford Madox Hueffer's magazine had been in existence only since the previous December, the same month Lewis had returned to England from Paris. It is possible that T. Sturge Moore, whose poem 'Noon Rise' also appeared in the May 1909 issue, had recommended the publication to Lewis. After Lewis began writing his Breton stories in December 1909 he made several visits to Sturge Moore and his wife during which he read much of his material aloud to them. The Sturge Moores were particularly keen on what they called Lewis's 'Brittany sketches' and encouraged him to pursue this particular line of interest: 'The Brittany sketches often return to my mind and always strengthen my conviction of their value', Sturge Moore wrote. 'Bring some more please' (quoted in *SSG* p. 92).

'The "Pole"' was less a story and more an observational commentary exploring the presence of 'Poles' – young men of Polish or Russian origin – within 'the many *pensions* that are to be found on the Breton coast' (*CWB* p. 209). With its description of the inhabitants and etiquette of Breton guesthouses, it was drawn from Lewis's experience of the boarding houses he had encountered during his 1907 and 1908 visits to Brittany. The presence of 'The "Pole"' in the May 1909 issue of *The English Review* was in keeping with this particular issue's focus on the travel writing genre, with Perceval Gibbon's 'Afrikander Memories' placed on the pages immediately after and J. G. B. Lynch's 'Some Sidelights on Modern Greece' appearing at the end of the issue.

However, Lewis's sweeping generalisations about 'Poles' and Poland – 'one of the most perilous countries, on the whole, that has ever been heard of' (*CWB* p. 215) – unflattering remembrances of a particular Pole he had met named Isoblitsky, and zoomorphic delineation of the eponymous 'Poles' as 'strange creatures' (*CWB* p. 212) who 'curled up in the corner near the fire' (*CWB* p. 216) and sat like 'fish in an aquarium' (*CWB* p. 218) suggest a superficiality in his travel writing that continued in 'Some Innkeepers and Bestre'. A short sketch divided into two parts, the first dealing with the general traits of hoteliers of different nationalities and the second an extended reflection on the character of 'Bestre', an imagined Spanish hotel proprietor who was in fact based on 'Peron', the Spanish hotel-owner who operated the boarding house Lewis stayed in at Doelan in July 1908, the piece appeared in the June 1909 issue of *The English Review*.

While the first part repeats the flaws of 'The "Pole"', the second reflects Lewis's growing maturity in terms of his delineation of character. His outward description of Bestre as 'a large man, grown naïvely corpulent', whose 'Spanish origin is visible in his face ... Sunburnt, with a large yellow-white moustache' (*CWB* p. 228), presents a vivid rendering of his central character, while the attempt to explore Bestre's 'common impulse of avenging that self that was starved and humiliated by the reality, in glorifying and satiating the self that exists by his imagination' (*CWB* p. 232) charts Lewis's attempts to explore character motivation and internality a year and a half before the modernist reconsideration of 'human character' Woolf suggested had occurred around December 1910.[2]

At this point, Lewis also began to develop his unique and lifelong interest in the theme of primitivism, arguably an extension of his increasing desire to delve into the nuances of human character. 'Some Innkeepers and Bestre' marvelled at the strange Breton 'primitive feeling of hospitality' (*CWB* p. 227) and 'The "Pole"' enacted a proto-modernist equation of dance with the primitive in its recollection of one particular performance by a Breton landlady and her Polish tenant:

> After one of their quarrels, they organised a dance to celebrate its completion; their two gaunt and violent forms whirling round the narrow room, quite indifferent to the other dancers, giving them terrible blows with their driving elbows, their hair sweeping on the ceiling. (*CWB* p. 217)

As Bernard Lafourcade argues, by 1909 Lewis was developing his personal 'combination of mystical primitivism and Picasso-esque "misérabilisme"' (*CWB* p. 236) fuelled by the new developments in anthropology and sociology of which Lewis, as an avid attendee of lectures by Henri Bergson and reader of Emile Durkheim and James George Frazer, was distinctly aware. This atavistic quality is evident in Lewis's next piece of pre-war writing, the short sketch 'Les Saltimbanques', which constituted Lewis's third and final piece for *The English Review*, appearing in August 1909. The sketch begins with a description of a gypsy circus Lewis saw perform at the small town of Quimperlé in July 1908. For Lewis, the circus had 'a psychology of its own' and was a form of life both alien yet compelling, an intrigue that reveals itself further in Lewis's astonishment at the 'proximity of these bulging muscles, painted faces and novel garbs' (*CWB* p. 241).

In his Breton Journal, Lewis had marvelled at a *pardon* he witnessed in July 1908:

> It is the renunciation and dissipation . . . of everything . . . that will not be contain'd [sic] in ordinary life; all that there is left of rebellion against life, fate, routine in the peasant . . . they come here and fling all to the winds. (Quoted in *SSG* p. 88)

His retelling of the *pardon* in 'Les Saltimbanques' – the peasants '[c]rowded in the narrow and twilight pavilion of the Saltimbanques . . .

moving themselves as though they had just woken up . . . shaking off a magnetic sleep' (*CWB* p. 242) – reiterates Lewis's seemingly antithetical fixation with and detached disdain for the ritualistic ceremonies. His ultimate conclusion that these Bretons 'are spiritually herded to their amusements as prisoners are served out their daily soap' (*CWB* p. 245) embodies the classic construction of primitive cultures as 'other'.

Between 1910 and 1911, Lewis departed from *The English Review* and published in two other periodicals: *The New Age* and *The Tramp*. His first periodical publication for 1910 was 'Our Wild Body', which appeared in the 5 May issue of *The New Age*, a distinctly modern-ist weekly magazine that reprinted works by Nietzsche and had Ezra Pound, T. E. Hulme, and Katherine Mansfield among its contributors. Despite remaining critically overlooked, 'Our Wild Body' witnessed Lewis's continued employment of the body and the 'primitive' as the-matic concerns, offering a profound attempt to expose, partly as a reac-tion to Victorian inhibitions, the centrality of the body to human life, an early modernist trope that anticipated Joyce's pioneering association of *Ulysses* (1922) with the human body or Lawrence's privileging of the body as the instrument of the unconscious. Although Lewis grounded his 'championing of the real body' (*CWB* p. 253) within the context of his Breton experiences, remembering the French 'hospitality of the body – making another at home in one's body' (*CWB* p. 251), this piece of writing, in keeping with the more critical, exploratory tone of *The New Age*, was Lewis's first foray into critical writing, setting the blueprint for the 'turn' from fiction writing towards the more serious debate pieces Lewis produced in 1914.

The practical realities of magazine publishing meant that Lewis could not complete this turn in 1910. As an emerging young writer he needed to establish himself and earn a more substantial income. He had balked at Hueffer's apparently paltry payment of four pounds and ten shillings for each *English Review* article, calling it a 'dirty little cheque' (*SSG* p. 94), and instead turned his attentions to a new magazine. Established in March 1910, Douglas Goldring's *The Tramp: A Magazine of Open Air Life* was an ambitious, if conflicted, little magazine. Steeped in a Victorian love of nature and 'tramping' (hiking), *The Tramp* was also modernist in its fascination with the commercial trappings of a nascent modernity characterised by cars, technology, and foreign travel, a contradictory ethos reflected in Goldring's editorial assertion that he wanted *The Tramp* to combine 'the literary distinction of the *English Review* . . . with the commercial success of *Country Life*'.[3]

Lewis made five contributions to *The Tramp* between 1910 and 1911: 'A Spanish Household' in the June/July 1910 issue; 'A Breton Innkeeper' in August 1910; 'Le Père François' in September 1910; a poem – 'Grignolles: Brittany. A Poem' – in December 1910; and 'Unlucky for Pringle' in February 1911, a month before *The Tramp*'s last issue in March 1911. These pieces, with the exception of 'Grignolles', a rather unskilled, yet compellingly juvenile poem, were vignettes; more 'Brittany sketches' offering snapshots of Breton life through the focal point of the character of the hotelier or English traveller.

As with his *English Review* contributions, Lewis's characters in *The Tramp* stories were taken from first-hand experience. 'A Spanish Household' was based on the Hotel Europa at which Lewis resided during his May 1909 visit to Vigo, in Spain, with his lover La Flora, described as a 'tall, lithe and handsome fisher girl' (*CWB* p. 264). The eponymous 'Breton Innkeeper' of Lewis's next vignette, the 'restless and vociferous mass' (*CWB* p. 269) whom Lewis named Roland, was, in the style of 'Some Innkeepers and Bestre', another rendering of Lewis's favourite stock character: the European landlord. He would employ this character again in the form of Monsieur Chalaran in 'Unlucky for Pringle', a story that saw Pringle, an Englishman, return to London from Paris only to rent a room from a French host.

Yet it was Lewis's third *Tramp* contribution, 'Le Père François', that represented a more mature attempt at 'drawing' character. This piece, a brief yet affectionate sketch of a drunken old 'French vagabond, hoisting a box up under his arm . . . and brandishing three ruined umbrellas' (*CWB* p. 277), appears as one of Lewis's most vivid exercises in character delineation. Its subtitle, 'A Full-length Portrait of a Tramp', alludes not only to Lewis's increasing application of his skills as an artist to the writerly 'drawing' of characters, but also to the contemporary vogue for the nostalgic, romantic employment of the figure of the tramp or vagabond as a counterpoint to the increasingly mechanised and dehumanised direction in which modern life appeared to many observers to be heading.

It was this vogue that Goldring had in mind when he established *The Tramp* and it is likely that Lewis, picking up on the new magazine's ideology, deliberately targeted his contributions at it, partly because of its ethos and partly because of its links with *The English Review*. By 1910, Lewis had an ambivalent relationship with Hueffer, who had failed to keep to Lewis his 'promise of keeping [him] on as a regular hand', probably because Lewis found the realities of periodical publishing – the keeping of deadlines and the 'hand-to-mouth' lifestyle that resulted from the 'uncertainties' of the publishing industry – all too 'troublesome' (*L* p. 40). It is plausible that Lewis only set about writing for *The Tramp* as an act of defiance and 'one-upmanship'. It was Hueffer whose 'Fathead' stories were promoted as the star feature of the first issue of *The Tramp*, and advertisements for *The English Review* appeared in its back pages.[4] In the small, networked world of modernist magazine production, Lewis, by writing for *The Tramp*, knew he would gain the satisfaction not only of having Hueffer see another magazine publish his work but also of receiving a respectable paycheck. (*The Tramp* was one of the few little magazines that offered 'payment for contributions at the ordinary rates'.[5])

Although *The Tramp* mainly featured work by pre-modernist writers like W. H. Davies and Arnold Bennett, in August 1910 Goldring published a copy of F. T. Marinetti's 'Futurist Declaration', describing it as 'such fun'.[6] Although Lewis's 'Breton Innkeeper' piece was placed several pages away from Marinetti's, the publication of Lewis and Marinetti in the same journal encapsulates a zeitgeist in which Lewis's work was becoming increasingly representative of an early type of alternative modernism. His publishing in *The New Age*, a magazine that was gaining for itself an esteemed status as an influential platform for the latest ideas in modern literature, art, and philosophy, with a very respectable weekly circulation of over 20,000, also cemented Lewis's position within the emerging modernist aesthetics of the early 1910s.[7] By 1911, Lewis, now part of the Camden Town Group formed in June of that year, and increasingly influenced by the impressive energy of Ezra Pound, whom he had met in 1909, was beginning to feel a new-found sense of confidence in his skills as a writer and a painter, but also an irrepressible desire to take those skills to a new level. Vorticism was a couple of years away, but after contributing 'Unlucky for Pringle' to *The Tramp* in February 1911, Lewis suggested that he was taking a break from his career as a writer and committed himself to developing his reputation as a serious artist: 'I shall now', he wrote, in an October 1911 journal entry, 'henceforth, devote myself to painting' (quoted in *SSG* p. 109).

Rebel Artist: 1914

By the time Lewis returned with his first piece of writing in three years, 'The Cubist Room', printed in the 1 January 1914 issue of Harriet Shaw Weaver's *The Egoist*, he was a relatively established painter. He had shown paintings at exhibitions for the Camden Town Group, exhibited *Kermesse* as part of the 5th Allied Artists Salon in July 1912, and also exhibited at the second *Post-Impressionist Exhibition* at the Grafton Galleries in October 1912. He had joined (and departed) Roger Fry's Omega Workshops in 1913, and in March 1914 he founded the

Vorticist Rebel Art Centre. It was only fitting that his first publication of 1914 should be art-related.

'The Cubist Room' was a reprint of the foreword to the catalogue of the *Exhibition of the Work of English Post-Impressionists, Cubists and Others* held in Brighton between 16 December 1913 and 14 January 1914. That 'The Cubist Room' was reprinted in *The Egoist* is unsurprising considering Lewis's close relationship with Pound. As Timothy Materer has recognised, although Pound did not become Lewis's 'agent' until 1916, by 1914 he was a major influence on the latter's writing style and publicity strategies. It was Pound who invented the term 'Vorticism' and who would go on to support Lewis in the establishment of *BLAST* (*P/ L* pp. 4–5). Pound never had an official title at *The Egoist*, but he was 'closely associated with the editors and tended to adopt a proprietorial attitude' towards the periodical.[8] It seems likely that Pound gained the 'gig' for Lewis and thus enabled the resumption of his writing career.

A discussion of the portraits in the room representing the Cubist contributions to the exhibition, 'The Cubist Room' charts Lewis's increasing confidence in using various terms such as Cubism, Post-Impressionism, and Futurism. Moreover, it charts the development of his personal thoughts and opinions on these labels: Cubism was 'the art of those who have taken the genius of Cézanne as a starting point', but Post-Impressionism was 'an insipid and pointless name invented by a journalist, which has been naturally ousted by the better term "Futurism"' (*WLA* p. 56). Lewis's descriptions of individual works by Jacob Epstein and David Bomberg are also important as they testify to the increased influence of Cubism and Futurism upon modern art: 'geometric bases', a sense of 'structure', the use of 'criss-cross pattern', and 'the rigid reflections of steel and stone' (*WLA* p. 57) were all features of The Cubist Room's paintings that Lewis found particularly intriguing. He also recognised that these artists, including others from the Camden Town Group like Edward Wadsworth and C. R. W. Nevinson, were aloof from mainstream British art and represented 'a vertiginous . . . island in the placid and respectable archipelago of English art' (*WLA* p. 56). This contention points to Lewis's growing awareness of himself and his peers as members of an alternative, modern scene, an awareness that undoubtedly led to his decision to found the Rebel Art Centre as an attempt to patent and promote a new modern aesthetic as an alternative to the 'terms and tags' (*WLA* p. 56) he had defined in 'The Cubist Room'.

In another sign of his growing self-confidence, the next set of writings Lewis produced in 1914 was not a collection of articles but a series of letters addressed rather soberly to 'The Editor of the New Age'. 'Epstein and his Critics, or Nietzsche and his Friends' set the trend for Lewis's 'response letter' genre, appearing in the 8 January 1914 issue of *The New Age* in reply to an article by its art critic, Anthony M. Ludovici, who had given a distinctly unfavourable review of the sculptures Epstein exhibited at the aforementioned *Exhibition of the Work of English Post-Impressionists, Cubists and Others*. Rather than considering the aesthetics of Epstein's work, Lewis instead launched a personal, if slightly comedic, attack on Ludovici for calling Epstein a 'minor personality', dismissing Ludovici as a 'cowardly and shifty individual' (*L* p. 54) who 'has the word "minor" on the brain' (*L* p. 55). It was in this personal, almost puerile tone that Lewis continued in his letter writing as the Ludovici/Epstein row rumbled on, sending 'Mr Arthur Rose's Offer' to *The New Age*. Published on 12 February 1914, the letter was a reply to one by a Mr Arthur Rose that asserted Epstein and Ludovici should sort their differences out by means of a fight that could, he offered, be held in his back garden. Lewis's letter was a jovial, sarcastic imagining of the fight taking place and, although unimportant in the context of Lewis's *oeuvre*, is nonetheless an early example of Lewis's playful, mocking, if slightly malicious style of penmanship.

'Modern Art' appeared next, also in *The New Age*. Published on 2 April 1914, it addressed Lewis's rift with Walter Sickert. Both men had clashed during their time in the Camden Town Group, and Sickert had published a letter on 26 March 1914 in which he criticised a painting – *Creation* – Lewis had shown at the exhibition in Brighton. Now it was Lewis's turn to reply and his response was predictably personal. Sickert, he said, had once been 'the scandal of the neighbourhood' but as an older, wiser man had 'sunk into the bandit's mellow and peaceful maturity' and made it his mission to 'get hold of the Brighton catalogue' and shout 'pornography' (*L* p. 58). Yet Lewis was on the offensive too. His writings in early 1914 were not the carefully crafted short stories of Brittany for which he had become better known, but a series of letters and publications that only cemented his now infamous status as something of a modernist tearaway. His writing in 1914 was almost deliberately controversial and continued in this vein. Lewis knew exactly how to attract maximum attention and exposure, conveniently just at the point at which he was busy launching the Rebel Art Centre.

Established in March 1914 by Lewis and Kate Lechmere, the Cubist painter and financial backer of the scheme, the Rebel Art Centre was an exhibition space at 38 Great Ormond Street, London. The epicentre of the Vorticist movement, the Centre exhibited works by artists like David Bomberg, Henri Gaudier-Brzeska, Jessie Dismorr, Jacob Epstein, Frederick Etchells, and Edward Wadsworth, and held lectures by figures such as Pound, Marinetti, and Hueffer.[9] Its 'Prospectus' promised 'public discussions, lectures and gatherings of people' to 'familiarise those who are interested with [sic] the ideas of the great modern revolution in art.'[10] To coincide with its launch, Lewis gave an interview to the *Daily News and Leader* newspaper in April 1914. Titled 'Rebel Art in Modern Life', the interview gave Lewis an opportunity to explain the thinking behind his Centre. The problem with modern art, he argued, was that it was simply not incorporated into modern life enough. He wanted, he said, to bring art into public buildings like hospitals and schools, rather than 'the ordinary living room.'[11] However, Lewis also recognised the fact that, for the most part, this ideal would not work: 'G. F. Watts offered to decorate Euston station and was refused. If I offered to decorate a working men's club or hospital, I should meet with similar difficulties.'[12]

Lewis knew that his aims would be hard to realise, thus making the successful establishment of the Rebel Art Centre as a space for the type of 'alive' art he envisioned all the more vital. He set about promoting his centre as soon as possible. 'A Man of the Week: Marinetti' was the first Futurism-related article Lewis wrote in 1914. It appeared in *The New Weekly*, a periodical (established in early 1914) that was dedicated to reviewing and publishing modern literature. It was edited by R.A. Scott-James, a literary editor and friend of Lewis. By 1914, Marinetti had given four lectures in England, the last of these being at the Rebel Art Centre on 30 May 1914.[13] Given Lewis's friendship with Scott-James, we can assume that the article's publication on the same date as this lecture was a deliberate publicity generator. It began negatively. Marinetti's 'claim to great notice is', Lewis argued, 'hardly an individual one' (*CHC* p. 29). However, after discussing the difference between 'Passéiste', 'Presentiste', and 'Futuriste', Lewis ultimately concluded that Marinetti was 'the intellectual Cromwell of our time' (*CHC* p. 30), a man whose 'revolution' attacked the 'crass snobbery' of English art (*CHC* p. 32).

If Lewis had seemed to endorse Futurism, the publication of Marinetti's 'Futurist Manifesto' in the 7 June issue of *The Observer*, in which Marinetti audaciously listed Lewis as one of the group's members, changed his attitude, sparking a return to his biting, critical writing style. Within a week, Lewis's responses appeared in three periodicals, the fact that he was able to get them published straight away reflecting his new-found status as a well-known figure within the emergent modernist scene. 'Futurism' appeared in *The New Weekly* on 13 June. Signed by several Vorticists, including Edward Wadsworth, Richard Aldington, and Lewis himself, it was a public dissociation of these figures from Marinetti's movement: 'We, the undersigned, whose ideals were mentioned or implied, or who might, by the opinions of others, be implicated, beg to dissociate ourselves from the "Futurist" manifesto which appeared in the pages of *The Observer* of Sunday, June 1.'[14] 'The Futurist Manifesto' was a slightly longer letter published in *The Observer* the next day, 14 June. Using the same 'undersigned' format, Lewis, along with the Vorticists who signed the previous letter, outlined Marinetti's 'assumption' of their participation in Futurism an 'impertinence' (*L* p. 62) and begged to be disassociated from it. *The Egoist* reprinted this letter on 15 June 1914, probably at Pound's insistence, as he and Lewis were at this point trying to launch and promote Vorticism as a movement independent of Futurism.

While Lewis enjoyed bickering with Marinetti publicly, the publication of G. K. Chesterton's 'The Asceticism of the Futurists', a highly critical article published in the weekly penny paper *T. P.'s Weekly* on 4 July 1914, brought a turnaround in Lewis's anti-Futurism. Although the paper had been edited by T. P. O'Connor since 1902, the 4 July 1914 issue was the first to appear under the new editorship of Holbrook Jackson, the one-time editor of *The New Age*. Chesterton's article was designed as a controversial 'crowd-drawer' for the paper's 125,000 weekly readers. In a public denunciation of Futurism, Chesterton declared that the movement was no more than an attention-seeking 'carnival' and 'practical joke.'[15] Having been asked to write a retort, Lewis responded in the next issue of 11 July 1914. Chesterton, he stated, was a man with 'Practical Joke on the brain' (*CHC* p. 35); he was a man who failed to grasp the Futurists' 'personal and logical vision' (*CHC* p. 36).

By July 1914, Lewis was a confident, outspoken artist and writer whose own periodical was about to come into being. This changed his negotiations with the periodical culture he had come to know well. Rather than having to send off endless query letters, Lewis now found himself being sought out by editors like Holbrook Jackson and Scott-James, and publishing within a broad array of mainstream periodicals, such as *The Observer* and *The Outlook*, rather than just within small modernist magazines. 'Kill John Bull with Art' and 'A Later Arm than Barbarity', which were published in *The Outlook* in July and September of 1914, respectively, reflect the fact that editors now wanted Lewis to write on more general topics. The first article was a semi-political piece in which Lewis argued for the death of 'John Bull', the imaginary figure he fashioned as the symbol of the rigid English 'nationality' and its apparent 'extermination of art' (*CHC* p. 40). The second was a profound consideration of the world's response to Germany's declaration of war: 'There is a new type of energy arrayed against them which they [Germany] . . . had not suspected the growth of.'[16]

At this point in his career, it was almost inevitable that Lewis would establish his own magazine. Having used the frequent periodicity of magazines as a convenient way of charting his changing, contradictory opinions on Futurism, and having explored some wider political issues through their pages, Lewis needed to assert his own movement. With its pages of manifestos and Vorticist art, and its 'bright puce colour' and 'general appearance . . . not unlike a telephone book' (*BB* p. 37), *BLAST* appeared on 2 July 1914 and gave Lewis the opportunity to engage in a more 'hands-on' role in publishing. Kate Lechmere had provided £100 to finance the magazine, and preparation began in late 1913, continuing through spring 1914.

Yet Lewis was not the most organised individual. It is telling that the roll call of professions he identified himself with included 'novelist, painter, sculptor, philosopher, draughtsman, critic, politician, journalist, essayist, pamphleteer' (*BB* p. 3) but not 'editor'. Rather than organising the 'back-room' business of the periodical's production himself, his first step was to assemble a meeting of people to whom he could delegate. Douglas Goldring, the editor of the now-defunct *The Tramp*, was brought in for his experience with the business of printing and publishing a little magazine, and secured Leveridge and Co. as *BLAST*'s printer. Lewis asked the journalist Henry Nevinson to contact publishers, and he deliberately selected John Lane, due to its status as 'a small, under-capitalized avant-garde publishing firm' as the future publisher of the magazine.[17]

Despite Lewis's limited interest in the production of the magazine, he was shrewd enough to negotiate terms by which John Lane would only receive a thousand 'free' copies, with Lewis receiving a shilling for any copies sold beyond that figure.[18] With links to *The Egoist*, *Poetry*, and the American *Smart Set*, it was Pound who was perfectly placed to advertise Lewis's little magazine within the right circles; it is no coincidence that advertisements in its back pages were for *The Egoist*, *Poetry*, and other alternative publications from John Lane, like the reprints of *The Yellow Book* (*B1* pp. 189–94).

Operating from the Rebel Art Centre, Lewis set about putting together his first issue, soliciting contributions from Pound, Hueffer, Wadsworth, Etchells, William Roberts, Rebecca West, Jacob Epstein, and Gaudier-Brzeska. Priced at 2/6, the magazine was intended to have quarterly periodicity and as such its total length was significantly longer than that of the average monthly or weekly modernist magazine. Lewis contributed several pieces and many excellent studies have explored these contributions in greater depth.[19] Although Lewis's writing in *BLAST* was characterised by his now well-honed pontifical style, his dramatic proclamation in 'Vorteces [sic] and Notes' that 'Reality is in the artist, the image only in Life' (*B1* p. 135) and his bold attempt to explain Vorticism in 'Our Vortex' – 'With our Vortex, the Present is the only active thing ... The Present is Art' (*B1* p. 147) – have, however, deflected attention from *Enemy of the Stars*.

While a full exploration of this complex text is not possible here, the play – with its use of two polar-opposite characters, a non-teleological plot, and the complex and almost existential consideration of human life at its core – demonstrates that Lewis had matured as a writer, finding time and conviction to develop his own interests rather than having to conform to the demands of other magazine editors.[20] Yet the play's 'Advertisement' shows Lewis reverting to his familiar thematic tropes. The 'TWO HEATHEN CLOWNS' and the 'BLEAK CIRCUS' (*B1* p. 55) at the centre of the story return to Lewis's fascination with the gypsy circus of Brittany some five years previously. The particular language he used to describe the clowns' 'dull explosive muscles' and 'sinewy energetic air' echoes the primitivistic lexicon he used to describe the 'bulging muscles, painted faces and novel garbs' (*CWB* p. 241) of the circus troupe in 'Les Saltimbanques'. The advertisement's carefully arranged page layout and meta-theatrical assertion that the play could be 'VERY WELL ACTED BY YOU AND ME' (*B1* p. 55) symbolise the fact that Lewis conceived *Enemy of the Stars* as a play within the wider 'play' of *BLAST*, the magazine whose materiality – its loud pink cover, bold, almost aggressive typeface, and eye-catching juxtaposition of attention-grabbing manifestos and Vorticist art – conferred upon it the status of appearing as a performance in itself.

This was Lewis's aim. *BLAST* was emblematic of the point at which Lewis and his pre-war writing career reached an early *crescendo*, representing a new phase of confidence and ability that was only cut short because Lewis joined the war effort in 1916. Robert Scholes and Clifford Wulfman have argued that *BLAST* folded after its second issue not just because Lewis went to fight in the war but because he had 'limitations as an editor that prevented his journal from reaching an audience that actually existed.'[21] Yet, in a zeitgeist in which few new movements possessed a lifespan of more than a couple of years, it seems inevitable that Lewis's periodical would fold in a relatively short space of time.

Lewis actively contributed to this zeitgeist, as my exploration of his pre-war writings demonstrates. His publications in *The English Review* and *The Tramp* helped to cement the status of both magazines as early icons of modernist literary production, while also inviting the important question of whether a magazine is defined as 'modernist' by its contributors or whether its contributors are defined as 'modernist' by the magazine in which their work appears. Lewis's letters and musings on Futurism act as indices of a developing sense of modernity that played out within periodicals like *The New Weekly*, *The Egoist*, and *The Outlook*. His writing shows that as both periodical editor and writer, Lewis engaged with many ideas that we now elide with the catch-all term 'modernism': from the invocation of the primitive, the body, and the new fascination for travel in his Breton sketches, to his more politicised writings on the intersections of art and nationhood or his musings on different modern movements, the propagation of Vorticism, and the purpose and future of art (and life).

However, in 1914 these ideas were not yet conceived of as hallmarks of modernism, the term itself being something of a nascent, undeveloped word, which was still rarely used. Lewis, then, was responsible for shaping the aesthetics and definitions of modernism in the early 1910s. His establishment of the Rebel Art Centre, his exhibiting of his works, and, most importantly, his creation of *BLAST* are all lasting contributions to modernism, but it is his periodical publications – his stories of Brittany, his stands against Futurism, and his letters to *The New Age*, in which various debates and tussles played out as he fought to establish himself and his opinions as more vibrant, more original, more urgent than those of his rivals – that most clearly show Lewis negotiating with and shaping the contours of a modernism not yet fully understood. In many ways this encapsulates the essence of the 'fight' that lay at the heart of the establishment of modernism. Long before Lewis found himself in the First World War he was enacting a battle of aesthetic values and competing practices, waging wars against Marinetti, for example, and negotiating the various artistic factions of the early modernist scene. It would be Lewis's first novel, *Tarr* (1918) that would finally cement his status as a modernist writer of serious standing. But, crucially, it was in the periodicals and modernist magazines of early British literary culture that the first round of the battle was won.

Notes

1. For a complete list of Lewis's periodical publications, see Omar S. Pound and Philip Grover (eds), *Wyndham Lewis: A Descriptive Bibliography* (Folkestone: Dawson, 1978).
2. Virginia Woolf, *Mr Bennett and Mrs Brown* (London: Hogarth Press, 1924), p. 3.
3. Douglas Goldring, *Odd Man Out: The Autobiography of a 'Propaganda Novelist'* (London: Chapman and Hall, 1935), p. 105.
4. See 'Contents', *The Tramp*, March 1910, p. xv.
5. Ibid., p. xv.

6. Filippo Tommaso Marinetti, 'Futurist Declaration', *The Tramp*, 1.5, August 1910, pp. 487–8.
7. Circulation figures are taken from Ann L. Ardis, 'The Dialogics of Modernism(s) in the *New Age*', *Modernism/modernity*, 14.3, September 2007, pp. 407–34: p. 420.
8. D. H. Lawrence, *The Letters of D. H. Lawrence – Volume II: June 1913–October 1916*, ed. George J. Zytaruk and James T. Boulton (Cambridge: Cambridge University Press, 1981), p. 131.
9. See *CVA* pp. 145–84 and Jane Beckett and Deborah Cherry, 'Modern Women, Modern Spaces: Women, Metropolitan Culture, and Vorticism', in Katy Deepwell (ed.), *Women Artists and Modernism* (Manchester: Manchester University Press, 1998), pp. 36–54.
10. See the 'Prospectus' reprinted in *CVA* p. 158.
11. 'Rebel Art in Modern Life', *Daily News and Leader*, 7 April 1914, p. 14.
12. Ibid., p. 14.
13. These were in April 1910, March 1912, November 1913, and May 1914. See Andrew Harrison, *D. H. Lawrence and Italian Futurism: A Study of Influence* (Amsterdam: Rodopi, 2003), p. 31.
14. Wyndham Lewis et al., 'Futurism', *New Weekly*, 13 June 1914, p. 406.
15. G. K. Chesterton, 'The Asceticism of the Futurists', *T. P.'s Weekly*, 4 July 1914, p. 5.
16. Wyndham Lewis, 'A Later Arm than Barbarity', *The Outlook*, 34.866, September 1914, p. 299.
17. See Peter McDonald, *British Literary Culture and Publishing Practice: 1880–1914* (Cambridge: Cambridge University Press, 2002), p. 13.
18. For more information on this deal see *SSG* pp. 151–2.
19. See William Wees, *Vorticism and the English Avant-Garde* (Manchester: Manchester University Press, 1972); Paul Edwards (ed.), *BLAST: Vorticism 1914–18* (Hampshire: Ashgate, 2000); Andrzej Gąsiorek, 'The "Little Magazine" as Weapon: *BLAST* (1914–15)', in Peter Brooker and Andrew Thacker (eds), *The Oxford Critical and Cultural History of Modernist Magazines – Vol. 1: Britain and Ireland: 1880–1955* (Oxford: Oxford University Press, 2009), pp. 290–313.
20. For an excellent study of the play see Scott W. Klein, 'The Experiment of Vorticist Drama: Wyndham Lewis and "Enemy of the Stars"', *Twentieth Century Literature*, 37.2, Summer 1991, pp. 225–39.
21. Robert Scholes and Clifford Wulfman, *Modernism in the Magazines* (New Haven, CT: Yale, 2010), p. 145.

Chapter 2

Vorticism and Avant-Gardism

Julian Hanna

Introduction: Wyndham Lionised

'When a man is young he is usually a revolutionary of some kind, so here I am speaking of my revolution' (*CHC* p. 378). Thus begins Wyndham Lewis's final reflection on his pre-war avant-gardism, 'The Vorticists' (1956). The essay, written to promote a major retrospective of Lewis and Vorticism at the Tate Gallery and published six months before Lewis's death, shows that the author's provocative edge had not dulled in the four decades since the movement was extinguished by the First World War. Known as 'The Enemy' from the late 1920s onwards, Lewis played the provocateur throughout his career. In 'The Vorticists', for example, he raised the hackles of his former comrades, especially the painter William Roberts, by suggesting that the movement was more or less a one-man show. Nevertheless, his avant-garde period remains distinct from his later career in several ways. First, the period saw Lewis behaving still as a leader or 'crowd master' and not yet as the 'solitary outlaw' he would become. Second, until he realised shortly after the war that Vorticism was truly over, Lewis remained optimistic about the role of art in society and the artist's ability to influence change. And finally, Lewis was still at this time relatively unguarded and open to new ideas – not unlike the Vortex itself, in fact, as defined by Ezra Pound ('a radiant node or cluster ... from which, and through which, and into which, ideas are constantly rushing').[1] Exploring these and other distinguishing characteristics of Lewis's engagement with the avant-garde, particularly in the shape of the 'Great London Vortex', will be the purpose of this chapter.

Lewis's Vorticist period saw his most successful collaboration with fellow artists and writers in a group dynamic, however independent its members claimed to be ('Blast [sic] presents an art of individuals' (*B1* p. 8), the first issue of the Vorticist magazine declared at the outset).

Shortly after the war, discouraged with his efforts to revive the Vorticist spirit in projects like Group X and his second magazine, *The Tyro* (1921–2), Lewis renounced all collective activities, associating collectives thereafter with his enemies in the Bloomsbury Group. But on the eve of war Lewis was at the centre of bohemian society, an artist celebrity who was lionised and ridiculed in the tabloid press. He was, in this sense, in his prime: 'on the right side of thirty' (*BB* p. 1), in his words, or near enough (he was thirty in 1912), and busy creating a public image. Lewis was very much a social animal before the war, frequenting popular haunts such as the Vienna Café, the Restaurant de la Tour Eiffel (where there was a 'Vorticist Room'), and Frida Strindberg's notorious Cabaret Club off Regent Street, the Cave of the Golden Calf, which featured abstract decorations by Lewis and the American-born sculptor Jacob Epstein.

Dressed in black with a broad-brimmed Left Bank hat, Lewis cut a dramatic figure at the time. But as Peter Brooker has argued, Lewis's bohemian image had a practical dimension as well. In order to make a living and exert an influence, the artist was forced to become a sort of commodity, to 'gain recognition in the public sphere'. The first six months of 1914 are filled with examples – 'the exhibitionist protests, the proclamations and the manifestos' – of Lewis's attempts to catch the public eye.[2] Lewis referred to these activities as 'games' but also described them as necessary labour on the part of the artist: 'I never had time to paint', he complained afterwards. 'I had been so busy massaging the British public' (*BB* p. 88). But it was an opportunity not to be missed: 'The Press in 1914 had no Cinema, no Radio, and no Politics: so the painter could really become a "star"' (*BB* p. 36). The heady days of the pre-war avant-garde, 'full of sound and fury', is the period in which Lewis achieved his greatest renown as a painter, writer, and public figure. (According to Lewis, even the prime minister questioned him on his Vorticist activities; see *BB* pp. 50–1.) As the Tate retrospective at the end of his life showed, he would always be first and foremost the leader of Vorticism and the editor of *BLAST*. As Brooker sums it up: 'The irresistible image for London's Modernist years is that of the Vortex'.[3]

Lewis thought of himself as a leader or 'herdsman' of the avant-garde. When he walked out of Roger Fry's Omega Workshops after a disagreement in October 1913, for example, he did not go alone. Instead he led a flock of fellow rebels – Edward Wadsworth, Frederick Etchells, and Cuthbert Hamilton – to his next project at the Rebel Art Centre, which opened the following spring in a house on Great Ormond Street. Here Lewis, as both 'manager' and 'director' of the Centre (according to the prospectus), collaborated with a group of artists and poets generally if not always strictly or exclusively associated with Vorticism. These figures included the Omega rebels (credited in the prospectus, with Christopher Nevinson, as 'associates'), Pound (who lectured on Imagism and brought in the poet and editor Richard Aldington), Kate Lechmere (who paid for the venture and was co-director with Lewis), as well as Jessica Dismorr, Helen Saunders, William Roberts, the photographer Malcolm Arbuthnot, the painter and poet Lawrence Atkinson, and many others. Marinetti was invited to lecture in May of 1914. Photographs of the Centre's striking geometrical designs, shown in murals and draperies, were published in the *Daily Mirror* and other popular media outlets, and advertisements for the Centre's activities were run in *The Times*. Under Lewis's direction, the Rebel Art Centre was to sponsor not only lectures and exhibitions, but also 'dances' and 'social entertainments' (*CVA* p. 158).

For Lewis the pre-war years were those of relative optimism. 'Optimism is very permissible. England appears to be recovering' (*CHC* p. 32). This seemingly oblivious remark, made just two months prior to the outbreak of war, nevertheless reflects the prevailing spirit of the first half of 1914, when the London avant-garde was at its peak. To Lewis and other avant-gardists before the war, as Alan Munton has argued, a 'transformation of life and culture throughout Europe' appeared imminent (they were right, of course, though not in the way they assumed).[4] Sentiments like these about the pre-war period stand in contrast to the pessimism and even paranoia with which Lewis viewed the world subsequently. Writing on the eve of the Second World War, he declared: 'it is unlikely the arts will again enjoy such a period of favourable calm as was experienced by those artists who came upon the scene between the French Revolution and the "Great War"' (*BB* p. 264).

Like many others, Lewis looked back on the pre-war years as a Golden Era: a period of relatively carefree creative production and the serendipitous exchange of styles and ideas between artists. Such openness to new influences is another point that sets Lewis's avant-garde period apart from his later work. These influences included, for example, the aestheticism of James McNeill Whistler (the American painter and rival of Wilde on whom Pound modelled himself at the time), the Cubism of Braque and Picasso, and the Expressionism of Kandinsky, as well as the highly contagious Futurism of Marinetti, who, despite becoming *persona non grata* when he and Nevinson launched their 'Vital English Art' manifesto using Rebel Art Centre stationery in June 1914, was praised by Lewis only the previous month for his energy and 'services' to an England still stuck in the Victorian period and mired in 'crass snobbery' (*CHC* p. 32). The influence of thinkers such as Henri

Bergson (*L'Évolution créatrice*, 1907), Wilhelm Worringer (*Abstraktion und Einfühlung*, 1907), and Georges Sorel (*Réflexions sur la violence*, 1908), each of whose work was mediated and diffused in the translations and criticism of T. E. Hulme, all contributed to the swirling pool of ideas that would form the basis of the London Vortex.

Paths to the Vortex

So when did Vorticism actually begin? The Vortex itself, coined by Pound in a letter to William Carlos Williams in December 1913, was only added to *BLAST* as a governing motif and used as a label for the Rebel Art Centre group on 13 June 1914, when the 'Manifesto of the Vorticists' was published in *The Spectator* in response to Marinetti's and Nevinson's manifesto. (It was Nevinson, in fact, who had come up with the name '*BLAST*'.) The night before, Lewis, Pound, and Hulme had heckled Marinetti and Nevinson during a performance at the Doré Gallery: the high-profile melee that followed was in a sense the first public outing of the Vorticist movement, as defined in opposition to Futurism. Until that time *BLAST* had been, in Pound's words, 'a new Futurist, Cubist, Imagiste Quarterly'.[5] In the narrowest terms, then, Vorticism lasted for a single year: from the summer of 1914 to the summer of 1915, when the only official group exhibition took place and the second and final issue of *BLAST* appeared.

Of course the origins of the London avant-garde that peaked in the summer of 1914 and of which Lewis was the leading 'lion' may be traced back much further – as early as 1908. In that year Lewis, Pound, and Hulme arrived in London from travels and study in France, Italy, and Germany respectively. Lewis had been in Europe – not only in France, in fact, but also Germany, Holland, and Spain – more or less continuously since 1902. This made him something of a foreigner in England: which he was anyway, having been born in Canada to an American father and a British mother. (The cosmopolitan influences and views on modern art and literature that he absorbed during his twenties were in this sense not unlike those of Marinetti when the Futurist leader arrived in London.[6]) In 1909 Futurism launched its first manifesto in *Le Figaro*, Roger Fry returned to London from New York, Hulme met Pound at the Poet's Club (of which Hulme was secretary), and Lewis began his writing career by publishing his first story in Ford Madox Hueffer's *English Review*. The pre-war avant-garde began to take shape.

In 1910, the year Fry joined Bloomsbury and organised the first *Post-Impressionist Exhibition* – and in the famous words of Virginia Woolf, 'human character changed' – Lewis met Pound for the first time in the Vienna Café near the British Museum. As Hugh Kenner describes it, they were an unlikely pair: 'Pound was a Beerbohm cartoon of the salon artist, beard, earring, green velvet, Lewis the black-hatted anarchist in a cape. Yet they became friends.'[7] In 1911 Hulme began holding his influential Tuesday salons in Frith Street, where the guests included painters of the Camden Town Group (of which Lewis was a member) and other future Vorticists, as well as a broad cross-section of London literary, social, and political life. Gaudier-Brzeska arrived from Paris, where he had recently met Epstein, who would be championed by Hulme and whose sculpture *Rock Drill* (1913–15) would become a centrepiece of Vorticist style. As a painter, Lewis's major breakthroughs leading to a recognisably Vorticist style came in 1912, notably in the series of illustrations based on *Timon of Athens*; six of the *Timon* series were included that year in Fry's *Second Post-Impressionist Exhibition*, and one was reproduced in the first issue of *BLAST*. When Lewis and others walked out of Omega in 1913 and Pound left Imagism to Amy Lowell the scene was set for the new movement to begin in earnest.

Pound chose to throw in his lot with Lewis and become a guiding force in the emerging movement for several reasons. In part he felt that Imagism had become a watered-down and superficial style, a victim of its own modest success. But he was also attracted to the pan-artistic nature of Vorticism, which, like Futurism, combined painting, sculpture, and literature, and could conceivably also include music, photography, cinema, and so on. Nor did Pound feel that he had to abandon his Imagist principles when he joined the Vortex. In his essay 'Vorticism', published in *The Fortnightly Review* in September 1914 (and subsequently included in *Gaudier-Brzeska: A Memoir*), he created a new definition that conveniently fused both his guiding concepts into one: 'The image . . . is what I can, and must perforce, call a VORTEX.'[8] Pound's Imagist principles, he had earlier claimed, originated in theories expressed by Hulme in the early days of the Poetry Club, and included direct treatment of the subject, precision, and an overarching rhetoric of masculine 'hardness' – an approach that would be taken up not only by men but also by women artists like Dismorr and Saunders, who sought to oppose the 'soft', 'feminine' aesthetic of Bloomsbury with a hard-edged, 'masculine' toughness. (Though Hulme's name does not appear anywhere in *BLAST*, Lewis acknowledged the critic's influential role in his memoir of the period, *Blasting and Bombardiering*: 'What he said should be done, I *did*'; *BB* p. 100.) In addition, Pound brought his interest in formalist principles handed down from aestheticism, as the first issue of *BLAST* shows: despite its 'blasting' of 'years 1837 to 1900'

(*B1* p. 18), 'Vortex Pound' declares its 'Ancestry' to include Pater and Whistler (*B1* p. 154).

Lewis's conception of the artist was influenced by several major European thinkers whose ideas he had been exposed to in his travels and who were starting to gain currency in London at the time. The ideas of the 'ego' and the 'will', for example, which originated in the philosophical writings of Max Stirner (see *Der Einzige und sein Eigenthum* of 1844), Schopenhauer, and Nietzsche, contributed to the rhetoric found throughout *BLAST*. 'The Vorticist movement', Pound confirmed in August 1914, was 'a movement of individuals, for individuals, for the protection of individuality.'[9] Vorticist art also sought to reflect a northern industrial work ethic: 'the Will that determined . . . the direction of the modern world' (*B1* p. 36). The dominance of Stirner's philosophy among the London avant-garde is evident in *The Egoist* magazine – London's leading modernist periodical in 1914, when the literary editor was Pound. Bergsonian 'Vitalism' or 'Dynamism', also in vogue at the time, emphasised characteristics such as energy and intensity that are clearly present in the pages of *BLAST*, although the influence is not consistent throughout. Lewis, who had attended Bergson's lectures at the Collège de France, was an enthusiastic supporter for a time, but would become an outspoken critic of what he called the 'time cult' in the 1920s.

In 1914 Lewis was just beginning to move away from Bergson in his formulation of a Vorticist aesthetic that was distinct from Futurism. Unlike Futurism, which was dominated by the principles of speed and dynamism, Lewis's Vorticism came to emphasise stillness, and, in keeping with the idea of a northern reserve, hard, sculptural form. 'Our Vortex', written by Lewis, states that there will be no more 'numbing displays of vitality' (*B1* p. 147). Instead, he declares: 'The Vorticist is at his maximum point of energy when stillest' (*B1* p. 148). In contrast to the 'automobilism' of Marinetti, which fawned too much over technology, Vorticism claimed: 'We hunt machines, they are our favourite game' (*B1* p. 148). The difference emphasised here and elsewhere is between uncritically embracing the 'Romance' of industrial modernity and merely reflecting, with a certain northern *sang-froid*, its everyday 'Realism'. '[T]he English', Lewis wrote in a piece called 'Automobilism' (20 June 1914), 'do not require a prophetic Milanese to tell them that Motor-cars go quickly' (*CHC* p. 33). Such appeals to national character, however, were limited to attacks on Futurism and sought primarily to encourage a domestic art industry. On the eve of war Lewis wrote (in 'Kill John Bull with Art', 18 July 1914): 'The national enemy of each country is its nationality' (*CHC* p. 40). He went further – further even than Marinetti had in his criticism of the English – singling out England as a disgrace among European nations:

> England has the great distinction of being different from other countries. She is a marked country in Europe: the great, unimaginative, cold, unphilosophic, unmusical bourgeoise!
>
> She has a terrific reputation from Tenerife to Tobolsk for strangling poets, putting artists in prison, and generally behaving like a land . . . committed to the extermination of art. Art is a red rag to her. (*CHC* pp. 38–40)

In fact the pre-war Lewis was nothing like the reactionary monster that he is too often characterised as being. He was a self-described 'literary militant . . . a painter up in arms against the dead hand of an obsolete authority' (*BB* p. 6). Far from seeking to protect the status quo, he called for a revolution ('A VORTICIST KING! WHY NOT?'; *B1* p. 8): because, to him, 'great artists in England are always revolutionary' (*B1* p. 7).

The targets of Lewis's militant outrage suddenly shifted, however, as the final pages of *BLAST* went to press. Following the dispute with Marinetti and the 'turncoat' Nevinson in June 1914, the aggression that had previously been aimed at the traditional targets of the bourgeoisie and philistine public, as well as the 'Victorian vampire' that was still sucking the blood out of contemporary London, now also became directed at other avant-garde movements. This is the moment, described in Bradbury and McFarlane, when 'ism' turned to 'schism'.[10] Last-minute advertisements of the new movement known as Vorticism declared: 'DEATH BLOW TO IMPRESSIONISM AND FUTURISM'.[11] Just weeks prior to the outbreak of war in Europe, the war among the European avant-gardes reached its peak. 'Life was one big bloodless brawl', as Lewis later put it, 'prior to the Great Bloodletting' (*BB* p. 35).

High Vorticism: The First *BLAST*

The first volume of *BLAST* was printed and assembled over several months leading up to its actual publication on 2 July 1914 (the date printed on the magazine is 20 June). What was initially planned as an intervention in the style of a European avant-garde 'little magazine' gradually took on a distinctly northern character: the recurring motif of the storm cone, for example, which was most likely a pre-existing design discovered on a printer's block at Leveridge and Co., the Harlesden printers used for *BLAST*, represents a 'storm from the North' (a black canvas cone was hoisted by the coast guard to warn ships of an approaching gale, or 'blast') and resembles the conical shape of a vortex.[12] Although it had been conceived earlier, only at the last minute was the movement behind *BLAST* officially named the 'Great London Vortex', or Vorticism. Lewis boasted in 1956 that Vorticism came from 'the brain of one man' (*CHC* p. 378), that is, himself, and it is true that as with his later periodicals *The Tyro* and *The Enemy*, if not quite to the same extent, much of the material in *BLAST* was written by Lewis: including (by his own admission) all the manifestos, the play *Enemy of the Stars*, and significant pieces of art criticism such as 'Vortices and Notes' (*B1* pp. 129–49) and 'A Review of Contemporary Art' (*B2* pp. 38–47). Nevertheless, Vorticism was still a collective endeavour.

The reason Lewis claimed the lion's share of the credit, so to speak, might not have been so much to do with his vanity as with his disappointment at the end result. Lewis lamented the fact that the 'Review of the Great English Vortex' was not more consistent. 'I wanted a battering ram that was all of one metal', he later wrote. 'A good deal of what got in seemed to me soft and highly impure. Had it been France, there would have been plenty to choose from' (*RA* pp. 138–9). The weakness, in terms of stylistic unity, was mainly in the literature: significant contributions came from Hueffer ('The Saddest Story', soon to become part of *The Good Soldier*) and Rebecca West ('Indissoluble Matrimony'), but they hardly represented a new 'Vorticist' literary style. Nor did Pound's poems live up to the promise of the manifestos; they were even at times embarrassingly puerile ('Salutation the Third'). Lewis's one-act play, *Enemy of the Stars*, though seemingly unstageable and almost unreadable, did at least push the boundaries, attempting to replicate in prose his painterly experiments with abstraction. In visual terms *BLAST* was more successful, featuring reproductions of works by Lewis, Wadsworth, Etchells, Roberts, Epstein, Gaudier-Brzeska, Hamilton, and Spencer Gore; the 'BLAST' and 'BLESS' sections; and Lewis's manifestos, which were composed primarily with visual impact in mind. Then there were the oft-remarked experiments in typography, the 'bright puce' cover, and the impact made by the magazine's sheer size and weight ('not unlike a telephone book'; *BB* p. 37).

But the 'mess' of the first volume of *BLAST*, as Edwards has pointed out, can also be read in a more positive way. It can be seen as a vivid reflection of an outpouring of artistic energy, which in turn reflected the social upheaval and the extremely rapid pace of change leading up to the summer of 1914.[13] Despite Lewis's claims to the contrary, Vorticism was not a top-down organisation: its members did not know quite what they were taking part in, except that it was a modern movement in some way analogous to the continental movements that were

Vorticism's acknowledged points of reference: Cubism, Expressionism, and Futurism. Shortly before the public announcement of Vorticism, Lewis called for 'A Futurism of Place': 'Artists in this country should attempt to find a more exact expression of the Northern character' (*CHC* p. 32), he declared, and he argued that much of Marinetti's vitality was 'untranslatable' (*CHC* p. 32). Vorticism was the name given to the avant-garde of a very specific place and time; as Kenner wrote in *The Pound Era*: 'The Future has no locale, an Image or a Cube may turn up in anyone's pocket, but any Vortex is somewhere on the map.'[14] More than any spurious notion of 'national character', however, the London Vortex reflected what was happening in London at the time. The changing social makeup, for example, of London's artistic life: expatriates from Europe and America, women as well as men, lower-middle class and provincial artists (and critics, like Hulme) as well as metropolitan ones.[15] *BLAST*, in that sense, fulfils its promise to the reader: it is a faithful representation of the Vortex, the concentration of artistic energy in a certain place and time, that it seeks to describe. For that reason, *BLAST*'s reputation as the central work of the London pre-war avant-garde is well deserved.

The visual aesthetic of the first issue of *BLAST* has one primary goal: to blast, like a gale, the cobwebs from contemporary England; to exorcise from the stubbornly 'Victorian' nation its 'timidity', its paralysing 'snobbery', and its 'FEAR OF RIDICULE' (*B1* p. 15). The criticism is not reserved for England alone, of course, but it is as a remedy to the nation's ills that *BLAST* excels (and still rings true). The 'expletive of whirlwind' – the 'blast' – is primal, primitive: everywhere in the magazine there are references to the primitivism advocated by Hulme in his lectures and which could be seen across the European avant-garde during the pre-war years. Vorticists are self-described 'Primitive Mercenaries in the Modern World' (*B1* p. 30); 'The Art-instinct is permanently primitive' (*B1* p. 33). Although Futurism had its own primitivist tendencies, Lewis drew a distinction between the true 'savage' nature of the Vorticists – the artist in the urban jungle – and the false notion of 'an "advanced," perfected, democratic, Futurist individual' (*B1* p. 33). Moreover, in keeping with Hulme's idea of primitivism, Vorticist primitivism did not equal wild, Romantic disarray: the humorous injunction to 'BLESS the HAIRDRESSER' (*B1* p. 25) was, in Lewis's own words, to promote 'formality, and order, at the expense of the disorderly and unkempt', to defend 'the classic standpoint, as against the romantic' (*BB* p. 38).

Beyond its use as a wake-up call, the magazine's task was also to show the nation and Europe that England could produce art and literature equal to if not greater than that of France, Germany, or Italy. The differences between Vorticism and Futurism, its nearest cousin, are significant: one has only to compare contemporary Futurist paintings by Balla (such as *Abstract Speed + Sound*, 1913–14) or Boccioni (*Dynamism of a Cyclist*, 1913) to Lewis's monumental canvas *The Crowd* (1914–15) to see how different they actually are. While the former paintings are dominated by the religion of speed and the resulting distortions and effects, in Lewis's composition where we might expect movement from the subject (a scene of large-scale mobilisation and the stirrings of revolt) there is stasis. The static arrangement of forms and colours, including buildings, flags, and stickmen, is watched over by a figure at the margins. In contrast to Boccioni's depiction of the cyclist's body as superhuman, in Lewis's painting massive architectural forms render human figures insignificant, almost futile. In a piece from *BLAST*, 'The New Egos', Lewis argued: 'THE ACTUAL HUMAN BODY BECOMES OF LESS IMPORTANCE EVERY DAY. / It now, literally, EXISTS much less' (*B1* p. 141). 'Dehumanization', he concludes, 'is the chief diagnostic of the Modern World' (*B1* p. 141). In the end, the fact that Lewis's movement was given its name in haste, at the last moment, and that the name supplied by Pound was something of a 'publicity stunt' (in Jameson's words), should not obscure the very real differences that exist between Vorticism and the other movements with which it shares certain obvious affinities.[16]

Another important characteristic of *BLAST* is its reflection of the social and political upheaval of the time. The famous 'BLAST' and 'BLESS' lists, for example, are full of nods and slights to contemporaries, and were intended primarily to stir up controversy. But the connection to the times went deeper, and by the highly politicised late 1930s Lewis had come to recognise the commonalities between art and war, and militant art and militant politics, which he claimed not to have been aware of at the time. In *Blasting and Bombardiering* Lewis devotes considerable discussion to the way in which 'war, art, civil war, strikes and coup d'états dovetail[ed] into each other' (*BB* p. 4) during the first half of 1914. The 'mature' Lewis admits that 'as an artist one is always holding the mirror up to politics' (*BB* p. 4): 'this organized disturbance was Art behaving as if it were Politics. But I swear I did not know it' (*BB* p. 32). Similarities are clearly present between, on the one hand, an artistic avant-garde issuing militant manifestos, and on the other, suffragettes, unionists, syndicalists, and anarchists making manifest their own radical platforms using radical new methods.[17] 'TO SUFFRAGETTES', a patronising note at the back of *BLAST* that begs Vorticism's 'BRAVE COMRADES' to 'LEAVE ART ALONE' (*B1* p. 152), reveals the anxiety that lurks beneath the magazine's masculine bravado, as well as the extent to which Vorticism was entangled with other militant movements. 'The editor of *Blast* [sic]', Lewis later acknowledged, 'would never have admitted that he was a suffragette' (*BB* p. 66).

Vorticism at War

On 2 July 1914 the first issue of *BLAST* appeared and Vorticism, a word that had only been introduced to the public weeks before, was truly on the town. Then, almost immediately, war broke out and threw the movement fatally off course. It brought the nascent movement to an end before Lewis, his fellow Vorticists, or the general public fully understood what Vorticism meant. As Lewis remarked at the end of his life: 'Wars have made it impossible to get on with anything for very long' (*CHC* p. 381). The catastrophic intervention of the First World War was a setback from which Lewis's career never fully recovered. On 28 June 1914, even before *BLAST* reached the bookshops, Archduke Franz Ferdinand was assassinated in Sarajevo by the Serb nationalist Gavrilo Princip, and on 4 August Britain declared war on Germany. Nevertheless, with the majority of Vorticists excluded from immediate service for one reason or another – Lewis was hospitalised with a venereal infection and first saw action in 1916 – the movement kept on, and in the summer of 1915 saw another significant moment.

That summer, however, was not without tragedy: Gaudier-Brzeska, who had enlisted with the French infantry in September 1914, was killed at the Front on 5 June 1915. His death occurred just days before the first *Vorticist Exhibition* was to open at the Doré Gallery, featuring work by Gaudier-Brzeska, Lewis, Dismorr, Etchells, Saunders, Wadsworth, Roberts, and invited artists (notably the Bloomsbury painter Duncan Grant, as well as Nevinson, Bomberg, Atkinson, and others in the orbit of Vorticism). The exhibition was the only proper Vorticist group show, although a second wartime exhibition, in January 1917, was organised at the Penguin Club in New York by the collector John Quinn, at Pound's urging, to promote the movement overseas. When the second issue of *BLAST* was published in July 1915, Gaudier-Brzeska's death was commemorated in a note to his own posthumous piece, a second 'Vortex'. Lewis also eulogised Gaudier-Brzeska in *Blasting and Bombardiering*, calling the 'sharp-faced, black-eyed stranger amongst us' (*BB* pp. 107–8) a true artist, and claiming that the death of this young sculptor, so full of vitality, filled him thereafter with a 'hatred for this soul-less machine,

of big-wig money-government, and these masses of half-dead people'
(*BB* p. 108).

Vorticism was, in a sense, always 'at war'. Lewis wrote in his memoir
of 'how like art is to war, I mean "modernist" art' (*BB* p. 4). The 'War
Number' of *BLAST*, however, is immediately distinguished from its
predecessor by its sober tone and its sombre brown-paper cover. Still,
at this point the optimism has not yet completely evaporated: in the
opening editorial Lewis is already looking beyond the war, hoping for
an early armistice and a resumption of business as usual. He tries to call
attention to – perhaps even to wish into existence – 'the serious mission
[*BLAST*] has on the other side of World War' (*B2* p. 5), as if the war
itself is merely a distraction. Whereas the first issue deliberately mocked
patriotism, vowing to 'fight first on one side, then on the other' (*B1*
p. 30), and was full of violent imagery, the second issue is by comparison
more measured and cautious. As Cork notes, Lewis 'struggled hard to
inject some of the old venom in the second issue' (*CVA* p. 286). There
is only a brief and listless rehashing of the 'BLAST' and 'BLESS' format
that was a comic highlight of the first issue. Moreover, the 'Notice to
Public' suggests a reluctance to even continue with the sort of militancy
that *BLAST* represents: 'as this paper is run chiefly by Painters and for
Painting, and they are only incidentally Propagandists, they do their
work first, and, since they must, write about it afterwards' (*B2* p. 7).
While still attempting to rise above the patriotic fervour, the editor
admits: 'Under these circumstances . . . it appears to us humanly desirable that Germany should win no war against France or England' (*B2*
p. 5). On the positive side, the 'battering ram', though lighter on the
whole, now seems to be much more 'of one metal'. In 'A Review of
Contemporary Art', Lewis writes confidently about 'the Vorticists' –
'Vorticism' having been mentioned as such only once in the first issue
– and makes his strongest attempt to differentiate the artists of his movement from 'the French, German or Italian painters of kindred groups'
(*B2* p. 38), though the resulting philosophy is still neither entirely clear
nor consistent. The visual works in the second issue show a greater
adherence to a recognisably 'Vorticist' style, while the literary works,
consisting of poetry by Pound, Dismorr, Hueffer, and T. S. Eliot, whom
Lewis had met through Pound the previous year, are kept to a minimum.
The second volume of *BLAST* also includes the first part of 'The Crowd-
Master': a counterpart in prose to Lewis's vast painting of the mobilisation, *The Crowd* (1914–15).

Blasting grew more difficult during the second half of the war, with
more Vorticists seeing action. Following the shock of Gaudier-Brzeska's
death early in the conflict, Vorticism suffered another blow with the

death of Hulme, its most important critic, who was killed by an artillery shell in 1917, not far from Lewis's position. Nevertheless, some activity continued. Lewis enlisted in 1916, at first as an artillery officer but then from December 1917 as an official war artist in a Canadian regiment, where he served alongside Bomberg. In fulfilling the documentary purpose of his wartime commissions his style sometimes takes a radical turn back to the figurative (*A Canadian Gun-Pit*, 1918), though in other works Lewis succeeds in fusing a Vorticist style to clearly recognisable subjects (*A Battery Shelled*, 1919). Wadsworth, meanwhile, was pioneering a new form of 'dazzle' camouflage. Rather than blending in with the environment, Dazzle ships, painted in striking Vorticist-inspired geometric camouflage patterns, sought to frustrate attempts by enemy spotters to discover their precise location, speed, and direction. Away from the battle, Vorticism was also breaking new ground: in 1916, for example, the American photographer Alvin Langdon Coburn invented a kaleidoscopic device called the Vortoscope in order to pursue his own experiments. The resulting 'Vortographs', including a number of portraits of Pound, were exhibited at the London Camera Club in February 1917. These and other activities were enough to keep the hope alive that the movement might continue once peace was restored.

The Death of Vorticism

In the February–March 1919 issue of *The Little Review*, Pound (then London editor of the magazine) ran a piece he wrote called 'The Death of Vorticism'. In it he insisted that, despite having been 'reported dead by numerous half-caste reporters', 'old ladies', and 'parasites', the movement was still very much alive. 'Vorticism has not yet had its funeral', Pound declared, citing as evidence the Vorticist-inspired wartime activities of Lewis, Bomberg, and Wadsworth, as well as the reception of a recent show of Gaudier-Brzeska's work.[18] In April Lewis added to Pound's efforts with 'What Art Now', an article in *The English Review* in which he still spoke of Vorticism as if it were alive among the other 'isms'. They both seemed to protest too much, however, and soon afterward Pound voted with his feet, abandoning London for Paris in 1920.

Lewis's first major post-war blast was *The Caliph's Design: Architects! Where is Your Vortex?* (1919), a lengthy pamphlet put out by The Egoist Press. Lewis later claimed it was 'another *Blast* [sic]' – a continuation in the same vein as the magazine – though he also admitted that, despite his use of the term in the subtitle, he was 'no longer a "vorticist"' (*WLA*

p. 129). One difference, of course, was that he was now working alone: *The Caliph's Design* is very much a one-man polemic on the state of contemporary art and the place of the artist in society. Another important difference is that the role of the artist has shifted: no longer hanging on to the art-for-art's-sake ideal of autonomy, Lewis displays an interest in the shaping of society that would continue for the rest of his career. '*You must get Painting, Sculpture, and Design out of the studio and into life*' (CD p. 12), Lewis tells his disciples. Other pieces written shortly after the war confirm Lewis's new stance: 'Art Saints for Villages' (1920; *CHC* pp. 62–3) and a *Daily Mail* piece called 'Why Picasso Does It' (1921), for example, attest both a desire for greater engagement with everyday life and a willingness to appeal to a broader public. In *The Caliph's Design* Lewis declares outright that he no longer has any desire to be seen as one of 'the queer wild men of cubes, the terrible futurists' (*CD* p. 39). Instead, he claims, the artist wishes to be a 'useful' part of society like anyone else.

Another 'bit of "blasting"' (*BB* p. 212) was carried out in 1920, when Lewis was part of an exhibition of painters, many of them ex-Vorticists, known as Group X. After his one-man show, *Guns*, at the Goupil Gallery the previous year, this marked a return to collective activities, but with an even greater emphasis than Vorticism on the independence of each member. Soon he was alone again, however, and his final attempt to resume his pre-war activities came in 1921 with *The Tyro*, a magazine that was intended to provide a counterbalance to Roger Fry's influence on the London art scene. Like *The Caliph's Design*, *The Tyro* attempts to enact a fresh start, declaring in its first issue: 'We are at the beginning of a new epoch' (*WLA* p. 195). When it became clear, however, that this new age was not forthcoming, or at least that Lewis would not be its leader, he abandoned the avant-garde and went 'underground' to write *The Man of the World* (which would eventually be published as a number of shorter books, including *The Art of Being Ruled*). When he emerged as a public figure again in the second half of the 1920s, he wore the mask of 'The Enemy'.

Hugh Kenner wrote appreciatively in the 1950s that in *BLAST* Lewis 'finds an appropriate tongue' (*KWL* p. 14). But Kenner also admitted with regret that Vorticism had become 'a lecture-room joke' (*KWL* p. 63). From this apparent low at the time of Lewis's death (and for at least a decade afterward), the reputation of Vorticism has steadily risen. Beginning with the pioneering work of William Wees and Richard Cork, to critical landmarks such as Fredric Jameson's *Fables of Aggression* (1979) and Paul Edwards's *Wyndham Lewis: Painter and Writer* (2000), through to the major Tate Britain exhibition, *The Vorticists*, in

2011, Lewis's avant-garde phase has, at its centenary, surpassed even the impact and influence of its spectacular debut.

Notes

1. Ezra Pound, *Gaudier-Brzeska: A Memoir* [1916] (New York: New Directions, 1970), p. 92.
2. Peter Brooker, *Bohemia in London: The Social Scene of Early Modernism* (Basingstoke: Palgrave Macmillan, 2007), p. 3.
3. Peter Brooker, '"Our London, my London, your London": The Modernist Moment in the Metropolis', in Laura Marcus and Peter Nicholls (eds), *The Cambridge History of Twentieth-Century Literature* (Cambridge: Cambridge University Press, 2004), pp. 117–31: p. 118.
4 Alan Munton, 'Wyndham Lewis: War and Aggression', in David Peters Corbett (ed.), *Wyndham Lewis and the Art of Modern War* (Cambridge: Cambridge University Press, 1998), pp. 14–37: p. 35.
5. Quoted in Hugh Kenner, *The Pound Era* (Berkeley: University of California Press, 1971), p. 237.
6. Brooker, *Bohemia in London*, p. 11.
7. Kenner, *The Pound Era*, p. 236.
8. Pound, *Gaudier-Brzeska*, p. 92.
9. Ezra Pound, 'Edward Wadsworth, Vorticist', *The Egoist*, 16.1, 15 August 1914, pp. 306–7: p. 306.
10. Malcolm Bradbury and James McFarlane, 'Movements, Magazines and Manifestos: The Succession from Naturalism', in Bradbury and McFarlane (eds), *Modernism: 1890–1930* (Harmondsworth: Penguin, 1976), pp. 192–205: p. 202.
11. Quoted in Brooker, *Bohemia in London*, p. 98.
12. Beyond suggesting an approaching storm in artistic terms, the metaphor could easily be interpreted as a reference to the looming threat of war. Rudyard Kipling's inter-war poem 'The Storm Cone' (1932) uses the metaphor in this way to warn of another conflict to come. One stanza in particular seems apt: 'Stand by! The lull 'twixt blast and blast / Signals the storm is near, not past; / And worse than present jeopardy / May our forlorn to-morrow be.' Rudyard Kipling, 'The Storm Cone' (1932), in Peter Washington (ed.), *Poems* (London: Everyman's Library, 2007), pp. 254–5: p. 254.
13. Paul Edwards, '*BLAST* and the Revolutionary Mood of Wyndham Lewis's Vorticism', in *VNP* pp. 199–219: p. 210.
14. Kenner, *The Pound Era*, p. 238.
15. Brooker, *Bohemia in London*, p. 8.
16. Fredric Jameson, 'Wyndham Lewis's *Timon*: The War of Forms', in *VNP* pp. 15–30: p. 26.
17. See Janet Lyon, *Manifestoes: Provocations of the Modern* (Ithaca, NY: Cornell University Press, 1999), pp. 92–123.
18. Ezra Pound, 'The Death of Vorticism', *The Little Review*, 5.10–11, February–March 1919, pp. 45–9: p. 48.

Chapter 3

'Harsh Laughter': Reading *Tarr*

Faith Binckes

Tarr (1918) was Wyndham Lewis's first novel. Its focus is the tangled intellectual and sexual fortunes of four protagonists: the young English artist Frederick Sorbert Tarr, the not-so-young German artist Otto Kreisler, Tarr's German girlfriend Bertha Lunken, and the 'beautiful and swankily original' (*T1* p. 189) German–Russian–American Anastasya Vasek. These protagonists inhabit the 'Knackfus Quarter', an area of Paris roughly equivalent to Montparnasse. The book features numerous satellite characters, notably the Russian–Polish art-dealer Soltyk; Butcher, one of Tarr's English friends; Volker, a more successful associate of Kreisler; and assorted members of an émigré group who gather around the well-heeled Fräulein Lipmann. Just as the terse black outlines in a Vorticist painting both delineated a visual object and held that object up for scrutiny, so *Tarr* presented a series of conspicuous generic and thematic templates to the reader. The book was self-consciously a tale of the 'Vie de Bohème' (*T1* p. 21) displaying features of a genre that had been popular since the mid-nineteenth century.[1] One of those features was an exploration of different national identities, as they rub up against one another with fractious sociability. It is impossible not to notice *Tarr*'s extended exploration of 'national character and the character of nations', as its discussions of aesthetic, intellectual, and even sexual conventions are frequently filtered through this lens.[2] Bohemian narratives tend to feature romantic and fraternal love, and Lewis's novel does too. However, Tarr's relationships with Bertha and with Anastasya are a long way from the tale of Rodolphe and Mimi, and Kreisler's violent entanglements with both women, and with his male 'rival' Soltyk (*T1* p. 150), push the novel even further from its generic comfort zone. Finally, Lewis's manipulation of the genre also facilitated an exploration of the comic, and of the tragic. For earlier authors, this balance had been struck through the contrast between high-spirited youthful adventures and the brutal realities of poverty, illness, and failure. Some of those outlines are visible in *Tarr*, principally by way of Kreisler. But Lewis's text devoted far more attention to the relationship between the two elements, as the novel used the comic to consider the most serious of issues. The titles of two sections – 'A Jest Too Deep for Laughter' and 'A Megrim of Humour' – signal this directly. In the epilogue to the initial, serial publication, Lewis was careful to quash any suggestion that Tarr was a veiled version of himself, but was happy to confirm that 'I associate myself with all he says on the subject of humour. In fact, I put him up to it.'[3]

Tarr is a complex, prickly text, and it emerged from an unusually convoluted process of composition and publication. In this respect, designating it simply as Lewis's 'first novel' does not really do the book justice. In one form or another, *Tarr*, or something like it, accompanied Lewis from the first chapter in his writing life until almost the last. He began to produce the first drafts of the story from which the novel developed as early as 1907 or 1908. The completed first version initially ran as a serial in *The Egoist* from April 1916 until November 1917. It then appeared in two almost simultaneous but distinctive British and American editions in 1918, by The Egoist Press and Alfred Knopf respectively. In 1928, a further British edition was published by Chatto and Windus, heavily revised by Lewis himself, and this formed the basis of a third edition, published by Methuen in 1951.[4] *Tarr*'s publication in *The Egoist* embedded the text in one of the central publishing networks of avant-garde modernism, encouraging comparisons with Joyce's *A Portrait of the Artist as a Young Man* (1916). The number for April 1916, in which the first instalment of the novel appeared, also provides a revealing glimpse into the text's earliest contexts. On the preceding page, Richard Aldington's short piece 'The Perfect Book' sang the praises of unpopularity: 'There could be no greater distinction for an author than to produce a book that everybody disliked.'[5] The article that followed *Tarr* was entitled 'Second-Rate Supermen', and was directed at the supposed confluence of Nietzschean philosophy and Prussian militarism.[6] It attacked the idea that aggression and military domination increased individual or national power, as 'to attain to lasting power individuals and nations must be able to think better, feel more', sentiments echoed in the novel.[7] Finally, at this point the title of the magazine still carried a reminder of *The Egoist*'s former incarnation as Dora Marsden's *The New Freewoman*. This radically modern figure rejected existing templates for womanhood – conservative and feminist alike – in order to pursue her own path with analytical energy. Anastasya springs immediately to mind. *The Egoist* also provided a ready-made reviewing culture when *Tarr* appeared as a book. T. S. Eliot's influential review appeared there in September 1918, closing with a memorable description of

Lewis's combination of 'the thought of the modern and the energy of the cave-man'.[8]

Tarr's appearance in the Phoenix Library series in 1928 put Lewis in very different company. The series, launched in that year, aimed for a selection of contemporary 'classics', attractively bound and moderately priced.[9] Tarr brought together two conspicuous themes within that remit. On one hand, it was a saleable, satirical comedy, which was published simultaneously with reprints of T. F. Cowper-Powys's Mr Weston's Good Wine and Aldous Huxley's Crome Yellow. But Tarr also contributed to the Phoenix Library's interest in art writing. Tarr appeared alongside Roger Fry's Vision and Design, and Clive Bell's Art. Chatto and Windus's inclusion of Tarr was, therefore, a marker of its status, and of the transition the novel had made – along with modernist writing more generally – into the book-buying mainstream. But it was also a reminder of the considerable tensions between authors of that generation, not least between Lewis and the Bloomsbury contingent so dominant in the non-fiction list. The coda to Tarr's visibility in the Phoenix Library is the largely neglected 1951 edition. If the years from 1916 to 1928 saw the rise and dominance of modernism, and the acknowledgement of Lewis's role in this process, the 1930s and early 1940s were a rather different story. It was only well after the war that Alan White's respect for Lewis led to Methuen reprinting Tarr, publishing The Human Age trilogy, and commissioning significant critical studies of Lewis by Geoffrey Grigson and Hugh Kenner.[10] The latter in particular confirmed Lewis's place in a second wave of modernist canon-building, which was still underway at the time of his death.

The first question a reader should ask, then, is: which version of Tarr am I reading? If you have a modern British paperback, the likelihood is that it will be the 1928 Chatto and Windus text.[11] However, the Black Sparrow edition, edited by Paul O'Keeffe and first published in 1990, is of the 1918 Knopf version. The differences between these editions are substantial, certainly too substantial to outline here. However, O'Keeffe's edition includes a comprehensive list of textual variants, and other more recent resources exist for the interested reader.[12] One of the most apparent differences is the use of what Lewis called 'those parallel lines' (P/L p. 107) – rendered as an equals sign (=) – as a mark of punctuation.[13] There has been some debate about the effect created by this convention, and about its origin. However, it was used in the correspondence between Lewis and Pound, where it appears routinely between 1915 and 1917, petering out by the early 1920s.[14] The presence of these disruptive little marks in the typescript and the Knopf version calls to mind an instruction Lewis issued to Pound in December 1915.

Tarr should be read out, he stated, 'in an incredulous and argumentative voice, full of mat [sic] harsh emphasis' (*P/L* p. 17). This tone suits not only the pugnacious character of Tarr, but the character of the book more generally. It stands – as the 'parallel lines' do – between the conventional structures to which the text adheres and its more unfamiliar, provocative, experimental qualities. This tension informs the novel all the way through, at the level of story, genre, and style. It is the latter that presents the most conspicuous challenge to the reader.

Later in his career, Lewis made several significant statements about *Tarr*, in which the style of the book was placed in context. In 1953, he presented the following account of his prose technique to Hugh Kenner:

> In *Tarr* . . . I was an extremist. In editing *Blast* I regarded the contributions of Ezra as compromisingly passéiste, and wished I could find two or three literary extremists. In writing *Tarr* I wanted at the same time for it to be a novel, and to do a piece of writing worthy of the hand of an abstractist innovator (which was an impossible combination). Anyhow it was my object to eliminate anything less essential than a noun or a verb. Prepositions, pronouns, articles – the small fry – as far as might be, I would abolish. Of course I was unable to do this, but for the purposes of the *novel*, I produced a somewhat jagged prose. (*L* pp. 552–3)

Here *Tarr* was presented as a failed experiment, the inevitably awkward marriage of novelistic convention with radically stripped-down, 'abstractist' innovation. In a different account, published in *Rude Assignment* (1950), Lewis connected the writing of the novel with his move away from visual abstraction:

> The writing of 'Tarr' was approached with austerity. I clipped the text to the bone of all fleshly verbiage. Rhetoric was under an interdict. Even so, it soon became obvious that in order to show the reader character in action, with its attendant passion, there was no way of reducing your text to anything more skeletal than that produced by an otherwise normal statement, even if abnormally harsh and abrupt.
>
>   In the course of the writing, again, I grew more interested with every page in the life of my characters . . .
>
>   So my great interest in this first novel – essentially so different a type of expression from more or less abstract compositions in pure form and colour – so humanist and remote from implications of the machine, turned me into other paths: one form of expression must affect the other if they co-exist within the confines of one brain. (*RA* p. 139)

Both these statements linked Lewis's literary and artistic selves, a connection echoed in the novel's own engagement with the lives of artists. But what was the 'abnormally harsh and abrupt', or the 'somewhat jagged' prose of the 1918 *Tarr*? How did it operate in relation to 'the life of [Lewis's] characters'? And how might a reader approach it?

The most striking and consistent feature of the narration is its interest in close observation. *Tarr* is as attentive to the minute calibrations of social situations, to psychological and physiological nuance, as a novel by Henry James. However, Lewis's technique deliberately deformed its realist inheritance. Norman Sherry borrowed from Alain Robbe-Grillet to pinpoint the effect: 'Nothing is more fantastic, ultimately, than precision.'[15] Some of Lewis's most distinctive writing possesses exactly this estranging, 'fantastic' quality, due to excessive descriptive precision, combined with curt syntax and strikingly original figurative language. Part 1, Chapter 4, is a good example. It is a blow-by-blow account of Tarr's abortive break-up with Bertha. Tarr has decided beforehand how the affair is to be handled. He has been reading Schopenhauer, and intends to adopt the recommended perspective of the male artist-observer – 'indifferent' and detached. Needless to say, things do not go according to plan. The passage below outlines what happens when Bertha suddenly realises that this might not be one of their routine cooling-offs, but a more definitive separation:

> She disengaged her arms wildly and threw them round his neck, tears becoming torrential. Underneath the poor comedian that played such antics with such phlegmatic and exasperating persistence, this distressed being thrust up its trembling mask, like a drowning rat. Its finer head pierced her blunter wedge.
> 'Oh! dis, Sorbet! Est-ce que tu m'aimes? M'aimes-tu? Dis!'
> 'Yes, you know. Don't cry.'
> A wail, like the buzzing on a comb covered with paper followed.
> 'Oh, dis; m'aimes-tu? Dis que tu m'aimes!'
> A blurting, hurrying personality rushed right up into his face. It was like the sightless clammy charging of a bat. More eloquent regions had ambushed him. Humbug had mysteriously departed. It was a blast of knife-like air in the middle of their hot-house. = He stared at her face groping up as though it scented mammals in his face. It pushed to right and then to left and rocked itself. = Intelligent and aware, it lost this intensity.
> A complicated image developed in his mind as he stood with her. He was remembering Schopenhauer. (*T1* p. 58)

Instead of the extenuations of James, the sentences are short. A couple of Lewis's 'parallel lines' break up the flow still further, suggesting a distinction between the phrase that begins 'He stared at her face' and the sentences on either side of it. Using her frequent corruption of his name, 'Sorbet', Bertha begs Tarr to tell her that he loves her, and he supplies a brief and unconvincing reply. In other words, the verbal communication is minimal and clichéd. But the narration is the opposite.

Far from being 'clipped to the bone', the language is both compressed and elaborate. Metaphors ricochet around, juxtaposing effects and implications. Is the bat-like 'sightless clammy charging' an element of Tarr's own personality, that has rushed 'right up into his face'? If so, does this deliberately mirror the 'drowning rat' of Bertha's? Or is the blurting personality hers too, since we know that their faces are close to one another's? Tarr's reading of Schopenhauer has led him to expect Bertha to be emotional, but, as the emotion is genuine, its power catches him off-guard. Similarly, while 'bat' and the 'rat' could be dismissive or debasing images, that inference does not seem to stick. The bat emerges from somewhere 'eloquent', displacing the 'humbug' of their mutual pretence with a 'blast' of 'knife-like air'. Even the distressed rat-like self has a sort of penetrating delicacy, as it pushes its 'finer head' through 'her blunter wedge'. Bertha's 'face' feels for something in his, with an action that might be predatory – something vampiric scenting its prey – or might simply be seeking comfort. Either way, the fact that 'it' appears semi-autonomous, more animal than human, is viewed as a sign of 'intensity', it has something of the 'wild body' about it (of which more later). Tarr's ensuing reflection on the 'complicated image' he has encountered via Schopenhauer exists in a curious relation to the similarly 'complicated image' that the narration has just provided. On one level, this image is a legitimate reflection on what has just taken place. But on another, Tarr's 'intelligent and aware' espousal of this theory – with its distinction between the female self and the behaviour of the rational male artist – is another form of potential humbug, and his mask of 'indifference' is revealed as a failure. In fact, at the end of the chapter, the situation between the two of them remains unchanged.

This sort of narrative complexity not only makes *Tarr* resistant to summary, it has generated conflicting critical opinions – sometimes within the same text.[16] For instance, it is obvious that early twentieth-century sexual politics play a key role in *Tarr*, and the meeting between Tarr and Bertha described above could be read as evidence of conventional modernist misogyny. The book's male characters frequently chew over the nature of 'women', and women are presented as sexualised objects of male desire. One of them (Bertha) is raped by Kreisler, another (Anastasya) offers herself up naked to Tarr. However, the narrator's descriptions of Kreisler's attitude to women are unambiguously critical. Kreisler's inability to perceive women as persons, rather than as a 'vast dumping-ground for sorrow and affliction – a world-dimensioned Pawn-shop' (*T1* p. 101) is compared to the more obvious violence of 'the drunken navvy on Saturday night, who comes home bellicosely towards his wife, blows raining gladly at the mere sight of her' (*T1* p.

102). Kreisler's rape of Bertha – an event torn into a space of the novel so roughly that we barely realise it has taken place at first – is presented in a series of fractured flashbacks, as she wrestles with its shattering physical and psychological effects. Similarly, while Bertha is characterised by tears and Anastasya by laughter, both are presented as intelligent and analytical. The difference is that Bertha, like the heroine of an earlier era of fiction, is preoccupied with social and romantic manoeuvring. In contrast, Anastasya rejects both confining women's fashions, and confining visions of Woman more generally. She rapidly sizes up the sexually opportunistic Kreisler, and befriends the equally pragmatic 'Impresario' (*T1* p. 150) Soltyk. She is Tarr's equal in both intellect and appetite, whether he realises it or not. Their extraordinary debate on the nature of art and life in the second chapter of 'Swagger Sex' produces some of the signal aesthetic statements in the novel – in particular Tarr's statement on the '*deadness*' (*T1* p. 299) and pure exteriority of art – before it collapses into drunken bad temper. Her appearance, naked, in the stark moonlight of Tarr's studio later that evening has been effected by her theft of his key, and plays upon his earlier assertion that '"naked men and women are the worst art of all"' (*T1* p. 299). In other words, the book does not simply present misogyny – both the text, and its characters, actively confront it.

This confrontational technique is equally visible in *Tarr*'s presentation of specific national identities. Lewis's 'Epilogue' to the serial publication, dated 1915, was quick to correct any assumption that *Tarr* had been written as a response to Germany's status as an enemy aggressor. Lewis did, however, align Kreisler with a faulty Nietzschean consciousness, as 'Germany's large leaden brain booms away in the centre of Europe.'[17] Throughout the novel, national identity is pushed centre stage, and placed under a forensic spotlight. The book opened with a description of the 'Knackfus Quarter' as a theatre of 'sluggish commonsense Germans' and 'Italian models', with 'Its rent . . . half paid by America' (*T1* p. 21). However, the earliest conversation is an awkward interview between two Englishmen who are conspicuous by their difference from one another: Tarr and Alan Hobson. Hobson is a satirical representative of Bloomsbury. He is Cambridge-educated, long-haired, louche, and affected. In a section removed from the 1928 edition, it was repeatedly pointed out that Hobson's family position has been derived from colonial wealth: 'His father was a wealthy merchant at the Cape' (*T1* p. 22), he is 'the Cape Cantabian' (*T1* p. 25). In one sense this emphasises the pose that Hobson is keeping up. In another, it draws attention to the novel's interest in a cosmopolitan complexity that competes with the simpler rubrics of 'English', 'Italian', 'German', or 'American'. As we have seen, several central characters have hyphenated national identities. Not only this, but almost every character participates in this complexity at the level of language, using French as an awkward lingua franca. 'He was a droll bird', Hobson muses, as Tarr launches himself into a monologue during their encounter. 'He wondered, as he watched him, if he was a *sound* bird, or homme-oiseau' (*T1* p. 27).

How should a reader approach *Tarr*'s presentation of this particular brand of identity politics? The options are numerous. In terms of Lewis's emerging literary career, his interest in national types links the novel not only to *BLAST*, but to earlier pieces such as 'The "Pole"', and 'Our Wild Body'.[18] The latter was a short article published in *The New Age* in May 1910, which used French, German, and Italian attitudes to critique 'a vast Anglo-Saxon conspiracy against the body', placing the physical self on the front line of both nature and culture.[19] There is also the question of Lewis's knowledge of, and interest in, Russian and German literary and philosophical traditions. Several notable early reviews of *Tarr*, by Rebecca West and Ezra Pound, as well as T. S. Eliot, noted Lewis's debt to Dostoyevsky. Alan Munton has argued for the novel's close connection with two Dostoyevsky novels in particular, the latter of which is *The Double*.[20] This theme of hostile doubles also connects *Tarr* to the work of German author E. T. A. Hoffmann, one of whose heroes is a suffering, alienated Romantic musician called 'Kreisler'. Towards the close of the book, when Tarr laughingly describes Kreisler's actions as 'Kreisleriana' (*T1* p. 312) he is ironically referring to Hoffman's collection of short texts of the same name, or perhaps to the Schumann piece based on them. The novel itself, in other words, enacts a sort of self-conscious cultural hybridity even as it meditates on the perceived nature of national difference. But it is important that this hybridity is 'jagged' and dissonant on every level, maintaining sharp outlines that enhance confrontation and contrast.

'Our Wild Body', with its meditation on curious English physiological traditions, also shares *Tarr*'s critique of various aspects of 'Englishness'. An important example of this, which connects directly with the novel's own use of the comic, is Tarr's lecture to Butcher on 'Humour' in Part 1, Chapter 2:

> 'The University of Humour that prevails everywhere in England as the national institution for developing youth, provides you with nothing but a first rate means of evading reality. The whole of English training – the great fundamental spirit of the country – is a system of *deadening feeling*, a prescription for Stoicism . . . It would be better *to face* our imagination and our nerves without this soporific.' (*T1* p. 42)

Evidently, as Pulley argued in 'Second-Rate Supermen', Tarr believes that one should be brave enough not only to 'think better' but also to 'feel more' and, as we know, Lewis stated that Tarr's ideas on the uses of humour closely approximated his own. The composition of and revisions to the *Tarr* narrative also bracket two further statements on the subject: the 'BLAST' and 'BLESS' manifestos in the first number of *BLAST* (1914), and Lewis's essay 'The Meaning of the Wild Body' (1927). The conversation above seems to resemble *BLAST*'s 'BLAST' manifesto most closely. 'Humour' and 'sport' – in the sense of 'playfulness' rather than football or cricket – had been blasted. Humour was denounced as 'Quack ENGLISH drug for stupidity and sleepiness. / Arch enemy of REAL' (*B1* p. 17). The 'FIXED GRIN / Death's Head symbol of Anti-Life' was equally damned in 'BLAST SPORT', which concludes: 'CURSE those who will hang over this / Manifesto with SILLY CANINES exposed' (*B1* p. 17). But the 'BLESS' portion of the manifesto is more difficult to align with Tarr's theories. Not only does it address the positive literary dimension of English humour, a subject of little interest to artist Tarr, but it praises a very specific aspect of laughter that Tarr criticises: '"Humour paralyses the sense for Reality and wraps people in a phlegmatic and hysterical dream-world"' (*T1* p. 43), he states. 'BLESS this hysterical WALL built round / the EGO. / BLESS the solitude of LAUGHTER' (*B1* p. 26), asserts the manifesto. So, while the two texts can certainly be considered in relation to one another, it is more difficult to view the novel as an exemplification of the manifestos, or vice versa.

'The Meaning of the Wild Body' presents several points of entry to *Tarr*. Most significantly though, it set out a theory of *'the absurd'* (*CWB* p. 157) that echoed the novel's exploration of the comedy in tragedy, and vice versa. The essay assumed 'the dichotomy of mind and body' as Lewis sought to establish the body as an essential territory of absurdity: 'There is nothing that is animal (and we as bodies are animals) that is not absurd' (*CWB* p. 157). Lewis argued that this absurdity can be recognised in others, but can be grasped only in flashes when it comes to oneself. Laughter is a product of such momentary self-awareness. He also noted that different national and cultural identities are an interesting index of the relationship between detachment from, and awareness of, absurdity: 'It is easy for us to see, if we are french [sic], that the German is "absurd," or if german [sic], that the French is "ludicrous," for we are *outside* in that case' (*CWB* p. 158). *Tarr*, with its ironic exploration of national typologies, could be viewed as a more thorough test of this theory.[21] The novel also tests the possibility of being 'outside' in one's own case, posing questions about the strategies and limits of objectivity. Lewis quoted a passage from William James's *Some Problems of Philosophy* (1911), in which James had imagined a subject reflecting on their 'queer bodily shape' and their 'fantastic character', letting their imagination 'steal over the detail as much as over the general fact of being' (*CWB* p. 157). James's assertion of the importance of 'detail' as a means of defamiliarising the self and encountering the actual, 'fantastic' nature of being – bodily and otherwise – seems highly reminiscent of Lewis's style in *Tarr*. The highest concentration of these specific absurd effects comes during the final chapter of the 'Bourgeois-Bohemians' section, when Kreisler disrupts the Bonnington Club dance.[22] With the exception of Tarr himself, this event assembles many of the major players in the novel: Kreisler, Bertha, Anastasya, Soltyk, and assorted members of the Lipmann circle. It has been preceded by a very pragmatic kiss between Bertha and Kreisler, and by the impoverished Kreisler's failure to raise the money required to buy his evening suit back from a pawn shop. The narration in this section is detached, remaining resolutely external until it gains access to Kreisler's consciousness towards the end of the chapter. The first part of this narrative is genuinely funny. First Kreisler bamboozles one English matron with a polyglot monologue delivered 'in a dialect calculated to bewilder the most acute philologist' (*T1* p. 147). Disconcerted and confused, she palms him off onto another woman, with whom he waltzes around the room with 'ever-increasing velocity' (*T1* p. 148) until:

> at the third round, at breakneck speed, [he] spun with her in the direction of the front door. = The impetus was so great that she, although seeing her peril, could not act sufficiently as a brake ... Another moment and they would have been in the street, amongst the traffic, a disturbing meteor, whizzing out of sight, had not they met the alarmed resistance of a considerable English family entering the front door as Kreisler bore down upon it. = It was one of those large featureless human groups built up by a frigid and melancholy pair, uncannily fecund, during interminable years of boredom. (*T1* p. 148)

This scene combines the kind of physical comedy familiar from pantomime (and, later, silent film) with both excessive, fantastic metaphor and deadpan verbal humour. The dynamic image of Kreisler and Mrs. Bevelage hurtling towards the exit is made even more amusing by its juxtaposition with the cruelly accurate description of the 'considerable English family'. At this point, it looks as if the whole chapter might be the most palatable sort of comic absurdity – but this is not to be the case. Kreisler is a renegade faction within the bourgeois-bohemian world, certainly, but he is still caught up in his own confected romantic drama, his 'solemn laughter-in-action' operating in tandem with 'the pleasant veil of his hysteria' (*T1* p. 151). This drama revolves around Anastasya, with whom he is determined to make contact. He does so by pouncing on her and her bewildered dance partner, before departing with significant glances in her direction. Anastasya is left:

looking after Kreisler curiously. She would have liked him to stop. He had done something strange and was as suddenly going away. That was unsatisfactory. = They looked at each other blankly. He showed no sign of stopping: she just stared. = Suddenly it was comic. She burst out laughing. = But they had clashed (like people in the dance) and were both disappearing from one another again, the shock hardly over. The *contact* had been brought about. (*T1* p. 153)

Anastasya's laugh is a moment of recognition, a flash or 'shock' of bodily contact. But Kreisler hears only mockery. 'His vanity was wounded terribly' (*T1* p. 157), the narrator informs us: 'In *laughing* at him she had puffed out and transformed in an extraordinary way, also, his infatuation' (*T1* p. 157). The dance suddenly seems '*infernal*' (*T1* p. 157) to him, and Kreisler comes to the conclusion that Anastasya 'was in fact evidently *the Devil*' (*T1* p. 157). He repeats to himself '"I *shall possess* her!" . . . seeing himself in the rôle of the old Berserker warrior, ravening and irresistible' (*T1* p. 157). Despite his struggles, Kreisler's 'lonely and comic Ego' (*T1* p. 121) is oppressed by absurdity, hearing only humiliating laughter around him and suffering self-disgust. It is this that stirs up a corresponding desire to regain the upper hand by sexual possession and violent conquest, precipitating many of the ridiculous yet terrible events of the 'Holocausts' section – Bertha's rape, Kreisler's duel with Soltyk, the farce of Soltyk's death, and Kreisler's subsequent suicide.

This Bonnington Club scene, with its demonic overtones, pantomimic physical comedy, and verbal excess, calls to mind a final template for the novel. It is one that T. S. Eliot noted in a 1923 appraisal of *Tarr*, in which he described the novel as possessing 'an element of that British humor, so serious and so savage, to which Baudelaire once devoted a short study'.[23] The 'short study' to which Eliot referred is the complex 1855 essay on laughter, 'L'Essence du Rire'. In this piece, Baudelaire used a vocabulary very similar to that of the Bonnington Club scene. He argued that laughter was inherently 'satanic' – based upon feelings of superiority and pride towards others that would, if taken far enough, verge on insanity. Only a 'philosopher', someone trained to watch 'as a disinterested spectator, the phenomenon of his ego', could truly laugh at their own fallen condition.[24] However, art rooted in the farcical, excessive, or the grotesque – what Baudelaire christened 'the absolute comic' – could evoke a similar sort of response in the rest of us. Such laughter is more uncontrolled and primitive, infinitely closer to the dangerous moment of self-revelation Lewis delineated in 1927. Baudelaire detected one strain of the 'absolute comic' in English pantomime traditions (the 'British humor' Eliot saw in *Tarr*), but he also considered that it had been perfected by none other than E. T. A. Hoffmann. Therefore, Eliot's deduction not only drew attention to the novel's place within a specifically 'British' tradition of serious and savage comedy. It also suggested a connection between *Tarr* and this foundational writer on the position of the artist in modernity, and on the rise of the bourgeois Paris in which the novel is set. But if we as readers glimpse the 'absolute comic' in *Tarr*, while as a character within the novel Kreisler cannot, what about the other artist figure, Tarr himself? Clearly, Tarr aspires to be a sort of 'disinterested' philosopher–artist, and he is able to edge closer to the sort of objectivity – or momentary exteriority – Baudelaire describes. But this move is not made without significant internal conflict. The principal example is not an aesthetic, but an ethical one, which comes when Tarr decides to embrace the absurdity of their collective situation by marrying Bertha to legitimise the child she is carrying (she presumes) as a result of Kreisler's assault. Lewis portrays this conflict in characteristic terms, pointing the reader once again towards the complexities and utilities of laughter:

> One after the other the protesting masses of good sense rolled up.
> He picked his way out of the avenue with a reasoning gesticulation of the body; a chicken-like motion of sensible fastidious defence in front of bouffonic violence. At the gate he exploded in harsh laughter, looking bravely and raillingly out into the world through his glasses . . .
> The indignant plebs of his glorious organism rioted around his mind.
> 'Ah-ha! Ah-ha! Sacré farceur, where are you leading us?' (*T1* p. 312)

Where indeed, we might ask, especially as only two short chapters of the book remain. Suffice it to say that Lewis managed to conform to, but also completely to undermine, the conventions of the happy ending. In fact, the end of the novel even defies the notion of an ending, as it introduces two entirely new characters, suggesting a pattern that will go on repeating itself.

As such, one of the extraordinary qualities of *Tarr* is its capacity, as a piece of art, to elucidate a theory of the dissimilarity of art to life in a novel that convincingly explores both the success, but also the failure, of what Baudelaire called 'the painter of modern life'.[25] In doing so, Lewis refused a presentation of Tarr as a kind of modernist superman, able to transcend the foibles of lesser mortals simply through a code of aesthetic discipline, egotism, and 'disinterest'. 'Is the artist-intellectual truly independent of the crowd-mind he satirizes, or is his humorous attitude actually an indication of his inescapable conformity?' enquires Michael North, of Lewis's self-portrait of the early 1920s *Mr Wyndham Lewis as a Tyro*.[26] We might ask instead whether humour, as it appears in *Tarr*, reveals this as a false opposition. The 'harsh laughter' of the character, and of the novel, illuminates both the participation of modern 'artist-intellectuals' in the conditions they share with others – including their cultural and aesthetic inheritances, and lived experiences as bodies – and the necessity of their attempt to view those conditions differently.

Notes

1. Henry Mürger is mentioned directly, but other tales of Bohemian life are equally relevant. George du Maurier's *Trilby* (1894) is a famous example. See Lisa Tickner's 'Bohemianism and the Cultural Field: *Trilby* and *Tarr*', *Art History*, 34.5, November 2011, pp. 978–1011.
2. The phrase is Seamus Deane's, from the second chapter of *Strange Country: Modernity and Nationhood in Irish Writing from 1790* (Oxford: Oxford University Press, 1997), pp. 49–99.
3. 'He [Tarr] is one of my showmen; though, naturally, he has a private and independent life of his own, for which I should be very sorry to be held responsible.' Lewis, 'Epilogue', *The Egoist*, 4.10, November 1917, pp. 152–3. O'Keeffe reprints this statement in *T1* p. 360.
4. O'Keeffe's 'Afterword' provides a detailed account (see *T1* pp. 361–85). See also *T2*.
5. R. A. [Richard Aldington], 'The Perfect Book', *The Egoist*, 4.3, 1 April 1916, p. 53.
6. Honor M. Pulley, 'Second-Rate Supermen', *The Egoist*, 4.3, 1 April 1916, p. 63.
7. Ibid., p. 63.
8. T. S. Eliot, '*Tarr*', *The Egoist*, 5.8, September 1918, pp. 105–6.
9. Andrew Nash, 'Sifting out "Rubbish" in the Literature of the Twenties and Thirties: Chatto & Windus and The Phoenix Library', in John Spiers (ed.), *The Culture of the Publisher's Series: Volume 1* (London: Palgrave Macmillan, 2011), pp. 188–201.
10. Maureen Duffy, *A Thousand Capricious Chances: A History of the Methuen List, 1889–1989* (London: Methuen, 1989), p. 135. Alan White, at that point the managing director of Methuen, had become very interested in Lewis in his youth.
11. This has been reprinted several times, most recently in *T2*.
12. In addition to the O'Keeffe and Klein volumes, other ways of reading *Tarr* are available for the curious reader. Stephen Sturgeon's doctoral thesis 'Wyndham Lewis's *Tarr*: A Critical Edition' (Boston University Graduate School of Arts and Sciences, 2007) is the most thorough comparative analysis of all three versions. The University of Victoria's online *Modernist Versions Project* has also explored versions of the novel.
13. Lewis to Pound, 12 October 1917: 'They occurred all through the book in the typewritten MSS. Could not they be disinterred, & used by Knopf?' (*P/L* p. 107).
14. Pound's last use of 'parallel lines' as a mark of punctuation seems to occur around April 1922 (see *P/L* p. 130).
15. Alain Robbe-Grillet, quoted in Vincent Sherry, *Ezra Pound, Wyndham*

Lewis, and Radical Modernism (New York: Oxford University Press, 1993), p. 106.

16. For instance, Bonnie Kime Scott's 1989 article 'Jellyfish and Treacle: Lewis, Joyce, Gender and Modernism' argued for *Tarr* as an expression of Lewis's misogyny, in contrast to his fellow modernist Joyce. But Kime Scott also conceded that the novel made a powerful point about 'the victimization of woman as art object', and featured 'substantial dialogs' on art between Tarr and Anastasya, an element lacking from Joyce's work after *Stephen Hero*. See Kime Scott, 'Jellyfish and Treacle: Lewis, Joyce, Gender and Modernism', in Morris Beja and Shari Benstock (eds), *Coping with Joyce* (Columbus: Ohio State University Press, 1989), pp. 168–79: p. 173 and p. 175. For a trenchant response to Kime Scott, see Kelly Anspaugh, 'Blasting the Bombardier: Another Look at Lewis, Joyce, and Woolf', *Twentieth Century Literature*, 40.3, Autumn 1994, pp. 365–78.

17. Lewis, 'Epilogue', p. 152.

18. 'The "Pole"', first published in *The English Review* in May 1909, deliberately apostrophised the questionable national identity of its protagonist.

19. Wyndham Lewis, 'Our Wild Body', *The New Age*, 7.1, 5 May 1910, pp. 8–10: p. 8.

20. The first is *A Raw Youth*. O'Keeffe draws on Alan Munton's doctoral thesis here – see Alan Munton, 'Wyndham Lewis: The Relation between the Theory and the Fiction, from his Earliest Writings to 1941' (University of Cambridge, 1976) – adding Timothy Materer's observations on other parallels between *Tarr* and *The Double* (*T1* p. 381). O'Keeffe presents an additional argument for the figure of Soltyk as Kreisler's 'double' (*T1* pp. 381–2).

21. Critics have been particularly drawn to Lewis's description of body as '*thing*', which marks out his subversive engagement with Henri Bergson's 1900 essay on laughter, 'Le Rire' (*CWB* p. 158). For a recent discussion, with reference to Lewis as a satirist, see Jonathan Greenberg, *Modernism, Satire and the Novel* (Cambridge: Cambridge University Press, 2011), pp. 5–7.

22. As Jessica Burstein has noted, the dance is another of the 'set pieces' of the nineteenth-century novel, which is 'rescripted' by Lewis and placed at the dead centre of *Tarr*. See Jessica Burstein, *Cold Modernism: Literature, Fashion, Art* (University Park, PA: Pennsylvania State University Press, 2012), pp. 44–5.

23. See Ronald Schuchard, *Eliot's Dark Angel: Intersections of Life and Art* (New York: Oxford University Press, 1999), p. 90. Schuchard is quoting from Eliot's 'Contemporary English Prose', which appeared in *Vanity Fair* in July 1923.

24. Charles Baudelaire, 'On the Essence of Laughter, and generally of the Comic in the Plastic Arts' (1855), in *Baudelaire: Selected Writings on Art and Artists*, trans. P. E. Charvet [1972] (London: Penguin, 1992), pp. 140–61: p. 148.

25. Baudelaire, 'The Painter of Modern Life' (1863), in ibid., pp. 390–436.

26. Michael North, *Machine-Age Comedy* (New York: Oxford University Press, 2009), p. 122.

Chapter 4

Lewis and War

Ann-Marie Einhaus

War is central to Wyndham Lewis's artistic and personal development, whether in the form of rhetorical violence or actual engagement with the two conflicts he witnessed as an adult, one as a combatant and one as an exile in North America. In the introduction to his 1937 autobiography *Blasting and Bombardiering*, Lewis boldly declared:

> One only writes 'biographies' about things that are past and over. The present period is by no means over. One couldn't sit down and write a biography about *that*. But the War and the 'post-war' are over long ago. They can be written about with detachment, as things past and done with. (*BB* p. 2)

Lewis's inter- and post-war career gives the lie to this assertion and bears ample witness to the fact that the First World War was anything but 'past and done with' for him. Having addressed the First World War in a number of short stories and in the 'war number' of *BLAST* in 1915, Lewis continued to engage with the legacy of war in his fiction, his autobiographical writing, and most prominently and controversially in his political analyses of the 1920s, 1930s, and 1940s. This chapter explores the bearing that Lewis's experience of war and his conception of the artist's role in society had on his political trajectory from 1914 to the early 1940s. Lewis's war experience and subsequent engagement with the First World War can be traced from his wartime stories and letters to a range of his later fiction, including *The Childermass* (1928) and *The Revenge for Love* (1937), but also political and autobiographical writings, such as *The Art of Being Ruled* (1926), his controversial volume *Hitler* (1931), *Left Wings over Europe: Or, How to Make a War about Nothing* (1936), the war memoir *Blasting and Bombardiering* (1937), *Count Your Dead: They Are Alive! Or, A New War in the Making* (1937), his recanting of much of his earlier appraisal of Nazism in *The Hitler Cult* (1939), the provocatively titled *The Jews: Are They Human?* (1939), and his reconsideration of Western democracy in *Anglosaxony:*

A League that Works (1941). Given the number of works directly addressing war, whether the war that Lewis experienced as a combatant and war artist, the potential war he saw looming in the middle distance during the late 1920s and 1930s, or the Second World War as it actually occurred, it seems more accurate to characterise Lewis's take on the First World War as a war that 'has made possible, nay, inevitable, all the odd things we see going on to-day' (*BB* p. 18) – in short, as a fundamental event that shaped the first half of the twentieth century and formed an 'integral part of Lewis's development as a writer', as an artist, and as a political commentator, prompting the production of his 'major critical books on culture, politics and philosophy in the 1920s' and beyond.[1]

Lewis's writing is characterised by a conflicted, continually evolving approach to war and violence. His combative rhetoric and the at times deliberate brutality of his prose style clash with a deep-rooted desire to avoid the renewal of actual war, prompted by Lewis's first-hand knowledge of war's physical, psychological, and economic impact. Lewis's *oeuvre* shows him to be a combative personality whose field of battle is art, but for whom real war proved to be little to his taste, declaring war a 'disappointing imitation' (*BB* p. 63) of art. The violence Lewis embraced is the 'inner violence' of polemic and satire, not the physical violence of war.[2] In 1914, Lewis had achieved his first significant success as the editor of *BLAST* and as the spokesman for Vorticism. Speaking retrospectively about the artistic scene before the war, Lewis later interpreted the lively rivalry between the various avant-garde groupings or movements, as well as their joint assault on the artistic establishment, as a world in which 'all the artists and men of letters had gone into action' over artistic manifestos and ideas in 'one big bloodless brawl, prior to the Great Bloodletting' (*BB* p. 35). Lewis dismissed Marinetti's violent Futurist aesthetic as a hollow fetishisation of progress and as a trailblazer for fascism. Yet his own Vorticist rhetoric in *BLAST* and the disturbing portrayal of the German artist Kreisler in his novel *Tarr* (whose first version Lewis wrote between 1909 and 1915) also seem to foreshadow the coming conflict. In the early stages of the war, Lewis cultivated a 'full frontal, high-booted, and aggressive' military persona reflected in a uniformed full-length studio portrait photograph of Lewis taken in 1916.[3] Indeed, Lewis deplored in retrospect what he regarded as the 'depressing' way in which his pre-war art 'prophesied' the advent of war and '[held] the mirror up to politics without knowing it', concluding that, for him, 'war and art [had] been mixed up from the start', and hoping that '[writing] about war may be the best way to shake the accursed thing off' (*BB* p. 4).

One can trace a noticeable ambiguity in Lewis's response to war, in that it came to combine the appeal of martial life in the abstract with disdain for its futility in the concrete. Despite Lewis's assertions that he embraced military duties with moderate enthusiasm (*BB* p. 28), however, he did not enlist until March 1916, partly due to illness in the early stages of the war, and partly due to unsuccessful attempts to obtain a commission prior to enlistment. As a result, Lewis first trained as a regular gunner (or 'bombardier') at Dover, before being accepted for officer training in late 1916 and sent to Exeter, where he obtained the rank of Second Lieutenant at Christmas that year. In the meantime, Ford Madox Ford (then Hueffer) had already been posted to France where he succumbed to shell shock and nervous breakdown after a stint in the firing line, events of which Lewis heard through Ezra Pound (*P/L* p. 56).[4] Lewis's own front line service began in late May 1917, when he was posted to France, moved to the Belgian front, quickly experienced intense bombardment, and was hospitalised with trench fever, returning to the front in late July. For roughly three months between July and November 1917, at which point Lewis was granted compassionate leave to visit his seriously ill mother in England and subsequently returned to the front as a commissioned war artist rather than an artillery officer, he experienced further heavy bombardment, including direct hits on his gun position in his fortuitous absence, and emerged with a particular disgust for the 'mud cum blood-and-thunder' (*BB* p. 151) of Passchendaele. However, his wartime letters to friends and fellow artists for the most part reveal any dismay he felt at the time only through the medium of his habitual flippancy, and present even ghastly scenes with sardonic detachment, demonstrating a noticeable refusal 'to draw upon a readily available rhetoric of destruction' while allowing the reader to glimpse at what is 'buried beneath techniques of bathos, comedy, and dismissal'.[5] In an unusually candid letter to Pound written in August 1917, shortly after his reunion with the battery he had trained with in 1916, Lewis described his position with a little more urgency than usual:

> My dear Pound. I am back now with my old Battery. I have come to a tedious spot. It is really extremely bad. The parapet of one of our guns was smashed last night. We were shelled and gassed all night. I had my respirator on for two solid hours. There is only one bright side to the picture: a good concrete dugout. (*L* p. 90)

In contrast to this description, his account of the same position to Helen Saunders reads rather differently and has an air of studied nonchalance. Where Lewis's account to Pound limits itself to the disquieting facts, his

letter to Saunders is peppered with whimsical expressions and incongruous statements, observing that in 'the more or less illusory security of
the concrete dugout (shortly full, however, of three different kinds of
gas) it is not too unpleasant to listen to the absurd enemy smashing the
parapets of your guns just outside' and casually declaring good books
a sufficient antidote to the somewhat greater unpleasantness of mortal
danger through shell fire: 'It is in fact, my dear Miss S., I know you will
be interested to hear, a bad place. I admit to being rather glad myself. I
have got many good books. *Le Feu* is worth reading' (*L* p. 91).

Lewis's wartime short stories similarly often operate on the level
of detached, quasi-anthropological observation, utilising 'a distance
between the mind and the body which allowed him to reflect on the . . .
character of humanity at war'.[6] Some of Lewis's war stories – including
the first Cantleman fragments – were begun in 1915, prior to enlist-
ing, and it is in fact 'The French Poodle', one of the stories written and
first published before the beginning of his military training, that offers
the most empathy and least sense of detachment in comparison with
later stories – or, as Wood suggests, a sense of 'confusion and anxiety'
about the war rather than first-hand knowledge.[7] Arguably, this greater
sense of empathy can be read both as a result of such pre-service
anxiety and of Lewis's own ill health at the time, which seems to shine
through his description of the protagonist's sense of being 'arrested in
a vague but troublesome maze of discomfort and ill-health' (*UP* p. 54).
Fundamentally, Lewis provides his readers with an early interpretation
of shell shock in the literal sense, as protagonist Rob Cairns has survived being hurled in the air by a shell and is now coming to terms with
the after-effects of this misadventure. It is shell shock as imagined by a
non-combatant, related to us at a triple remove from Lewis the author
to credit his position as a bystander: his narrator himself has the story
from another man, not Cairns himself.[8] Shell shock as Lewis envisages it
centres on the loss of agency, on the fundamental and traumatic experience of losing control and understanding one's own fragility in the face
of death, and the convalescent Cairns is shown to be fixated on this
loss of control, unable to 'accustom himself to the idea of insecurity'
(*UP* p. 53). It is to a large extent a similar sense of losing control, both
in terms of realising one's mortality and of experiencing the loss of
individual political agency of the civilian-turned-volunteer soldier, that
later prompted Lewis's vocal opposition to the war. Geoff Gilbert has
suggested that Lewis's depiction of shell shock in 'The French Poodle'
has productive as well as destructive elements, in that his trauma has put
Cairns into the 'position of awareness and refusal' that in Lewis's view
also characterised the artist as observer.[9] However, Gilbert also rightly

points to the difficulty of transforming the soldier's subordinate position and lack of agency into a platform for productive critical reflection.[10] To Lewis after the war, critical reflection on his wartime experiences meant the adoption of a passionately anti-war stance, already encapsulated in 'The French Poodle' in Cairns's blunt pronouncement: 'It is bad for men to beat and kill each other' (*UP* p. 55).

'Cantleman's Spring-Mate' – begun in 1915 but extensively revised later, prior to publication in October 1917 – continues this trend, albeit in a far more cynical tone. The story betrays clear anxiety over the likely impact of the war on humanity, and responds by adopting a thoroughly misanthropist stance. The story's narrator contrasts the cruelty of animals who 'showed their fondness for their neighbour in an embarrassing way: that is they killed and ate them' (*UP* p. 78) with humankind, concluding that the only thing which distinguishes humans from other animals is their unfortunate capacity for self-awareness: 'human beings anywhere were the most ugly and offensive of the brutes because of the confusion caused by their consciousness' (*UP* p. 79). Cantleman's attempts to thwart nature by unrestrainedly following his 'natural' urges fail precisely because he underestimates how much he is a part of the animal kingdom, in which war constitutes not an aberration, but merely a parallel to the merciless natural environment that he observes in the English countryside. His consciousness only serves to trouble and ultimately deceive him as to his ability to rise above nature.[11] Such a pessimistic view of humanity's ability to transcend its fundamental animal nature also characterises much of Lewis's inter-war political writing, and contributed significantly to his embrace of (proto-)fascist ideas in *The Art of Being Ruled* and *Hitler*, despite the fact that, as Andrzej Gąsiorek has pointed out, Lewis was 'critical of nationalism and imperialism' and 'viewed nationalist rhetorics as politically retrogressive'.[12] It resurfaces in 1939 in *The Hitler Cult* when Lewis resignedly declares war to be the unfortunate but inevitable consequence of humans being at all times 'half animal', possessed of 'a sort of bogus "freewill"' (*HC* p. 178), and traces German warmongering and political developments back to 'the immense vogue of Darwin's theories' and their impact on 'European thought' in the form of social Darwinism (*HC* p. 179). Lewis's view of his fellow veterans in the inter-war period echoes his depiction of Cantleman, in that he felt they had deceived themselves into believing in their own free will and democratic rights when they had in fact allowed themselves to be stripped of both (*BB* p. 26).

In the inter-war period, Lewis showed all the familiar symptoms of the shared post-war disillusionment of veterans of his class and artistic occupation: he highlighted the incommunicability of his war experience and specifically of the blasted landscapes of the Western Front (*BB* p. 131); remarked on the 'callousness' (*BB* p. 185) of the civilian population towards those who had fought after the war; and stressed his anxiety at having effectively lost several years of work to military service. His political writings were, among other things, explicitly driven by the same sense of responsibility towards the dead and solidarity with some (if not all) fellow veterans that informed much of the post-war work of other veteran writers such as Siegfried Sassoon and Richard Aldington. Although these sentiments ring familiar from a variety of classic war texts, such as Sassoon's scathing poem 'On Passing the New Menin Gate' (1928) and Aldington's vitriolic attack on civilian callousness in *Death of a Hero* (1929), they are tempered in Lewis's case by his irreverent, sardonic sense of humour. Similarly, Lewis's political trajectory in the inter-war years is by no means unusual, and has much in common with that of substantially different artist veterans such as the nurse-volunteer and writer Vera Brittain. Lewis and Brittain alike emerged from the war as firm believers in its destructive effects and as opponents of the Treaty of Versailles; they were determined to prevent renewed conflict, although it is hardly surprising – given their disparate backgrounds – that they differed radically in their appraisal of the underlying causes of the war and their motivation for wanting to prevent another. Whereas Brittain was driven by a desire to memorialise the dead through her pacifist activities, seeking to prevent future wars by promoting greater international unity through the young League of Nations, Lewis came to feel strongly that the League of Nations and its internationalist outlook would in fact be to blame for the next war.[13] He condemned the League for what he saw as its unjustified interventionism, controlled by 'the "Great Powers" which won the war of 1914–18' in order to 'defend the "victory", or what is generally referred to as the *status quo* – that is the principle of *no change*' (*LWE* p. 32). The League of Nations doctrine of no change, Lewis asserted, was far from being the means of keeping peace; rather, it acted in his opinion as 'the sufficient *casus belli* in the present international crisis' (*LWE* p. 33).

Lewis's desire to avoid another war was, like Brittain's, based on his direct experience of the destructive effects of the First World War. But where Brittain focused on the loss of life, Lewis increasingly highlighted the economic destruction in the war's wake that affected those who survived. He linked the destruction of civilisation with economic collapse, as in the ongoing inter-war crisis, and predicted a second, much worse collapse after a second world war (*LWE* pp. 47–9). This does not mean, of course, that Lewis did not also refer to the inhumanity of war itself.

For him, the most heartfelt blow the First World War had occasioned was possibly the death of his mother from pneumonia in the immediate post-war epidemic, following closely upon his own illness. Even earlier, in his account of Cantleman's fictional journey from Edinburgh to London, Lewis had homed in on the figure of a 'mother, a burly woman, with a kind square face' (*BB* p. 73) taking leave of her naval reservist son as the most humane and touching encounter in the midst of a deeply cynical, offhand view of Britain under mobilisation. The death of his own mother – 'not', as Lewis pointed out, 'an old woman' – certainly appears to have significantly influenced his anti-war stance, and he notes that it gave him 'a peculiar feeling about the Great War which I have not noticed in most War Books, because it had worn her down and killed her: and I swore a vendetta against these abominations' (*BB* p. 211). Although perhaps a little too keen to chime in with the established tragic discourse of remembrance, Lewis's wife Anne characterised *Blasting and Bombardiering* well when she stated in her preface that the 'style of this book is light and sardonic but contains the essence of this tragic war embodied in the Serviceman's reticence in relating horrors seen and endured at the Front' (*BB* n.p.). Lewis reworked his war experience with his characteristic mix of detached sardonic humour and provocative statements, but allowed some room for humane observations, particularly with regard to the men fighting the war. Having entertained a less than favourable opinion of a number of fellow officers during the war (see *L* p. 91), Lewis nevertheless had a strong regard for many of the men he fought with, whom he described as for the most part 'unmilitary' idealists who kept 'telling themselves that this was a war-to-end-war' and, he felt, were 'helpless in the hands of all these doctors, drill-sergeants, padres and "Officers"' even while still in training (*BB* p. 26). One instance in the memoir is particularly pertinent in this respect. Lewis describes how he narrowly escaped death when he left his position to accompany a staff officer to group headquarters over a trifling errand. After highlighting the absurdity of the situation, he proceeds to describe the outcome of the bombardment he has missed:

> When over an hour later I got back to the battery position my gunpit . . . was like a small quarry. The sergeant and a half dozen men had been in it: it had been a direct hit, a few feet at the side of the gun. He and the six men were all killed or wounded. I wrote to the widow of my sergeant, saying what a popular man he was, and got a new N.C.O. for my gun and the necessary reinforcements. As this is written, so it happened. But that is obviously not how men's lives should be taken away from them, for nothing at all. (*BB* p. 146)

Lewis may state boldly earlier in the volume that he is much more concerned 'with ideas than . . . with people' (*BB* p. 8) and 'a fanatic for the
externality of things' (*BB* p. 9), but this seemingly sober description of
carnage shows him to be quite interested enough in individual lives. The
understatement of the passage, with its reference to the standard letter
of condolence penned by junior officers and its oblique yet evocative
reference to a 'direct hit', with unspoken associations of severed limbs
and eviscerated bodies, calls upon the reader to read between the lines.
Lewis's own opinion shines through his curt description in his blunt
comment that 'obviously' men should not be killed 'for nothing at all' –
as clear a statement of perceived futility as the most disillusioned veteran
could wish for.

By the mid-1930s, Lewis felt that the war had paved the way for a
relinquishing rather than a saving of democracy, describing the common
soldiers on the Western Front as 'properly entrapped and . . . cowed and
worried' and observing that 'they shed their historic "rights" overnight
like philosophers. Sophists of the school of Bairnsfather! Of course that
was a wretched hypocritical philosophy, but in this sudden emergency
it was all they had' (*BB* p. 26). In Lewis's view, army service amounted
to 'assisting at the assassination of Democracy' (*BB* p. 28). Although it
is hard to establish exactly how much of this he felt at the time and how
much was retrospective reflection, by the time he wrote his war memoir
Lewis certainly did feel a noticeable 'scepticism regarding the reality of
this Democracy which had bestowed upon [him] such a high opinion
of [his] skin', and a decided 'inability to accept the theory that [he] was
making the world any more "safe" by [his] present activities' (*BB* p. 28).
Given this scepticism, however, it is not surprising that Lewis's political writing from the 1920s onwards is concerned fundamentally with
two issues: (1) a questioning of Western democratic values and political
alternatives to democracy, including a championing of the sovereign
state over internationalisation; and (2) the role of art and the artist in
relation to the political field. Lewis's thoughts on both of these issues are
crucially shaped by his experience of and attitude to war.

References to the First World War are ubiquitous in Lewis's political
writing. Whether he used the war as a reference point or as a means
of comparing present and past circumstances, cited it as a validation
of particular views, or employed war reminiscences as embellishment,
these frequent intrusions of the war demonstrate clearly how formative
an experience the First World War was for him. In his first and most
controversial account of National Socialism, *Hitler*, he introduces Hitler
immediately as a fellow veteran, 'an austrian [sic] house-painter, just
over forty years old' who 'served in a bavarian [sic] regiment during

the War with distinction' (*H* p. 7). It is not least Hitler's veteran back-ground that prompts Lewis's initial faith in him as a 'Man of Peace', albeit 'certainly not "a pacifist," of the order of the regulation pacifist best-seller Remarque', but 'the typical german [sic] soldier' whose 'Iron Cross, conspicuous upon his bosom, signifies that he is a brave soldier, not that he is a bravo or a pugilist' (*H* p. 32). Correspondingly, once Lewis turns against Hitler, he does so by focusing strongly on Hitler's self-declared intense desire for war rather than peace, drawing closely on *Mein Kampf* to portray Hitler as a wildly misguided disciple of the 'prin-ciple of force' who not only 'sank down upon his knees to thank Heaven for the beautiful war that Providence had provided for him' (*HC* p. 82) in 1914, but had previously 'really despaired of ever having a war in such a rotten time as he had got into' (*HC* p. 83). Prior to this change of outlook, Lewis also repeatedly blamed the fact that Germany had been 'tested beyond endurance by the vast losses and sufferings of the most inhuman and meaningless of all wars' (*H* p. 34) as a blanket explanation for any objectionable German political decisions, and even declared the German re-militarisation of the Rhineland 'a desperate gesture of self-defence' (*LWE* p. 110) following the crushing and unfair treatment he felt Germany had received under the terms of the Treaty of Versailles. In a fine example of Lewis's ostentatious falling back on his war experience for rhetorical effect, he compared the notion of a disarmed Germany trying to attack France with 'a naked unarmed man [making] a frontal attack upon a machine-gun nest (with a cloud of bomb-bearing aero-planes circling overhead)' (*H* p. 56). The war to come he regularly inter-preted in the light of the war already witnessed as 'Great War No. 2' (*LWE* p. 18), and Lewis also noted in 1936 just 'how easily one drops, these days, into the slang of the trenches!' (*LWE* p. 46). Lewis's precari-ous political position for most of the 1930s, although more publicly and controversially expressed than many others, was no isolated stance. His political trajectory was perhaps so similar to that of many of his contemporaries because veterans and civilian survivors of his generation alike shared the first-hand knowledge of what war was like and what its consequences could be. Lewis's gradual move from a persistent endeav-our to advocate an avoidance of war at (almost) all costs, to a desire to fight the war as quickly and efficiently as possible once it had become patently unavoidable, mirrors not only the private sentiment of many inter-war pacifists, but also the government's appeasement strategy that Lewis came to chastise harshly. Even in 1939, Lewis stuck to his guns, as it were, declaring that '[as] for winning a real war, *nobody* wins that, not in the twentieth century' (*HC* p. 80). His violent opposition to communism was equally motivated at least in part by a desire to avoid war, which throughout most of the 1930s he felt was more likely to be prompted by communist rather than fascist aggression.

Lewis's experience of the First World War not only fuelled his appeasement stance prior to 1939 and contributed to his embracing of fascism as a means of avoiding a communist war, but also served him subsequently when he revised and explained his previous views once he realised his error of judgement with regard to Nazi 'peacefulness'. In *The Hitler Cult*, Lewis deliberately linked his stance on the new war to his First World War experience to rehabilitate himself and acceptably explain his political trajectory since the late 1920s, showing that the First World War was not only 'a trauma that was for him unassimilable', but also a strategic argumentative tool he employed to validate a range of evolving political positions.[14] Discussing his former pleas for neutrality and appeasement in late 1939, Lewis declared that, at this point, 'to be neutral [was] to be anti-British', even 'anti-European culture' (*HC* p. vii), and that his sympathy for the German population, whom he had previously cast as oppressed victims, had dwindled in the face of their overwhelming support for Hitler's warmongering. His erstwhile neutrality, Lewis pointed out – and this claim does not in fact contradict his earlier account in *Hitler* – was motivated not by sympathy for Nazism, but adopted 'because another war like the last one is hardly an event lightly to repeat' (*HC* p. vii). Lewis declared that after his 'efforts at "appeasement" beside which those of Mr Chamberlain pale in comparison' (*HC* p. viii), and despite the fact that 'it is "humanely desirable," too, that no war should have broken out at all' (*HC* p. vii), the war so unfortunately begun must be fought to prevent 'England or France suffering defeat at the hands of Germany' (*HC* p. viii). Nevertheless, Lewis's embrace of war was grudging. Dedicating a whole chapter to comparing the situation in 1939 to 1914 in *The Hitler Cult*, he came to the rather unfavourable conclusion that '1939 in comparison with 1914 [was] a much less favourable year to start a world war for Great Britain' (*HC* pp. 157–8) in the face of a rise in air over sea power, and in light of the diminished support that Britain could hope for from its colonial allies (*HC* p. 159). Having devoted the best part of at least three book-length political analyses – *Hitler*, *Left Wings over Europe*, and *Count Your Dead* – to expounding the need for appeasement, Lewis now summarised British foreign policy over the past decades perhaps a little unfairly as a

> spectacle of an anything but masterly inactivity: an inactivity which cloaked a great deal of mild and half-hearted interference: a 'non-intervention' which went from bad to worse until Munich, when it came to a dead stop. Then it slowly and reluctantly changed into a belated bellicosity. (*HC* p. 137)

Lewis's fear was that as a result of British hesitancy, a 'limited war' between France and Germany might ensue, in support of which he once again drew on his own experience of the war, citing Canadian and German arrangements on the Vimy Ridge in 1917, where military action was suspended because both sides 'were satisfied that nothing was to be gained by attacks' (*HC* p. 151) – a situation he felt might arise in this new war to the detriment of Britain, as all it was in France's interest to do was defend its own territory (cf. *HC* p. 153).

Both *Left Wings over Europe*, which draws attention to its own topicality in Lewis's foreword, and *Count Your Dead* read like frantic, hastily written repeat attempts to avert war at all costs, and clash notably with Lewis's own criticism of appeasement policy in *The Hitler Cult*. Whereas he attacks English political hesitancy to strike early in the latter volume, *Left Wings* still vehemently defends Germany's 'most elementary right' to 'fortify its own territory against attack' (*LWE* p. 23). However, the irony of his misguided attempt to endorse, in the name of securing peace and the further existence of what he saw as endangered (white) Western civilisation, the very man and regime that brought this civilisation very nearly to its end, had certainly begun to dawn upon Lewis when he re-evaluated National Socialism in *The Hitler Cult*. By the time he wrote *Anglosaxony*, he fully embraced the need for a war of ideas in which democracy was pitted against the brute 'religion' of fascism. Lewis at this point dismissed flaws in the democratic system that he had pointed out earlier to temper easy dismissals of fascism – such as the possibility for groups or individuals to still be discriminated against on the basis of their skin colour or creed, or of a corrupt legal system – as flaws that are outweighed by having a near-enough ideal system in place, arguing that it would be foolish to reject a political system that at least in principle allows a great deal of impartiality and freedom without serious consideration (*ALW* p. 14). He compares democracy to what he calls the principle of '[t]raditional psychology' (*ALW* p. 14) that holds that if one assumes the air of happiness, then happiness will follow. By the same token, Lewis argued,

> [the] fact that in a democracy we affect, from morning till night, to be 'fair' and 'just,' as well as equal and free, is already a very substantial safeguard against an absolute and downright disregard of fairplay [sic] and of justice. (*ALW* p. 15)

Having previously declared going to war futile in both 1914 and 1939, he now once again equated both scenarios and declared war equally necessary in both cases:

> The general notion that attaches in the public mind . . . to totalitarianism or fascism, is of a cult of Force, of physical compulsion. And that is undeniably accurate. That characterized Kaiserism as much as it does Hitlerism. And that way of going about one's business outrages men today as much as it did in 1914, on the Anglo-Saxon side of the fence. (*ALW* p. 17)

Previously opposed to the League of Nations as an interventionist prompter of war for much of the 1930s, Lewis now, in 1941, advocates a different League, international and parochial at the same time, declaring that 'Anglo-Saxony *is* a League of Nations that *works*' (*ALW* p. 75). Lewis's Anglo-Saxon League, however, is meant largely to be based on the principle of non-intervention, one in which Anglo-Saxon democrats let other political systems take their course, in the spirit of a 'true democratic path, of live-and-let-live' (*ALW* p. 29), albeit with some humanitarian caveats:

> We are democrats – which is fine and dandy. Let other people be anything their instincts tell them to be, provided they do not try and coerce us: and provided, of course, they do not insist upon their right to commit murders every night in their own house, while we neighbours have to lie awake and listen to the screams of their victims. (*ALW* p. 30)

Lewis's stance on war and his experiences in the First World War are also intricately connected with his theories on art and the artist. To Lewis's mind, the artist served a crucial function as the urgently necessary reflexive mechanism of society (*BB* p. 259), as 'a kind of moral arbitrator in an ordered and structured society' – a function which war could interfere with, but could equally be necessary to preserve.[15] Just as Lewis had declared in the second volume of *BLAST* that Germany stood for the objectionable Romantic principle in art (*B2* p. 5), communism became for a time his number one enemy of art by virtue of its repressive attitude towards artistic expression after the First World War.[16] Similarly, Lewis chastised Marinetti for having created an art form that paved the way for fascism, and ultimately argued that National Socialism had to be fought also – though not exclusively – because of its take on the arts and its curtailing of artistic freedom. Fredric Jameson has suggested that art served Lewis as a withdrawal spot, an excuse for 'his unwillingness to identify himself with any determinate class position or ideological commitment' and an

> ultimate fall-back position, which asserts the ultimate critical standard and Archimedean point of the pure eye and attempts to justify his immense and wide-ranging cultural critiques in terms of the defense of the rights of the visual and the painter's practice. (*JFA* pp. 17–18)

Whether this stance was 'untenable' (as Jameson felt it was) or not, Lewis's inter-war belief in art, particularly avant-garde artistic expression, as 'the best hope for cultural renewal' certainly seems sincere.[17] The thought of a German hegemony dominated by what he saw as the Nazi ideal of a 'uniformed athlete bank clerk' (*HC* p. 253), a 'Spartan robot beyond the Rhine' (*HC* pp. 253–4), was repellent enough for Lewis to overcome his opposition to renewed war. He predicted that Germany, under Hitler's ascetic rule, must ultimately become a 'Sunday School of sunburnt state-paupers, armed to the teeth' (*HC* p. 254) unless something was done to prevent this. It is significant that the closing paragraphs of *The Hitler Cult* deal specifically with the *cultural* threat posed by Germany, disparaging German 'Kultur' in an uncanny echo of mainstream First World War propaganda as a 'nation . . . to-day culturally extinct' (*HC* pp. 254–5), vying for dominance with 'French and Celtic culture generally, allied to the genius for tolerance of the Anglo-Saxon' (*HC* p. 255).

As we have seen, Lewis felt that for him 'war and art [had] been mixed up from the start' (*BB* p. 4), and he deplored the fact that 'as a result of the War . . . artistic expression [had] slipped back again into political propaganda and romance' rather than aspiring to 'the detachment of true literature' (*BB* p. 250). Nevertheless, Lewis did not think that artists could remain aloof from war, and, despite his belief in the critical distance of the artist as cultural observer, he realised that 'the artist in warfare was part of "life" in all its immediacy'.[18] Accordingly, he directed considerable rancour at the pacifist Bloomsbury group for having 'exempted themselves' (*BB* pp. 184–5) from military service during the First World War and for having survived where others – like Gaudier-Brzeska and T. E. Hulme – had died. While he did pin some hopes on the unsettled state of society in the aftermath of violent conflict, hoping it might be conducive to radically new artistic endeavours (*BB* p. 251), he also concluded that, between the two dominant ideologies of communism and National Socialism, the artist's position did not look overly auspicious, as 'neither [promised] the requisite conditions for an improvement in the position of the arts' (*BB* p. 264). In the face of Lewis's disdain for the National Socialists' essentialist 'teutonic' notions of art (*JAH* p. 83) and his intense dislike of fascist art as embodied to him by Marinetti (*ALW* pp. 38–45), Lewis's identity as an artist made his eventual change of direction somewhat inevitable. Despite Lewis's protestations that he did not object to Hitler purely because he offended his artistic sensibilities (*ALW* pp. 45–6), his views on art and his views on war mingle closely in shaping both his initial objection to a new war, and his eventual grudging acceptance of it. Despite Lewis's awareness of the cost of war based on personal experience, which prompted such lengthy and vocal opposition to renewed armed conflict with Germany, his artistic integrity, as well as his fundamental regard for human rights, were arguably bound to gain the upper hand over his war-induced scruples. If Lewis championed the artist as 'a bearer of civilised cultured values' and if his 'cultural theory and philosophy . . . forced him to view warfare as the betrayal of human civilisation',[19] then he ultimately had no option but to regard totalitarian disregard of human rights and cultural freedom alike in the same way.

Notes

1. Robert E. Murray, 'Wyndham Lewis and His Fiction of the First World War', *Journal of the Short Story in English*, 14, Spring 1990, pp. 41–62: p. 58; Paul Edwards, 'Wyndham Lewis and the Uses of Shellshock: Meat and Postmodernism' in *WLC* pp. 223–40: p. 223.
2. Alan Munton, 'Wyndham Lewis: War and Aggression', in David Peters Corbett (ed.), *Wyndham Lewis and the Art of Modern War* (Cambridge: Cambridge University Press, 1998), pp. 14–37: p. 14.
3. Jamie Wood, '"A Long Chuckling Scream": Wyndham Lewis, Fiction, and the First World War', *The Journal of Wyndham Lewis Studies*, 1.1, 2010, pp. 19–42: p. 19.
4. See also Alan Munton, 'The Insane Subject: Ford and Wyndham Lewis in the War and Post-War', in Andrzej Gąsiorek and Daniel Moore (eds), *Ford Madox Ford: Literary Networks and Cultural Transformations* (Amsterdam: Rodopi, 2008), pp. 105–30.
5. Munton, 'Wyndham Lewis: War and Aggression', p. 20; Wood, '"A Long Chuckling Scream"', p. 28.
6. Tom Normand, 'Wyndham Lewis, the Anti-War War Artist', in Peters Corbett (ed.), *Wyndham Lewis and the Art of Modern War*, pp. 38–57: p. 42.
7. Wood, '"A Long Chuckling Scream"', p. 27.
8. See also ibid., p. 25.
9. Geoff Gilbert, 'Shellshock, Anti-Semitism, and the Agency of the Avant-Garde', in Peters Corbett (ed.), *Wyndham Lewis and the Art of Modern War*, pp. 78–97: p. 78.
10. Ibid., p. 82.
11. See also Murray, 'Wyndham Lewis and His Fiction of the First World War', pp. 49–51.
12. Andrzej Gąsiorek, 'War, "Primitivism," and the Future of "the West": Reflections on D. H. Lawrence and Wyndham Lewis', in Richard Begam and Michael Valdez Moses (eds), *Modernism and Colonialism: British and Irish Literature, 1899–1939* (Durham, NC: Duke University Press, 2007), pp. 91–110: p. 97.
13. Brittain's work for the League of Nations Union is detailed in Chapter XI ('Piping for Peace'). Vera Brittain, *Testament of Youth: An Autobiographical*

Study of the Years 1900–1925 (London: Victor Gollancz, 1933), pp. 535–605.

14. Edwards, 'Wyndham Lewis and the Uses of Shellshock', p. 227.
15. Normand, 'Wyndham Lewis, the Anti-War War Artist', p. 43.
16. See also Paul Peppis, '"Surrounded by a Multitude of Other Blasts": Vorticism and the Great War', *Modernism/modernity*, 4.2, April 1997, pp. 39–66: pp. 40–1.
17. Gąsiorek, 'War, "Primitivism," and the Future of "the West"', p. 95.
18. Christine Hardegen, 'Actors and Spectators in the Theatre of War: Wyndham Lewis's First World War Art and Literature', in Peters Corbett (ed.), *Wyndham Lewis and the Art of Modern War*, pp. 58–77: p. 59.
19. Normand, 'Wyndham Lewis, the Anti-War War Artist', p. 45 and p. 38.

Chapter 5

Lewis and Cultural Criticism

Alan Munton

Wyndham Lewis is modernism's critic of culture. Secular (compare T. S. Eliot), continuously engaged with his times (contrast Ezra Pound), his critiques mattered at the time they were made, and retain their significance. His earliest and most spectacular intervention is *BLAST*, in 1914 and 1915. That publication excited the avant-garde, and animated the serious press. Today, *BLAST* defines our historical sense of British artistic radicalism, but it can be read historically both as a critique of the culture of its time and as a vivid alternative to it. A different kind of cultural engagement occurred in the mid-to-late 1920s: the political-revolutionary text *The Art of Being Ruled* was published in 1926, and *Time and Western Man*, which is both literary and philosophical, appeared in the following year. Lewis intended these works to be read by 'the general educated man or woman' (*TWM* p. xi), but he did not understand how far he had written beyond the likely interests of those figures-of-reference. His hope that *Time and Western Man* might be sold in its thousands 'to college students' caused astonishment (*SSG* p. 278), and suggests that Lewis did not understand the difficulty of his own work; equally, he may not always have understood the significance of what he achieved in cultural criticism.

In 1928 *The Childermass* appeared, a fiction set in the afterworld. It uses ideas about ideology and hegemony to make a satirical attack on James Joyce that develops into a critique of cultural control. *The Apes of God* (1930) is different again, a satire on the Sitwell family and others that interprets the worlds of art and literature as a set of networks and relationships, and which again emerges as a critique of the ways cultural dominance is achieved and enforced. In *The Revenge for Love* (1937) Lewis explores contemporary politics through the consciousness of a woman character, Margot, in a way that gives her primacy over the novel's male characters in understanding what is occurring. In a different mode, by 1948 Lewis has becomes an internationalist, and conceives 'the global village': the phrase remains active to this day.[1]

Lewis's engagement with the 'present' through which he lived far exceeds that of any other of the foremost modernists, whether Eliot, Joyce, Woolf, or Pound. He failed, nevertheless, to identify some of the most troubling developments of his time, and this was culpably true of his politics during the 1930s. This failure is transcended by his success in identifying matters of significance: questions of cultural authority and ideology, developments in feminism, an interest in technology and its consequences, an early recognition of the importance of George Orwell, and a sense of globalism long before it was widely recognised. His work may appear to engage with too many things, notably his varied responses to the movement of history and culture. His most persistent concern was the relation between art and the conditions of its production, and it is from this significant concern that the present discussion derives. In what follows, I shall attempt to identify and describe Lewis's cultural criticism as it engages with power and control, and specifically with concepts of ideology and hegemony.

Lewis is rightly considered to deal with 'the external' in art and life, and often asserted this against the damaging internalisations of what he called 'Time-philosophy': his view that the work of Henri Bergson destabilised the sense of self, for example. The difficulty here, however, is that Lewis is as concerned with states of consciousness as any other modernist, Woolf included. For Lewis, as the material world changes, so too does consciousness. In *BLAST* he writes that in cities 'Society is sufficiently organised for his [the artist's] ego to walk abroad' (*B1* p. 141), and – in an opposite and indeed an oppressed sense, but still in the city – 'One feels the immanence of some REALITY more than any former human beings can have felt it' (*B1* p. 141). Such external–internal relationships – society / ego, or material world / consciousness – define Lewis's thinking on the question of what the artist *endures* (in the material world), and what the artist *experiences* (when making art). A moment that defines *consciousness* occurs early, in *The Caliph's Design* of 1919, where Lewis argues for the artist's primacy in changing the actual world on behalf of the people living in it, here primarily through architecture. This argument 'is one of Lewis's most unequivocally positive statements of the importance of creative art in the invention of new modes of consciousness' (*CD* p. 147), as Paul Edwards puts it. The artist suffers under an oppressive reality, immanent to the mind, which must be resisted even as it is represented; at this point such cultural forms as the satirical novel and the polemical critique are mobilised in opposition. New writing, and in art 'new beauty', emerge from positive aesthetic and creative impulses, but these are operated from within a wider context where – as Lewis understands it – the artist endures a sense of oppression or domination.

This discussion does not have the space to engage equally with both sides of the culture-consciousness debate, however. I shall to a degree set aside a consideration of consciousness, so that Lewis's cultural criticism can be specified and assessed; but states of consciousness are always present, and will recur in this discussion. In what follows I shall take up separate, diverse, and often incompatible moments in Lewis's cultural criticism. An account of how the word *culture* is used in different ways in the novel *Tarr*, in its first version of 1918, is followed by a discussion of *BLAST*, which I interpret as the moment when Lewis first identifies the culture of his time as a field of potential activity, and as a 'whole' entity that may be the proper object of criticism. The assertiveness of *BLAST* is, to use terms developed by Pierre Bourdieu, an exercise of symbolic power within existing culture. In the 1920s, very different questions of ideology and hegemony are raised, and these situate Lewis on the political left for a period. Aspects of his cultural critiques in the unfortunate years of the 1930s have been adequately discussed elsewhere, but changes at the end of that decade lead to versions of socialism and internationalism in the years during and after the Second World War, and to Lewis's engagement with Orwell. Each encounter has its own particular cultural formation.

'Culture' in *Tarr*

Lewis was alert to the possible uses of the word 'culture' from early in his writing career. His novel *Tarr* is a story of artists, art, love, social exclusion, and absurd deaths in Paris before the First World War; begun in about 1908, it was published in 1918. Towards the end, Lewis uses the words *culture* and *cultural* three times within two pages. All concern the relationship – social and imminently sexual – between Tarr and Anastasya. They drink in a café, kiss, argue, and she leaves: 'The drinks of the evening were a culture in which his disappointment grew luxuriantly' (*T1* p. 305). Without his realising it, she has stolen his key, and awaits him at his apartment, undressed. When he arrives he situates the event: 'This impulse to take her clothes off had the cultural hygienic touch so familiar to him' (*T1* p. 306). She asks if Tarr, as artist, requires a model; he says that he never uses nude models, and she remarks ironically that she supposes she must dress again. When he shouts '"I accept, I accept!"' the event is again situated: 'Tarr had learnt the laws of cultural emancipation' (*T1* p. 306).

This first use of 'culture' refers to growing plants, an organic meta-phor that tells us about Tarr's state of mind; the second refers to the fashion for 'natural' diets and 'natural' behaviour that might include nudity, and helps Tarr situate (surely mistakenly, and therefore comi-cally) what is happening; the reader too must know about a then-recent popular-cultural activity.[2] The third use gets its significance from the energy of the debate between Anastasya and Tarr, which is conducted on equal terms. Anastasya acts purposively to make a sexual relation-ship possible, and it is Tarr who is so far from being dominant in this situation – he hardly seems to get the point – that he cannot act as Anastasya desires without first finding a culturally recognisable element by which to locate himself. This turns out to be the feminism prevalent in their bohemian milieu, something that Tarr has internalised: he has 'learnt the laws' of emancipation *within this micro-culture*. Once he has located the cultural referent, both lovers can act with a new freedom. This is a significant moment in modernist writing, when the woman acts to seize meaning and the man concurs. Contemporary readers can see that their shared emancipation, exultantly named 'Swagger Sex' in the novel, is not the encounter of two egoistic subjectivities but the represen-tation of a personal and cultural relationship that we can identify as an aspect of early twentieth-century feminism.

BLAST as Recognition

BLAST was a major intervention in the cultural activity of its time. The magazine was conceived and named in about November 1913 and formally released by its publisher John Lane on 2 July 1914 (*VEA* pp. 157–63).[3] Lewis learned about culture during those eight months. He realised that a culture could be understood as a whole, that advanced modernist culture consisted of elements in conflict, and that change was structured as the interplay of dominant and dominated forces. *BLAST* was the voice of new, but excluded, forces. It was necessary to persuade the surrounding culture, largely dormant as it was, to recognise what was occurring.[4] Until 1912, Lewis had been in many ways a ruralist: his short stories are set in French villages or small towns in Spain, and his art often shows pairs or trios of thoughtful or frenetic modernist-inflected figures in rural isolation. The influence of Futurism took him towards the city as a subject, and towards a realisation that discussion of art could be – indeed, should be – polemical, oppositional, and driven by ideas.

Lewis asserted as late as 1949 that '*vorticism* was purely a painters

[sic] affair' (*L* p. 492); Ezra Pound picked this up at the time, and wrote to James Joyce that *BLAST* 'is mostly a painter's magazine with me to do the poems'.[5] These artists were in a difficult position because their work was experimental, radical, disruptive, and indebted to European modernism – and was little understood by the British public. The artist and organiser Roger Fry had given critics and public a partial opportunity to catch up through the two Post-Impressionist exhibitions he curated in London in 1910 and 1912: Lewis featured conspicuously in the latter, and was extravagantly praised by Fry.

Fry was important to the genesis of Vorticism in another, less creditable respect. In October 1913 the 'Ideal Home Rumpus' occurred at the Omega Workshops, where Lewis and several other artists worked on craft and design under Fry's direction. Fry appropriated a commission from the *Daily Mail* for paintings at the *Ideal Home Exhibition* by ensuring, in almost certainly improper ways, that the work be done by himself and his friends Duncan Grant and Vanessa Bell: all minor artists. On 5 October Lewis, Edward Wadsworth, Frederick Etchells, Cuthbert Hamilton, and (a little later) Jessie Dismorr walked out of the Omega (see *VEA* pp. 65–7).[6] *BLAST* was conceived during the month following this incident, at a time of conflict among British artists. Marinetti visited London that same November, when his lectures and spectacularly dramatic readings of poetry about war contributed to the sense that modernist culture had to be oppositional to be meaningful. As late as May 1914 Lewis wrote in *The New Weekly* that 'England has need of these foreign auxiliaries to put her energies to rights and restore order'.[7] Nevertheless, he was to break with Futurism, and the question of cultural power became insistent as Lewis developed the ideas that would distance Vorticism – named by Pound in about May 1914 – from Futurism (see *VEA* p. 160 and p. 161).

We can say that the Bloomsbury group, to which Fry had only recently become attached, won the long-term power game over Lewis by exercising its influence against him. A much later remark by Leonard Woolf shows this: 'He was employed by Roger Fry in the Omega Workshops and I don't think Roger ever wrote anything against him or indeed about him.' Woolf, who is responding to an academic enquirer, wrote in a second letter: 'Can you quote a single instance in which any of us [in Bloomsbury] ever wrote anything about Wyndham Lewis?'[8] That, of course, was the problem: damaging silence. In recent years Bloomsbury's artists have lost decisively: the exhibition curated by Richard Shone, *The Art of Bloomsbury: Roger Fry, Vanessa Bell, and Duncan Grant* (Tate Gallery, 1999–2000) received disastrous reviews from which these artists' reputations have not recovered.[9]

Since the word 'Vortex' was not adopted until May 1914, and the artworks published in *BLAST* had been photographed before that, there were consequently no 'Vorticist' artworks in the first *BLAST*; but there was the work produced up to that time by seven artists familiar with the new modernist art of Paris and elsewhere.[10] In the second *BLAST*, of July 1915, there are eighteen illustrations; Lewis's cover design, 'Before Antwerp', is a response to war, and inescapably Vorticist in its assertive diagonals. C. R. W. Nevinson's 'On the way to the Trenches' and Edward Wadsworth's 'War-Engine' would have been thought of as Vorticist. Other works in *BLAST* 2 belong to the development of particular artists (notably Helen Saunders, Jessie Dismorr, Frederick Etchells, William Roberts, and Henri Gaudier-Brzeska); these are Vorticist only in that they were so named for publicity purposes. A closer definition would ask how far particular works agree with Lewis's definition of Vorticist art in 'A Review of Contemporary Art' in *BLAST* 2. Here, Lewis distinguishes the Vorticist movement from Cubism, Expressionism, and Futurism. Vorticism is in some sense 'northern': this separates it from Marinetti, coded as 'southern'. Vorticism was opposed to trivial subject matter, such as still life as it appeared in Picasso's Cubism; instead it worked with significant topics, such as Wadsworth's industrialism or David Bomberg's East London; or it attempted to situate what was represented: Lewis's *The Crowd* (1914–15) celebrates urban revolution at the same time as it makes a critique of the idea of the city as an environment.

The Vorticist polemics by Lewis and Pound use vivid images, but they do not describe the new art. For Lewis, 'Our Vortex rushes out like an angry dog at your Impressionist fuss' (*B1* p. 149), while Pound writes, more or less meaninglessly, that the Vorticist relies upon 'the primary pigment of his art' (*B1* p. 153). Gaudier's Vortex is an imaginary history of art, mostly Chinese and Middle-Eastern (*B1* p. 157). In the first *BLAST*, the 'Vortex' is an idea without a referent, and Vorticist art is not there defined in any way that can be grasped in art-historical or pictorial terms; but that was not the intention. The intention was speculative, cultural-aggressive, dramatic, imaginative: an act of publicity and provocation, and an attempt to occupy cultural space by pushing aside both Omega and the Futurists. When Lewis wrote in 1956 that 'Vorticism, in fact, was what I, personally, did, and said, at a certain period' (*WLA* p. 451) he is referring to the publicity that made him so well known: for you cannot 'do' or 'say' a work of art. The artworks existed already, but 'Vorticism' was notoriety, publicity, what Lewis in a letter of 1914 called 'my (alas!) undeniable political activity' (*L* p. 61). To get 'Vorticism' – at that time a concept without substance – into the newspapers was a skilful exploitation of what the culture offered in enabling the occupation of cultural space.[11]

All the distinctive aspects of Vorticism are the outcome of shared or collective cultural activity. The famous 'MANIFESTO', thirty-five pages of BLASTs and BLESSes, immaculately designed and wittily and incisively written, is what critics have taken to embody Vorticism – even though it was written and set in type before the term was conceived. The opening words – 'BLAST First (from politeness) ENGLAND' – possess iconic status today, and are sometimes appropriated for other uses.[12] The words are Lewis's, but it is probable that some or all of the design was done by William Henry Leveridge, head of Leveridge & Co., who printed both numbers of *BLAST*.[13] The structure BLAST / BLESS is not original, but is taken from Guillaume Apollinaire's (possibly pastiche) Futurist manifesto *L'Antitradition Futuriste: Manifeste=synthèse*, first published in French (dated '29 Juin 1913', p. 3).[14] This uses two antitheses, 'Destruction' against 'Construction' and 'Merde Aux' against 'Rose Aux'. Destruction is urged upon 'l'harmonie typographique' (p. 1), a hint that Lewis may have taken. The lists of those to be BLASTed or BLESSed were put together at a meeting over tea at Lewis's studio in Fitzroy Street in London, possibly in December 1913 or January 1914, when Pound, Nevinson, and Roberts were present, together with 'the oddest collection of *rapins* in black hats, girls from the Slade, poets and journalists' (*VEA* p. 43), according to Douglas Goldring.[15] This definition of what the London avant-garde admired and detested was the result of a collective activity, and should be read as showing what a wide range of engaged individuals, including Lewis, believed to be the conspicuous features of the culture of their time.[16]

The BLASTs identify spheres of public influence: well-known painters, musicians, and religious figures are peremptorily disposed of; all were conservative figures of cultural, political, and religious authority. The BLESSes are qualitatively different and go the other way: to Kate Lechmere for her support of *BLAST* itself, to Leveridge its printer, and to writers who supported recent developments, such as *The Observer*'s art critic P. G. Konody, the critic Frank Rutter, or Frida Strindberg, founder of the Cave of the Golden Calf nightclub. Joyce is blessed, as is the erotic autobiographer Frank Harris, and the publisher Leonard Smithers, another eroticist. The suffragist Lillie Lenton, who burned buildings, is blessed. Several boxers are named, as are aviators, and music hall entertainers such as Gertie Millar and Harry Weldon: these are not powerful figures within the culture, but they are also much more than random 'likes', for together they define the magazine's transgressive and anti-authoritarian tendency as it recognises alternative cultures.

BLAST, indeed, *is* recognition. Lewis recognises that advanced culture is structured antagonistically, but also that it can be understood as a whole. After the Omega debacle, 'BLAST First' attacks Roger Fry as 'AMATEUR / SCIOLAST [i.e. Scholiast] / ART-PIMP' (*B1* p. 16).[17] This is divisive, but is a response to Fry's initial aggression, his timely demonstration that the institutions of culture are not inclusive and gentle but are opportunities to assert dominance or contrive success. Lewis now brings in the psychic or internalising tendency that so often accompanies his discussion of the external appearances of culture. The Vorticists will refuse to endure 'abasement': 'But there is violent boredom [among English artists] with that feeble Europeanism, abasement of the miserable "intellectual" before anything coming from Paris, Cosmopolitan sentimentality, which prevails in so many quarters' (*B1* p. 34). Lewis is resisting what we now call abjection. Here, 'abasement' identifies a willingness to internalise dominant forces and submit to them. Inner resistance to external power is essential for the success of any new cultural activity. *BLAST* exemplifies the confidence derived from refusing abjection. The manifestos have little to do with any supposed egotism on Lewis's part; that is to misread its typography. A newspaper editor who uses huge typefaces on the front page is not an egoist; he is trying to influence his readership (usually politically). Lewis was attempting to influence his readers towards new developments in visual art: that was why he needed his battering ram. The buoyant aggressivity of *BLAST* asserts a newly conceived symbolic power within the existing culture. The magazine was an act of culturally grounded assertion that defined a cultural field where new creative and critical intelligences could perform.

Ideology and Hegemony

Lewis's first use of the term 'hegemony' in relation to the arts appears to be in *The Caliph's Design* in 1919, where the term is used in a way that suggests there is truth in his claim that he was reading Proudhon and Marx during and after the First World War (*BB* p. 144 and p. 150). Lewis is discussing how artists were trying to maintain the 'great new vivacity' of ten years before – the years of Cubism and Futurism from about 1907 onwards – but in these difficult post-war years, they struggle. Politics, however, may come to the rescue and deliver the best conditions for art:

> This local effort [of art in Paris and London] has to contend with the scepticism of a shallow, tired and uncertain time; there is no great communal or

personal force in the Western World of to-day, unless some new political hegemony supply it, for art to build on and to which to relate itself. (*CD* p. 120)

This desire for a *political* hegemony to ensure the success of art in its social and economic aspects is both desirable and dangerous. Here, it seeks a benevolent communality; but this desire also points forward to an unfortunate development in Lewis's thinking: by 1926, and subsequently, he will specify the fascist regimes as potentially offering greater security for art and artists than the more conventionally capitalist states. This expectation is abandoned in 1937, but it damaged Lewis's reputation.

It is an aspect of Lewis's diverse thinking, or his creative inconsistency, that an entirely different use of the term 'hegemony' occurs during the later 1920s. In his discussion of James Joyce's *Ulysses* (1922) in *Time and Western Man* the term recurs as part of an argument about the ways in which certain ideas achieve dominance in culture. This is a subjective process of internalisation that has material consequences, involving 'any of the hundred ways and degrees in which assent is arrived at, and an intellectual monopoly or hegemony consummated' (*TWM* p. 87). *Ulysses* is dominated by philosophies of Time: 'I regard *Ulysses* as a *time-book*', Lewis writes, because it emphasises and often manipulates 'the self-conscious time-sense, that has now been erected into a universal philosophy' (*TWM* p. 81). The 'time-philosophy' was not, of course, universal; but it was extremely influential, and Lewis is correct to point to the influence of theory (Bergson, Einstein, and others), and the prevalence of a literary response (Proust, Gertrude Stein) that shared identifiable characteristics with that theory.

Lewis's account of ideology appears to arise from his agreement with the way the term is used by Napoleon Bonaparte. But this is not the case. He writes: '[An] analysis of the domination achieved by an idea and how it ceases to be an idea, and becomes an *ideology*, as Napoleon called it, an instrument of popular government, has to be undertaken' (*TWM* p. 85). Here, Lewis misunderstands how the French ruler used the word *idéologue*, which was to dismiss intellectuals holding liberal views as 'de phraseurs et d'idéologues' ('windbags and ideologues', in Rehmann's translation).[18] Napoleon can be better understood from the chapter on ideology in Raymond Williams's *Marxism and Literature* (1977). Here Napoleon is quoted at greater length: '"It is to the doctrine of the ideologues – to this diffuse metaphysics . . . to which one must attribute all the misfortunes which have befallen our beautiful France."' This was, Williams says, an influential reactionary account of ideology 'as "impractical theory" or "abstract illusion"' that was used in the later nineteenth century to argue against liberalising change.[19] It is striking that Lewis and Williams should share an interest in Napoleon's version of ideology – they were fifty years apart, and the more recent book is a defining account of the theory of Marxist cultural studies. While Lewis misunderstands Napoleon, he instead attributes to him his own theory of how ideology may work. It is, for him, a programme of research that would identify the hegemonic processes by which an idea becomes an ideology, and in turn 'an instrument of popular government' that makes political dominance possible. In *Marxism and Literature* Williams writes: 'A lived hegemony is always a process. . . . It is a realized complex of experiences, relationships, and activities', one that 'does not just passively exist as a form of dominance'.[20] This is very close to Lewis's understanding of hegemony as a process that becomes instrumental '[in] popular government'. Lewis is not invoking Napoleon's reactionary views, but replacing them with his own interpretation of hegemony, which – in its insistence on process – is close to Williams's Marxist version.

Lewis uses the terms 'hegemony' and 'ideology' to propose that the creative activity of his (and Joyce's) time is provoked by impulses that are political, 'and its stimuli are masked ideologies' (*TWM* p. 88). That is why Joyce, and others, should be subjected to what we can legitimately call ideological criticism. Here, Lewis is primarily interested in literature and art, with philosophy a sometimes suspect transitional medium that makes possible certain forms of hegemonic process. At this date, the mid-to-late 1920s, such a theorisation of the arts shows an extraordinary originality.

Although the arts have primacy, Lewis is almost as interested in how the state performs its ideological purposes by facilitating the internalisation of ideas and beliefs. In *The Art of Being Ruled* (1926), he argues that the electoral system is made problematic by ideological forces: the free citizen's vote is 'cancelled' by 'the imposition of the will of the ruler through the press'. The ordinary citizen 'is gradually made into a newspaper reader, it could be said, rather than a citizen' (*ABR* p. 105). Lewis summarises this argument in a striking formulation: 'So what we call conventionally the *capitalist state* is as truly an *educationalist state*' (*ABR* p. 106). The ideology of the liberal-democratic capitalist state is taught, not only (or even primarily) in schools, but through the press and in public discourse. This process establishes a form of internalisation, one that encourages acceptance and passivity in the public sphere.

When he writes satiric fiction, Lewis returns from the wholly public world of politics to that area where fiction and art encounter the processes of internalisation and hegemony. In a mildly paranoid fantasy of what it might mean to be a reader of radical works in oppressive circumstances, he imagines Tolstoy's *War and Peace* having to be read in secret ('*en cachette*': but compare the conclusion of Ray Bradbury's *Fahrenheit 451* (1953)) as if it were pornography, because it was 'written to rouse the consciousness of the oppressed', and might be dangerous; he concludes that the 'people who read such books, after all, should be the rulers' (*ABR* p. 112). This phrase dramatically conceives the extinction of hegemonic power. It is serious, and not serious – but it is only unserious in terms of practicality. For people today, enduring rulers for whom culture is an absence, it speaks truth.

These ideas are enacted in Lewis's satirical fiction, notably in *The Childermass* (1928), *The Apes of God* (1930), *The Revenge for Love* (1937), and *The Vulgar Streak* (1941). All, in differing ways, enact the processes by which ideas are internalised and eventually emerge as instruments of political control or cultural power. The most difficult, but most fundamental, of these texts is *The Childermass*. Here, in a post-death landscape set 'outside Heaven', suppliants have to establish their *reality* before being allowed into the Magnetic City. Their reality is in question because the entire environment – the Styx-like river, the flatlands around it, the mountains, pathways, distant views, and the inhabitants – behaves as if particular theories of time and space (for Lewis, outlandish ones that diminish the autonomy of the subject) were true in reality and enact themselves there. Two friends endure this: James Pullman is a version of James Joyce, and his companion Satterthwaite ('Satters') is an apparently dim schoolboy figure whose common sense slowly emerges as the most reliable interpretation of their surroundings. Pullman ('Pulley') believes in the truth of those theories of time for which Lewis criticises Joyce in *Time and Western Man*; indeed, Pullman wants the untruths of this world to be true because he has accepted the interpretation of reality that is offered by the controller of this afterworld, the Bailiff, 'the irritable magistrate' (*C* p. 235) who embodies the zeitgeist. This Mr Punch-like figure questions and explains and bullies; but Pullman submits his intelligence to him in a process of voluntary internalisation. When he explains their surroundings to Satters, his deference towards the Bailiff can be heard in the language he uses:

> 'He's really not so black as he's painted. Haven't you ever gone down there and listened to him? I mean for a whole morning, say? . . . I was very surprised at first to find – you hardly expect to find a sense of humour in such a person.' (*C* p. 48)

The defensiveness, the hesitations, and the attribution of an unlikely humour all tell the reader that Pullman knows the Bailiff is evil, but is willing nevertheless to submit to him. When Macrob, an articulate and intelligent Scot who objects to the 'reality' test, grabs the Bailiff's nose and pulls it hard, the Bailiff's men tear him apart. An executioner's basket is brought, 'and the fragments of Macrob are stuffed and stamped into it' (*C* p. 235). The Bailiff declares a fifteen-minute interval, and as the filled basket passes him, Pullman says of the Bailiff: '"He's always massaged during the interval, the Bailiff's gone you see, let's stretch our legs shall we?"' (*C* p. 236). This is complicity.

It is in the *Prison Notebooks* of Antonio Gramsci that the terms 'hegemony' and 'ideology' were theorised in ways that would much later be developed in cultural studies, notably in the work of Stuart Hall. Are there any aspects of Lewis's thinking that might be thought compatible with Gramsci, even though he did not know his work? In her essay 'Hegemony and Ideology in Gramsci', Chantal Mouffe argues that what ideology does is to create subjects. Ideology is spread by '*hegemonic apparatuses*' such as schools, churches, the media, 'and even architecture', a point that would have interested Lewis as author of *The Caliph's Design*. Subjects are not given, but produced by an ideological field 'so that subjectivity is always the product of social practice'. It follows that 'it is ideology which creates subjects and makes them act'.[21] It must be apparent that Lewis is engaged to a significant degree in exploring how subjectivity is created, in both his works of theory and in his fiction. The theory tends to identify hegemonic practices, and the fiction to mobilise subjects acting ideologically. This is done most complexly in *The Revenge for Love*, where ideology may refer to political belief (Percy Hardcaster's communism) or to the gentler internalisation of the values of Bloomsbury by Margot, the novel's most perceptive character. Despite the way she is partly constructed as a subject by her internalisation of the values of Virginia Woolf's *A Room of One's Own*, it is she who understands the emotional chaos into which she and her partner Victor have been drawn by the imperatives of left-wing politics: and she interprets the situation far better than any male character represented in the novel. This is probably the finest outcome of Lewis's uncertain, incomplete, and yet decisively effective exploration of hegemony and ideology within high modernism.

Lewis and Gramsci meet in another respect, in a shared understanding of how hegemonic practices within political culture perform as preferable alternatives to state violence. I shall quote Lewis's early formulation of 1926, tentative as it is, and follow it with Gramsci's confident assertion from 1932. In *The Art of Being Ruled* a discussion of the role of intellectuals leads Lewis to consider (and deplore) the 'enregimentation' of women through the imposition of fashion in dress as a mode of conformity, a 'smooth-running process' which encourages 'the image of a political state in which no legislation, police, or any physical compulsion would be required' (*ABR* p. 362). Lewis then reformulates the same idea, but refers this time to an entity less tangible than fashion but more powerful: the Hebrew God. The teaching of righteousness, the citizen's own active conscience, and ritual: all merge to make an example of 'moral rule'. This is 'rule by opinion as opposed to rule by physical force: of much more effective *interior*, mental, domination, in place of a less intelligent *exterior* form of government' (*ABR* p. 363).

Gramsci's version occurs in a letter of 2 May 1932 in which he defines the active term as 'that moment in politics that is called the moment of "hegemony", of consensus, of cultural direction, to distinguish it from the moment of force, of coercion, of legislative, governmental, or police intervention.'[22] Lewis's 'rule by opinion' is close to Gramsci's 'consensus', just as the latter's 'cultural direction' (i.e. control from outside through power and violence) is present as the object of criticism in all Lewis's significant work of the 1920s. This convergence is remarkable; 'hegemony', in its cultural version, is usually attributed to Gramsci, but Lewis evidently formulated a working version of the concept some years before the Italian Marxist did so. When each speaks of the notionally democratic state, there are undoubted convergences between their thinking on the question of cultural control.

George Orwell: A Case Study

The publication of *The Mysterious Mr Bull* in 1938 marked Lewis's move to the political left. George Orwell reviewed the book favourably, and said: 'I do not think it is unfair to say that Mr. Wyndham Lewis has "gone left."' Lewis has declared himself 'a "revolutionary" and "for the poor against the rich"', which is unexpected, Orwell says, given the nature of his earlier writings.[23] The 'Mr Bull' of the title is the invented John Bull, the supposedly 'typical Englishman': forthright, straightforward, not radical, but representing the generality of the English. Lewis's strategy in the book is to show that in his time there is no such figure, not least because the class system has made it impossible: 'class is what disintegrates any coherent picture of John Bull' (*MMB* p. 286). Cultural control is still a predominant concern: 'In every branch of English life you find paternalism and authoritarianism prevails' (*MMB* p. 93), particularly in the media: 'in no country is the standard of information and amusement so low as in the Anglo-Saxon countries' (*MMB* pp. 94–5). The remark quoted by Orwell – 'I, too, am for the poor against the rich'

(*MMB* p. 199) – is followed by Lewis's argument that the potential freedoms of ordinary people ('the plain workman') were greater before the First World War than they are now: 'Thirty years ago [c. 1908, a time of workers' agitation] the prospects for their liberties were rosier than they are now' (*MMB* p. 199). There is even a contemporary aspect to Lewis's theorisation: 'The liberties of the manual workers are much more *our* liberties than are the liberties of the select personnel of the great finance-rackets' (*MMB* p. 199).

Orwell was in a good position to assess Lewis's move to the left, for he had been reading him closely for several years. In 1932 he read Lewis's journal *The Enemy*, and remarked in a letter that Lewis has 'evidently got some kick in him', adding: 'whether at all a sound thinker or not, I can't be sure without further acquaintance'.[24] Orwell's review of *The Mysterious Mr Bull* shows that further acquaintance took place, and that he was fully aware of the dramatic change that took place in Lewis's thinking in 1937. In 1941, the relationship between Orwell and Lewis becomes one of mutual recognition. In that year Lewis published a novel about class in England, *The Vulgar Streak*, and wrote to ask his publisher to send a copy to, among others, 'Mr Orwell (I dont [sic] know his first name) author of "Lion and Unicorn"' (*L* p. 307). Orwell evidently received the book, for he quotes from it in a major essay, 'The English People': 'The English working class, as Mr Wyndham Lewis has put it, are "branded on the tongue"', he writes, and adds later: 'No one should be "branded on the tongue". It should be impossible . . . to determine anyone's status from his accent.'[25] This episode shows that Orwell could absorb Lewis, and that Lewis recognised Orwell's importance in British culture long before the successful publication of *Animal Farm* in 1945.

In 1946 Orwell blundered, writing in the Trotskyist-edited New York journal *Partisan Review* that Lewis had become a communist.[26] This gaffe did not affect the long discussion of Orwell in *The Writer and the Absolute*, published in 1952. In Lewis's reading, after the war Orwell threw off the conventional left-wing thinking of the 1930s, and 'finished his literary life in a burst of clairvoyance' (*WA* p. 155). That clarity arose because Orwell entered a *public* realm where the satire of *Nineteen Eighty-Four* (1949) is most full of meaning:

> His hideous palaces of Truth and Love are first-rate political creations. His elaborate bureaucratic monstrosities will quite likely one day be historical facts: this is one of those rare books in which we may actually be looking at something existing in the future. (*WA* p. 190)

That, of course, is one of the primary ways in which *Nineteen Eighty-Four* is still read (though such readings are also contested). Elsewhere,

Lewis's discussion is sceptical, sometimes off-track (as in his speculations about Orwell being essentially on the right politically: again, others have proposed that view), but is still concerned with questions of power. He remarks of *Burmese Days* (1934) that its criticism of imperialism – itself an exercise of power that Lewis regards as 'disgusting' – differs in no essential respect from the way power is exercised at home: 'But man was not ruling man more oppressively in Kyauktada than he was in London, Leeds, Liverpool, and Birmingham' (*WA* p. 175).

The clarity that Orwell finally achieves is to go beyond the 'party' politics of the 1930s: 'Every writer should keep himself free from party, clear of any group-pull: at least this is *my* view of truth' (*WA* p. 193). This move towards 'objectivity' is – as we by now expect – accompanied by an inward turn towards a subjective account of how the writer exists in culture. Lewis defends a certain kind of egoism, for himself as much as for Orwell, by saying that – distinct from any party line – it involved writers saying 'what they thought'; Lewis then dissolves the idea of the writer as an egoistic individualist in an extremely interesting move that throws light upon his sense of himself as a participant in culture:

> [T]he *individual* cannot signify one person because there is no such thing as one person. Intellectually, you and I are a great number of people, alive and dead. The individual . . . is anything but an isolated speck, rigidly detached from all coeval minds. My opinion on most subjects is more or less shared by a respectable number of people. (*WA* pp. 194–5)

That being the case, and whatever 'machine' may exist to ensure 'conformity of opinion' – hegemonic forces, that is – any individual opinion is also a group opinion, so that 'it is quite incorrect to regard me as an abstraction called the *individual*' (*WA* p. 195). The writer stands in relationships with others that are shaped by a knowledge of, and an internalisation of, a history of ideas in the widest sense; this joins with actual experience and shared opinions, also internalised: 'individualism' in the proud and isolated sense is not possible because any particular person partakes of other people, as of ideas not their own; these accumulations appear to situate the individual in what we call culture, but because that individual does not really exist, she or he might be more accurately described as dissolved within culture.

By the 1950s, Lewis writes: 'Our intellectual consciousness has shrunk' into 'a private and exclusive mode', art is constrained, as is authorship: 'the writer is not free, he is ideologically restricted' (*WA* p. 197). The term 'ideology', which Lewis first used in 1919, developed so interestingly in the 1920s, and allowed to be submerged by the political dross of the 1930s, here reappears with renewed force. That it does so as part of a discussion of George Orwell as a public intellectual (a phrase not then in use, but the essentials are here) confirms that even in his latter years Lewis continued to have a valid perception of how the culture he worked in was itself functioning. The critique of culture is still based upon radical theory.

Conclusion

This account of Lewis as a cultural critic is necessarily incomplete; but enough has been said to show how his approaches varied as the times changed. In the *BLAST* years Lewis learned that culture can be performed antagonistically and has to do with relations of power. In the 1920s a holistic interpretation recognises the working of ideology in culture, enforced by hegemonic strategies. Lewis's later recognition of Orwell's significance shows how important it is to discuss writers in their public roles.

Julian Symons, who knew both Lewis and Orwell, wrote:

> The modern writer with whom he [Lewis] had most in common was, it seems to me, George Orwell. Like Orwell he maintained intellectual independence in a time favourable to one or another sort of conformity; like Orwell had an itch for politics; like Orwell was ignored, because of his ideas, by some people in important positions; like Orwell was utterly informal, without a trace of literary or social affectation. Yet although he was so easy to talk to Lewis was inhuman, in a way that Orwell was not; he was a man devoured by a passion for ideas, which he wished to put to the service of art.[27]

It is not clear why a passion for ideas should be thought 'inhuman', but – that apart – these remarks humanise both men: to work, and to think, in the service of art, is honourable, particularly as a project within modernity. What Symons has missed are Lewis's arguments about ideology and hegemony. They define his achievement as a satirist and as a critic of culture: the refusal to be abject before power.

Notes

1. '[N]ow that the earth has become one big village' (*ACM* p. 16).
2. The activity is blasted in *BLAST* as 'SENTIMENTAL HYGIENICS' (*B1* p. 18).
3. For the date, see *VEA* p. 242, n. 21.
4. For example, *The Studio* for February to May 1913 (Vol. LVIII, 342 pages) shows no Impressionist or Post-Impressionist work.
5. Forrest Read (ed.), *Pound/Joyce: The Letters of Ezra Pound to James*

Joyce (New York: New Directions, 1970), p. 26. Dated '[c. 1 April] 1914' (p. 25).

6. The Bloomsbury version of events avoids discussing Fry's culpability by deploring the satirical 'Round Robin' that the departing artists wrote later (see *L* pp. 47–50). For example, S. P. Rosenbaum begins with the polemic and never investigates whether Fry might have carried out 'discreditable actions'. See S. P. Rosenbaum, *Georgian Bloomsbury: The Early Literary History of the Bloomsbury Group 1910–1914* (Basingstoke and New York: Palgrave Macmillan, 2003). Lewis wrote the 'Round Robin' letter 'after his explosion' (p. 145) at the Omega Workshops in 1913.

7. Wyndham Lewis, 'A Man of the Week: Marinetti', *New Weekly*, 1, 30 May 1914, p. 329.

8. Leonard Woolf, 'To Roy Thornton', in Frederic Spotts (ed.), *Letters of Leonard Woolf* (London: Weidenfeld and Nicolson, 1989), p. 543 (letter of 17 February 1966), and p. 545 (16 March 1966). Woolf describes Lewis as 'practically insane with persecution mania' (p. 543).

9. See, for example, Tom Lubbock: 'This large show is a waste of space . . . Nobody seems to admire [Fry, Bell, and Grant] very highly, and nobody is likely to.' Tom Lubbock, 'Jack of All Styles, Master of None', *Independent*, *Review* section, 9 November 1999, p. 10.

10. See *VEA* p. 159 and p. 242, n.12 for a date in the spring of 1914.

11. For example, *Daily Express*, 14 June and 2 July 1914; *The Observer*, 5 July 1914.

12. The record label 'BLAST First' was founded c. 1985 in the UK.

13. See Michael E. Leveridge, 'The Printing of *BLAST*', *Wyndham Lewis Annual*, 7 (2000), pp. 21–31: p. 20. '[I]t was Leveridge who showed him what might be done': Paul Edwards, '*Blast* and the Revolutionary Mood of Wyndham Lewis's Vorticism', in *VNP* pp. 199–219: p. 204.

14. See http://gallica.bnf.fr/ark:/12148/bpt6k70494p/f5.image (accessed 24 November 2014). Later translated into Italian.

15. A *rapin* means both a trainee artist and a bohemian painter of doubtful talent.

16. The names are identified in *VEA* pp. 217–27. The present writer carried out the initial research for a seminar led by Professor Wees at McGill University in 1970.

17. A scholiast is a scholar who writes in the margins of (usually) ancient manuscripts: a marginal and dependent activity, therefore.

18. Jan Rehmann, *Theories of Ideology: The Powers of Alienation and Subjection* (Leiden: Brill, 2013), p. 19.

19. Raymond Williams, *Marxism and Literature* (Oxford: Oxford University Press, 1977), p. 57.

20. Ibid., p. 112.

21. Chantal Mouffe, 'Hegemony and Ideology in Gramsci', in Chantal Mouffe (ed.), *Gramsci and Marxist Theory* (London: Routledge, 1979), p. 186 and p. 187.

22. Antonio Gramsci, *Letters from Prison: Volume II*, ed. Frank Rosengarten, trans. Raymond Rosenthal (New York: Columbia University Press, 1994), p. 169. Gramsci is arguing against Benedetto Croce at this point.

23. George Orwell, 'Review of *The Mysterious Mr. Bull* by Wyndham Lewis;

The School for Dictators by Ignazio Silone' (1938), in Peter Davison (ed.), assisted by Ian Angus and Sheila Davison, *The Complete Works of George Orwell Volume Eleven: Facing Unpleasant Facts 1937–1939* (London: Secker and Warburg, 1998), p. 353. First published in *New English Weekly*, 8 June 1939.

24. George Orwell, 'Letter to Brenda Salkeld (extract)' (1932), in Sonia Orwell and Ian Angus (eds), *The Collected Essays, Journalism and Letters – Volume 1: An Age Like This 1920–1940* (Harmondsworth: Penguin, 1970), pp. 125–6: p. 126.

25. George Orwell, 'The English People' (written 1944, published 1947), in Sonia Orwell and Ian Angus (eds), *The Collected Essays, Journalism and Letters – Volume 3: As I Please 1943–1945* (Harmondsworth: Penguin, 1970), pp. 15–56: p. 19 and p. 51.

26. See George Orwell, 'London Letter to *Partisan Review*' (1946), in Sonia Orwell and Ian Angus (eds), *The Collected Essays, Journalism and Letters – Volume 4: In Front of Your Nose 1945–1950* (Harmondsworth: Penguin, 1970), pp. 219–25: p. 223.

27. Julian Symons, 'Meeting Wyndham Lewis', *London Magazine*, 4.10, October 1957, p. 53.

Chapter 6

Lewis, Satire, and Literature
Jamie Wood

In a rather neglected essay, written on the death of the acerbic column-
ist Charles Whibley, T. S. Eliot described Wyndham Lewis's satire in
terms that have come to dominate our understanding of the relationship
between Lewis and his chosen genre. Eliot proposed that Lewis, 'the
most brilliant journalist of my generation . . . often squanders his genius
for invective upon objects which to every one but himself seem unworthy of his artillery, and arrays howitzers against card houses'. While
we might detect a cold irony in the term 'brilliant journalist', Eliot's
critique is of content rather than genre. By 'journalism' he means a very
particular neoclassical tradition of invective prose, of Jonathan Swift's
letters, the 'pamphleteering' of Daniel Defoe and, more importantly, the
work of Léon Daudet and Charles Maurras, central figures in the anti-
democratic and monarchist Action Française movement, some of the
principles of which Eliot hoped to help foster within England.[1]

Eliot's critique of Lewis is that having seemingly made the right genre
choice, the man failed the art. Notice how Eliot so deftly achieves this
by yoking together biography and text: his analysis is built upon a metaphorical reference to Lewis's service with the Royal Garrison Artillery
during the First World War, leading out into the implication that Lewis
is solipsistic, perhaps delusional, in his manias. There is that sense of a
wasted and sterile talent, past its best while tilting at windmills. Eliot's
deftness, particularly the repetition of the gun image, slips together text
and artist so easily that Lewis's failure appears to stem from a neurological source, all the more worrying because unnamed. What differentiates
Whibley from Lewis, indeed what determines whether any work of art is
'cogent or not' in Eliot's analysis, is whether the artist's 'mind is *serré*',
tight, woven, and strong, 'or *délié*', loose and fluid, indeed 'whether the
whole personality is involved' or not. Such yoking together of the language of psychiatry with molecular imagery taken from the chemistry
laboratory is characteristic of Eliot, providing a metaphorical apparatus

of vesicle, reaction, and absorption in which text and author merge, as if osmotically, from their unique entropic states. Whibley stands apart from Lewis because 'he modulated his thunders according to the tree, shrub, or weed to be blasted'. Again, the sly image of Lewis as if at perpetual war with *BLAST* (1914–15). Whereas Whibley was selective, Lewis simply cannot seem to stop blasting. 'There is a kind of saturation in the text of an author, more important than erudition', Eliot proposes, and Lewis, it seems, has too much personality for the job.[2]

That today we tend initially to detect the irony in Eliot's 'journalist' epithet, rather than the imagery of warmongering, owes a great deal to how remote the neoclassical tradition has become and to how we read literature, how saturated we feel texts are with their authors. This notion of reading helps demonstrate the persistence of what Catherine Belsey has called the 'commonsense view of literature' in which Aristotelian mimesis is combined with the Romantic conviction that poetry expresses powerful feelings, so that 'the text is seen as a way of arriving at something anterior to it: the convictions of the author, or his or her experience as part of that society at that particular time'.[3] Eliot saw himself, of course, as precursor for the move away from this model, away from the author to a textual practice consolidated in the work of I. A. Richards, F. R. Leavis, and, later, the American New Critics. But the model of sincerity set out by Eliot in the essay on his patron Whibley, in which there must be a consistency between the printed word and speech, that is a consistency between art and life, plump full of a sort of moral integrity and fearlessness, sets up a problem in which there is a continuous sliding back to the author in order to defend, or even erect, the conclusions found in the text. Nowhere is this clearer perhaps than in the reception of Lewis's satire.

A quick glance down the title list of Lewis criticism shows the extent to which Eliot's original critique has come, perhaps indirectly, to saturate studies of Lewis's satire through tropes of aggression, arrogance, pitilessness, mockery, and enmity.[4] Robert Chapman categorises Lewis's satire as the product of a 'violent age', the literary equivalent of T. E. Hulme's legendary knuckle-duster carved in brass by Henri Gaudier-Brzeska, while William Pritchard proposes that we can better understand Lewis's satire, his 'very personal, interested base', if we understand him as a paranoiac who took to receiving his mail at the Pall Mall Safe Deposit.[5] Although Lewis encouraged such readings in the aliases behind *The Tyro* (1921–2) and *The Enemy* (1927–9), these features have largely been transcribed from the titles of paintings, novels, journals, and pamphlets as if they were barcodes. Kenneth Burke tentatively proposes a medical approach to Lewis's condition: 'There are symptoms to indicate that his excoriations arise from a suppressed fear of death.'[6] According to Ernest Hemingway, Lewis always reminded him of something 'medical'. He tactlessly described Lewis later in life as 'a frog', always looking 'nasty' in his 'wide black hat' with the eyes of an 'unsuccessful rapist'.[7] In the very special case of Wyndham Lewis, we appear to want to make an exception to much of literary theory's attempt to prise apart text and author: the man and the genre choice seem too perfectly aligned for the correlation to be ignored: Lewis's satire appears to arise from the combination of an intensely adversarial spirit, a series of psychopathologies, and 'a continuous want of ready cash'.[8]

In contrast, I want to propose that Lewis's theory of satire, when we can untangle it from its own crude socio-economic analysis and a ludicrous theory of alterity (particularly in relation to gender), can best be thought of as an alternative theory of literary practice to the one proposed by Eliot, Richards, and Leavis, a theory which continues to be such a powerful influence on the ways we read and teach literature today. Although these three theorists of literature reached subtly different conclusions, Lewis, I believe rightly, assessed their common theoretical base in a Romantic ideology of the aesthetic which was unfit for the challenges of modernity. Lewis's mature theory of satire, set out in *Men without Art* (1934) and its predecessor *Satire & Fiction* (1930), was after all developed, formalised, and published in the very midst of the frenetic period of activity which saw the principles of English Literature as a discipline set out for the first time. Richards published *Practical Criticism* in 1929, his pupil Q. D. Leavis followed with *Fiction and the Reading Public* in 1932, the year that saw her husband's *New Bearings in English Poetry* and the launch of the journal *Scrutiny*. The years around 1930 also saw important works of literary criticism from Max Eastman, D. S. Mirsky, John Middleton Murry, Mario Praz, Laura Riding and Robert Graves, Stephen Spender, and Edmund Wilson, each of which attempted to establish a genealogy of modernist literature, codify patterns of interchange between England and the continental avant-gardes, and determine what was and what was not worth reading. As Terry Eagleton neatly puts it, 'in the early 1920s it was desperately unclear why English was worth studying at all', but 'by the early 1930s it had become a question of why it was worth wasting your time on anything else'.[9] It is within this context that Lewis's theory of satire ought properly to be considered.

It is unsurprising then that there is much that is similar between Eliot, Richards, Leavis, and Lewis. They each proceeded from an essentially pessimistic assessment of where the world and literature had arrived in

1930, and, more importantly, from a conviction that the time had come
to remedy the situation. Richards summarised the situation best: by the
late 1920s the century was, he said, 'in a cultural trough rather than
upon a crest', a situation 'sufficiently serious to force' consideration
of the available 'remedies'.[10] These theorists would, as I will describe
later, differ in their remedies, but this affiliation of origins should not be
missed. Lewis, never one to shy away from accreditation, even went as
far as proposing that Richards had adopted his method of isolating the
'the affiliation of the sublime and the ridiculous' in the modern world
from his own work (*MWA* p. 16).

What is most obviously consistent in these socio-economic critiques
is the idea that the impersonal forces of science, technology, and a
form of advanced capitalism had combined in the post-war world to
create a culture of commodities that threatened to consume both art
and the individual. F. R. Leavis repeatedly mapped out the impact of a
'"technologico-Benthamite" civilization' concerned solely, as Gary Day
outlines, with 'productivity, a higher standard of living, and technical
progress'.[11] Lewis saw a 'British "Bankers' Olympus"' (*MWA* p. 30)
mysteriously controlling affairs at the centre of the state. Where Leavis
saw 'a process of standardization, mass-production and levelling-down'
and viewed civilisation as 'a solidarity achieved by the exploitation
of the most readily released responses', Lewis similarly proposed that
English society had become 'finely homogeneous, very thoroughly *lev-
elled*', a 'pell-mell confusion' (*MWA* p. 16).[12] In Leavis's work we find
the idea that the division between work and labour in the modern state
had created a crude advertising industry that undermined the self, that
the apparatus of the media had undermined social relations, and that the
proliferation of popular fiction had undermined reality with fantasy.[13]
Lewis sniffed a giant conspiracy in the superstructure too, proposing 'it is only by means of the gigantic smoke-screens of Lotteries and
Sweepstakes, Football Matches, Beauty Contests, Cross-Word Puzzles,
Sensational Crimes – the Smoke-screen put up by the Daily and Nightly
Press' (*MWA* p. 201) that the dire state of England was hidden from
view. It could quite easily be Lewis ghost-writing Q. D. Leavis's 1932
description of the emergence of English mass culture at Woolworths
with its 'cheap crockery, strings of beads, lamp-shades, and toffee, toys,
soap, and flower-bulbs' alongside which the 'customer is beguiled into
patronising literature.'[14] Lewis himself bemoaned how the war had
allowed 'the Jolly Roger of "Romance"' to keep flying and propelled a
'veneration for the violent' (*MWA* p. 148) in detective novels and gang-
ster fiction. Indeed, Lewis's main complaint throughout *Men without
Art* is that mass culture, 'proletarianization', and the '"Americanizing"

process [was] far advanced' (*MWA* p. 30) in 1930s England. This is the basis of the critique of Hemingway: his is 'a poster-art', a *'cinema in words'* (*MWA* p. 33).

There is then in each of these writers a common root in the attempt to determine what art could do to redeem the historical situation. There is a pessimistic assessment of the world, of literature's place in the world, of the 'monstrous impersonality' that results from the 'commercial and economic machinery'. There is even agreement on the need for 'conscious and directed effort' to remedy the situation, for an almost militaristic 'resistance by an armed and conscious minority'.[15] There is consensus on the value of craft, of art as a craft, 'in the sense that mathematics, cooking, and shoemaking are crafts'.[16] Genius is to be prioritised. For Leavis, the poet is 'at the most conscious point of the race in his time'.[17] Up to here, then, we could even say that Lewis and Leavis shared with each other, and with Eliot and Richards, what amounts to an essentially Romantic critique of the individual in relation to the formation of modernity, of the emergence of a callous industrialism, and of a philistine empiricism. But there the similarities end. On the one hand, it is clear that Leavis and *Scrutiny* were both strongly opposed to Lewis. Douglas Garman, reviewing a number of Lewis's satirical works in 1932, proposed that Lewis's 'eye, so bitterly critical when it is turned upon the world at large' was 'blurred by a narcissistic film'.[18] T. R. Barnes, concluding a review of one study of Lewis in 1933, likened Lewis's satire to the story 'of a German tailor, who, annoyed with his employer, had the latter's portrait tattooed on his behind' which he exhibited 'to the delight of his friends, and the discomfiture of his enemy'.[19] Leavis appears to have agreed, choosing his former student's article for inclusion in *A Selection from Scrutiny* in 1968 and dismissing Lewis later as '"the brutal and boring Wyndham Lewis"'.[20] Objecting in one essay to Lewis's criticism of D. H. Lawrence, Leavis took up Eliot's own vocabulary, proposing that Lewis's 'pamphleteering volumes are not books; their air of sustained and ordered argument is a kind of bluff'. Like Eliot, he proposed that Lewis's 'remarkable satiric gift is frustrated by an unrestrained egotism'.[21]

Perhaps more importantly, *Scrutiny*'s opposition to Lewis was founded on a deeper moral and artistic opposition to the satiric neoclassical tradition. Here Leavis departs from Eliot. Whereas Eliot saw invective as the direct route to the plain-speaking modern man, for Leavis satire posed an immediate and direct threat to the coherence of both the unified personality and the organic community, both of which he felt had been lost at the very birth of the modern. H. J. Edwards complained, in a *Scrutiny* review of the work of the eighteenth-century satirist Charles Churchill, that 'presumably to-day [Churchill] would have been a mere journalist'.[22] Here, 'journalist' really is ironical. In his essay on Swift, Leavis found that in satire 'the positive itself appears only negatively – a kind of skeletal presence, rigid enough, but without life or body'. Leavis found Swift's work 'probably the most remarkable expression of negative feelings and attitudes that literature can offer – the spectacle of creative powers ... exhibited consistently in negation and rejection'. Like Lewis, Swift's problem appears neurological: he is a force 'conditioned by frustration and constriction; the channels of life have been blocked and perverted'.[23] In this way, Leavis was able to transform Eliot's sponsorship of neoclassical invective into a kind of negative force that typified the dissociation of the modern sensibility.

For his part, Lewis makes it clear in *Men without Art* that he was attempting directly to counter the Eliot–Richards–Leavis axis. Lewis did not differentiate between the three, seeing them as essentially interchangeable, Richards having performed the 'task of definition, and of *exposure*, for his partner' Eliot (*MWA* p. 58), and the Leavises being Richards's 'appendix' (*MWA* p. 16). It was an axis Lewis believed had developed the 'most important literary theory, upon the English scene, since that of Walter Pater' (*MWA* p. 64). As is typical with Lewis, the critique is digressive, at times frustratingly inconclusive, and often poorly structured, but we can attempt a rather colourless summary. In the work of Eliot, Richards, and Leavis, Lewis argues, there is a retreat from the world into the 'saturated' and mystical text. The approach advocated by Richards in *Practical Criticism* ensured that while we might be able to quarrel about the aims of a poem 'we cannot legitimately judge its means by external standards'.[24] The poem as a result becomes a self-supporting structure, although, as we have seen, Eliot and Leavis both frequently used it as the home base from which to slide back to the author when convenient. What Lewis, I think rightly again, detected in the essence of these approaches, although in practice the matter is more nuanced, was an eventual retreat into the solitariness of the artist's mind, nostalgia for what had been lost replacing political solution. The source of this for Lewis was the Romantic aestheticians Immanuel Kant and Friedrich Schiller, who, in conceiving an unchanging useless thing called art invented for its own purposes, merely reinforced the extent of the artist's isolation from the world.

Lewis saw that the theories proposed by the Eliot–Richards–Leavis axis merely represented a 'new aesthetic of *art pur*', what he termed a 'stylists' evangel', another move by the '*art-for-art's-sake*' movement no matter how '*disguised*' it might be as something else (*MWA* p. 64). What Lewis derided in the axis was the extent to which an essentially valuable

Romantic critique of modernity had deployed an essentially wayward aesthetics of romanticism as an antidote. He saw the work of Eliot, Richards, and Leavis as being too deeply entrenched in the Victorian legacies of John Ruskin and Pater, especially in Matthew Arnold's attempt to use literature to Hellenise a philistine middle class who had failed to underpin their economic ascendancy with a viable ideology. Arnold's proposal, like that of the Leavises and Richards, was to insert literature as a moral standard into education as a means of defraying anarchy. Indeed, like Arnold before him, the major culprit in Leavis's work is the machine, which functions in his work as a synecdoche for 'any systematic, external, abstract approach to social problems which does not take account of individual human circumstances or needs or of traditional wisdom'.[25] In response to 'the incessant rapid change that characterizes the Machine Age', the consequent 'uprooting of life', Leavis was left with a retreat from the world into a lost organic community of unified personalities in which literature would act as a sort of moral glue.[26] Lewis, in contrast, saw the machine as a much more problematical object. It had changed the world and there could be no going back in art or in life. Things must be faced; humankind must be stiffened. Such a task required literature to bypass romanticism entirely.

There are two essential features of Lewis's alternative theory of satire: one, a theory of origins, contained in Lewis's definition of satire as a form of classicism, and one, a theory of artistic practice, contained in 'the method of *external* approach' (*MWA* p. 105). The first of these, the opposition of classicism to romanticism, is perhaps the easiest to deal with. According to Aristotle, poetry was borne from two alternative tendencies, one which 'represent[ed] noble actions, and those of noble personages' in 'hymns and panegyrics', and one, 'the meaner sort', which focused on 'the actions of the ignoble' in the form of 'invectives'.[27] These invectives were a form of ritual magic in which the good was invoked and evil expelled. The satirist was thereby a crucial force for holding together public order in classical societies, although such force was often overshadowed by, and held in tension with, the anarchic way in which he exercised his practice. Although such phallic fertility rituals seem a long way removed from Lewisian satire, these origins help explain how, as the satirist's role is altered by the introduction of law in the modern urban society, wit came to function as an essential means to challenge the established order, through modes such as irony, burlesque, innuendo, fable, and allegory.[28] It is in this tradition, of the magical disorderly power of the satirist to disturb the social order, in order to cleanse and to heal, that Lewis's satire operates: 'It is what is behind the Façade' that is interesting in the 'pantomime' as Lewis himself says

(*MWA* p. 103). Rather than looking back nostalgically to a lost community, it looks behind the world as it is. It is spatial rather than temporal.

According to Lewis, what lay behind the 'Façade' of modern England
was romanticism, an all-encompassing ideology of escapism that he
believed underpinned politics, economics, science, and culture. In effect,
wherever Lewis saw a retreat into the self from the world of action,
he saw romanticism. In this way, Lewis was able to bring together a
somewhat vulgar assessment of the socio-economic situation of England
in the 1930s, with his opposition to the modern state's self-professed
intellectual advancements: Henri Bergson's theory of *durée*, Gertrude
Stein's theory of composition, Virginia Woolf's stream of consciousness,
A. N. Whitehead's use of relativity, and J. B. Watson's behaviourism. As
here, Lewis was often highly selective in his targets, setting up straw men
that served his purpose, but as Anna Burrells explains, he was at least
consistent in that his 'key objection to these approaches was that they
effectively reduced the mind to a receptor that registered, rather than
acted upon, the operations of the outside world'.[29] To this list I would
add the Eliot–Richards–Leavis axis. After all, Lewis's major criticism
is that Eliot is insincere in his model of sincerity: 'Sincerity is precisely
what Mr. Eliot is afraid of – sincerity in the sense of integral belief of
any sort' (*MWA* p. 66). What Eliot actually demonstrates for Lewis is
a 'dogmatic hostility to the *individual*' (*MWA* p. 66), and to individual
patterns of belief, in lieu of which Eliot recommends certain communal practices, Catholicism being the most obvious, in which belief is
'disinfected . . . by the mere fact of possessing general assent' within 'a
great multitude passively sheltered in their consciousness' (*MWA* p. 66).
Perhaps Lewis sensed what Eagleton makes explicit, namely that the
Eliot–Richards' model of poetry, supplying pseudo-answers to pseudo-
questions, emotive rather than referential, seeming to describe the
world but actually organising our feelings about the world in a pleasing
way, is actually a kind of 'behaviourist model of the mind' based upon
quantification.[30]

Aristotle's distinction between 'invectives' and the 'hymn' is important also in fully understanding Lewis's very peculiar opposition of
classicism to romanticism. Lewis's principal point of difference from
the theories that precede him by Eliot and Hulme is in seeing religion
as part and parcel of the entire humanistic and Romantic tradition.
Using Herbert Grierson's work, Lewis traces the origin of the Romantic
spirit to the blood of Christ and to those regimens of controlling the
spirit (against the desires of the flesh) that feed from Platonism to Saint
Paul. Lewis follows Friedrich Nietzsche here: Christianity is figured
as a power structure, a slave-ethic in which a life beyond the grave is

promised as salvation from the horrors of the everyday. Such an analysis allowed Lewis to link up Grierson with another major theorist of romanticism, Mario Praz, who, in *The Romantic Agony* (1930, trans. 1933), had described romanticism as essentially based in a deviant bourgeois imagination focused on the beauty of the Medusa and the transformative power of Satan, and codified in the work of the Marquis de Sade. De Sade's erotics of pain and Christianity's focus on the destruction of flesh to exalt spirit, are then the opposite sides of the same coin for Lewis: a kind of 'calculated perversity' (*MWA* p. 143), a clear temptation to become more sinful, to '*prove* the Fall' and 'tearfully to invite the graces of the Atonement' (*MWA* p. 73). In such a state, Lewis believed men were free to leave their human nature behind and place all their 'pride in an hypostatized intellectual contraption' (*MWA* p. 73). Eliot's literary theory was just one such contraption; a piece of art-for-art's sake that was purely self-referential, making Eliot 'the last of that line of romantics' (*MWA* p. 67). In this way, Lewis's Romantic critique was able crudely, and in quite suspect reductionist terms, to envisage in one sweeping historical panorama how 'a satanic culture' of sexual perversion had worked its way through Christianity, romanticism, and the 'Naughty Nineties' (*MWA* p. 67) of Pater and Oscar Wilde, to the bourgeois humanist tradition infesting 'the tables and mantelpieces of Kensington and Mayfair' and, of course, Bloomsbury (*MWA* p. 96).

Lewis termed this artistic practice 'the method of *external* approach'. 'In contrast to the jelly-fish that floats in the centre of the subterranean stream of the "dark" Unconscious', set out in the work of Virginia Woolf, Lewis proposed that he preferred '*the shell* of the animal': 'The ossature is my favourite part of a living animal organism, not its intestines' (*MWA* p. 99). This, Lewis proposes, belongs properly to 'the "classical" manner': it relies on the eye rather than the more emotional organs of sense and can thereby make sense of the grotesque nature of the new world-order, making of it 'a healthy and attractive companion' rather than retreating from it (*MWA* p. 103). It stands as a result in contrast to most of the rest of Western art, which traces its roots to the Greek naturalist canon, and against the likes of James Joyce and Henry James who tell the story from the inside. The terms are again strongly gendered: the classical is based on a masculine formalism of action, solidity, permanence, and universality. It is public and concrete, based in the intellect and upon reason. In contrast, the Romantic is private, weak, it 'falls to pieces', it is 'a drifting dust' (*MWA* p. 153), gaseous without pattern or order. It focuses on fantasy, on the sensuous, and the nerves.

The crucial problem here is how to make classicism relevant in an age of such rampant romanticism. Lewis proposes the paradox that 'in a romantic age the most classically-minded artist would also be the most *personal*' (*MWA* p. 155), resulting in one of the most problematical issues in Lewis's theory: the question of the artist's own detachment. At the level of art, Lewis was concerned that Eliot's biochemical model of the mind, text, and society that aimed at a separation between author and text, achieved nothing of the sort. For Lewis, such separation was neither possible nor desirable: the artist is not depersonalised, he argued, '*he* is a seething mass of highly *personal* fine-feelings' (*MWA* p. 225). This might appear to be a contradiction, but there are two alternative concepts of individuality at stake here. Lewis is not interested in the Romantic personality, declamatory and struggling to find expression, but rather the author in the text, that personality that aims for 'a constancy and consistency in being, as concretely as possible, *one thing* – at peace with itself, if not with the outer world' (*MWA* p. 62). It is a vulgar classicism that proposes no interest in the inner life: but whereas romanticism starts from the inside to move out, classicism tends to set the inner life in the context of kinship, history, and the public world.

We can perhaps illustrate this point by looking at the figure of Pierpoint, the supposedly absent narrative presence behind *The Apes of God* (1930). Many critics have proposed that Pierpoint is the safe artistic vantage point from which the naive exploits of the novel's central character, Dan Boleyn, can be exposed as moronic.[31] But this surely misses the point of Pierpoint's own entanglement. The clue is perhaps in the name: the Pierrepoint family were British executioners for over fifty years from 1900 and well known to the popular British imagination. Pierpoint might hang the Apes he exposes, but how implicated is he then in the crimes of the criminals he exposes? In this respect, the satirist is, as Jonathan Greenberg points out, part of a class of moral menials – alongside bailiffs, butchers, garbagemen, paid executioners, and their like – who get metaphorically dirty on behalf of the societies they represent.[32] Lewis, as moral menial, uses the text consistently to remind the reader of the text's opacity, of the manipulation of the characters by the author, of the presence of the author in the text despite the tactics of disguise. His model is, he alleges, more sincere as a result.

How then would we summarise this opposition between Leavis and Lewis? One important difference is clearly the issue of genre. One of Lewis's real innovations lies, I think, in his manipulation of genre, the way he bends traditional genres as a means of communicating the trauma of modernity, rather than using the techniques we often associate with the modernist project, for example the fragmentation of language, non-linearity, temporal disruption, and ambiguity. Leavis really never had any interest in genre: he saw the best novels as dramatic poems and was dismissive of any game or formal experimentation that opened up a gap between words and experiences.[33] Equally important is the difference related to form. As Belsey suggests, if we want to imagine the opposite of the Leavisite tradition, we need to look to the work of writers such as Georg Lukács, who, in seeing the basis of art as resting in a constant striving after reality, aimed at sympathy with the suffering of people.[34] Such a comparison might seem strained: Lewis appears to show little sympathy with the people in *The Apes of God*, and he was strongly opposed to using art in the name of an exterior cause like Lukács, seeing in it a betrayal of the essential truth-telling basis of art. But Lewis's satire was attempting something similar, particularly in the manner in which it was ruthlessly focused on the real and on how 'the "visual" intelligence' focuses on 'the geographic background – the *visual medium*, as it were, in which men exist' (*MWA* p. 123). It seems odd for an artist so associated with the abstract shapes of Vorticism to return here to notions of realism, but the post-war Lewis wanted an art focused on the here and now, avoiding Pound's exotic historical slippage into 'the glamour of strange lands' (*MWA* p. 61). The classical was, Lewis thought, the expression of the 'the man who lived firmly in the present', of the artist who recognised the materiality of words (*MWA* p. 61). His satire was conceived as a powerful mode of truth-telling, similar, as several critics have noted, to the work of theorists in the Lukács-influenced Frankfurt School, particularly in the way it attempted to use an aesthetics of alienation as a means of telling the truth about the world, about the tactics of capitalism, about the way mass culture threatened art.[35] Indeed, Lewis had proposed as early as 1917 that 'life is invisible and perfection is not in the waves or houses that the poet sees' (*CWB* p. 319). And as Tyrus Miller suggests, Lewis's satiric mode functions almost as a consistent negotiation between satire and realism.[36] Where the two genres meet and part, Lewis says, is in the way satire chooses the people it wants to magnify with deliberate care:

> once these figures have been so magnified – not as "realism" works, but in an heroical manner of its own – whatever they may have been to start with, they become really important, they occupy space. With this magnification they undergo also a subtle change, they develop more energy. (*MWA* p. 113)

However, I want to conclude by suggesting that the way to best unite the points I have made might be to put aside the term satire altogether. Lewis pushed, strained, and developed the concept of satire so far that another sister-term is, I think, more appropriate: the grotesque. What, after all, is a non-moral satire but the grotesque? The grotesque shares with the satiric the pull of both the real and the fantastical, and the impulse of

creating alienation in the audience, but it revels in the opposites themselves, in their lack of resolution, the lack of any ethical closure: it is
'*the unresolved clash of incompatibles in work and response*', or '"*the
ambivalently abnormal*"' as Philip Thomson concludes.[37] Frances S.
Connelly goes further, suggesting that we should think of the grotesque
as a kind of anti-form, an 'aberration from ideal form', that refutes fixed
positions, resists prediction, and rebels against the stable: 'The grotesque
is a boundary creature', defined by what it does to boundaries, 'trans-
gressing, merging, overflowing, destabilizing them'.[38] This is a radical,
not a conservative, artistic practice.

The grotesque is, then, akin to the satiric bone hollowed of moral
marrow. Indeed, the one key feature in Lewis's satire we have not so
far considered is its non-ethical nature. Lewis argued that the greatest
satire could not be moralistic: good minds cannot be taken in by a purely
moral code, he proposed, 'the artistic impulse is a more primitive one
than the ethical' (*MWA* p. 89). Shorn of morality, satire can be pursued
purely '*for its own sake*' since even the best of men 'is only a shadow
. . . of some perfection; a shadow of an imperfect, and hence an "ugly,"
sort' (*MWA* p. 89). This non-ethical satire aims to speak of the real in
the cleanest possible fashion; it laughs at everyone, tilting at '*perfect
laughter*', an 'inhuman' impulse that selects 'as the objects of its mirth
as much the antics dependent upon pathologic maladjustments, injury,
or disease, as the antics of clumsy and imperfectly functioning healthy
people' (*MWA* p. 92). Satiric laughter is '*tragic* laughter' (*MWA* p. 92),
which, in lacking both pity and terror, aims to strengthen modern man.
As Lewis says, 'there is a stiffening of Satire in everything good, of "the
grotesque," which is the same thing' (*MWA* p. 99). This is closer to a
form of psychotherapy rather than a revelation of psychopathology.

Thinking of Lewis's style as the grotesque rather than as satire helps to
explain why he continues to find such a polarised community of critics
and supporters. For on the one hand, it is possible to see Lewis's rogues
gallery of grotesques as a form of conservative ridicule, an anti-human-
istic assault by genius upon mass culture.[39] But the grotesque can also
be seen, as I have proposed, as a form of brutal authenticity, a means
of representing and, possibly, diagnosing a disordered world. Thomas
Mann suggested that the grotesque is '"the genuine anti-bourgeois
style"', and it is something of this manner in which Lewis's satire functions.[40] It rightly belongs 'to an "expressionist" universe which is reeling
a little, a little drunken with an overdose of the "ridiculous" – where
everything is not only tipped but *steeped* in a philosophic solution of
the material . . . of the absurd' (*MWA* p. 232). In truly grotesque style,
what Lewis wants to achieve with this genre is to leave 'upon [the] retina

a stain of blood', to cause the reader 'to associate a little more . . . with [their] own entrails' (*MWA* p. 204). The angle of approach may be unusual, but Lewis's concern here is genuinely with the suffering of the people: he feared greatly that 'linger[ing]' with Eliot in the 'chambers' of the mind would genuinely drown humanity, that the behaviourist view of man as 'great herds of performing animals' robbed life of all value (*MWA* p. 233).[41]

Marshall McLuhan's observation that 'Lewis was a visionary for whom the most ordinary scenes became the means of intense seeing' is suggestive. Such 'seeing' McLuhan proposed was 'a means of clairvoyance'.[42] The more mystical aspects of clairvoyance may well have sat awkwardly with Lewis, but the word's French derivation, its root in a clarity of vision that comes from the eye, is I think appropriate. So too is the implication that truth might lie beyond ordinary human parameters. Throughout his life Lewis returned to images of the inhuman as a means of entry to vision. One thinks, for example, of Tarr's infamous '"deadness is the first condition for art"' (*T2* p. 265), that strange relationship between man and dog in 'The French Poodle' (1916), and the alien forms of *The Childermass* (1928) and the aborted 'Hoodopip' project. Look for example at Lewis's description of the true classical method developed by Oriental artists: 'It was not . . . anthropomorphic – it saw a bird or a frog as a bird or frog would see it, with the appropriate eye.' The artist is, he says, older than the fish: 'The intellect at its purest does not function in a specifically *human* way' (*MWA* p. 187). This is at the very core of Lewis's conclusion in *Men without Art*: modern man can opt to use language to humanise or to dehumanise ourselves: we can either accept our reason as 'a refinement, merely, of the mechanical animal condition' or we can look upon it 'as a *gift*' (*MWA* p. 233).

Notes

1. T. S. Eliot, *Charles Whibley: A Memoir*, The English Association Pamphlet series (London: Oxford University Press, 1931), p. 8 and p. 4.
2. Ibid., pp. 8–10.
3. Catherine Belsey, *Critical Practice* (London: Methuen, 1980), p. 2 and p. 13.
4. For example *JFA*; Mark Perrino, *The Poetics of Mockery: Wyndham Lewis's 'The Apes of God' and the Popularization of Modernism*, MHRA Texts and Dissertations series (London: Maney, 1995); and Geoffrey Wagner, *Wyndham Lewis: A Portrait of the Artist as the Enemy* (New Haven, CT: Yale University Press, 1957).
5. Robert T. Chapman, 'Satire and Aesthetics in Wyndham Lewis' *Apes of*

God', *Contemporary Literature*, 12.2, 1971, pp. 133–45: p. 133; William H. Pritchard, 'Literary Criticism as Satire', in *MWL* pp. 196–210: p. 198. Having his mail diverted was probably a matter of common sense: Lewis was in the process of moving house at this time.

6. Kenneth Burke, *Attitudes Toward History*, 3rd edn (Berkeley: University of California Press, 1984), p. 50 (first published in 1937).
7. Ernest Hemingway, *A Moveable Feast* [1964] (London: Arrow, 2004), pp. 63–4.
8. Pritchard, 'Literary Criticism as Satire', p. 197.
9. Terry Eagleton, *Literary Theory: An Introduction*, anniversary edn (Malden, MA: Blackwell, 2008), p. 27.
10. I. A. Richards, *Practical Criticism* (London: Kegan Paul, Trench, Trubner, 1930), p. 320.
11. Gary Day, 'F. R. Leavis: Criticism and Culture', in Patricia Waugh (ed.), *Literary Theory and Criticism* (Oxford: Oxford University Press, 2006), pp. 130–9: p. 133.
12. F. R. Leavis, *New Bearings in English Poetry* (London: Chatto and Windus, 1932), p. 214.
13. Day, 'F. R. Leavis: Criticism and Culture', p. 132.
14. Q. D. Leavis, *Fiction and the Reading Public* (London: Chatto and Windus, 1932), p. 17.
15. Leavis, *Fiction and the Reading Public*, p. 270.
16. Richards, *Practical Criticism*, p. 312.
17. Leavis, *New Bearings in English Poetry*, p. 13.
18. Douglas Garman, 'A Professional Enemy', *Scrutiny*, 1.3, 1932, pp. 279–82: pp. 281–2.
19. T. R. Barnes, 'Review of *Wyndham Lewis: A Discursive Exposition*, by Hugh Gordon Porteus', *Scrutiny*, 1.4, 1933, pp. 400–1: p. 401.
20. Leavis quoted in Chapman, 'Satire and Aesthetics', p. 134, taken from Leavis's 1963 Richmond Lecture.
21. F. R. Leavis, 'Mr. Eliot, Mr. Wyndham Lewis and Lawrence', *Scrutiny*, 3.2, 1934, pp. 184–90: pp. 187–8.
22. H. J. Edwards, 'Satire', *Scrutiny*, 2.4, 1934, pp. 416–19: p. 419.
23. F. R. Leavis, 'The Irony of Swift', *Scrutiny*, 2.4, 1934, pp. 364–78: p. 366 and pp. 377–8.
24. Richards, *Practical Criticism*, p. 204.
25. Richard Storer, *F. R. Leavis* (London: Routledge, 2009), p. 47.
26. Leavis, *New Bearings in English Poetry*, p. 91.
27. Aristotle, *On the Art of Poetry*, trans. Ingram Bywater (Oxford: Clarendon Press, 1988), p. 30.
28. Robert C. Elliott, 'The Satirist and Society', *ELH*, 21.3, 1954, pp. 237–48.
29. Anna Burrells, 'Satire Machines: Wyndham Lewis, Samuel Butler, and *Erewhon*', *The Journal of Wyndham Lewis Studies*, 1, 2010, pp. 62–80: p. 70.
30. Eagleton, *Literary Theory*, p. 39.
31. For example Chapman, 'Satire and Aesthetics', p. 136.
32. Jonathan Greenberg, *Modernism, Satire, and the Novel* (Cambridge: Cambridge University Press, 2011), p. 6.
33. Storer, *F. R. Leavis*, p. 67.

34. Belsey, *Critical Practice*, p. 14.
35. For similar parallels see Andrzej Gąsiorek, 'Wyndham Lewis on Art, Culture and Politics in the 1930s', in *WLC* pp. 201–21: p. 215; and Rebecca Beasley, 'Wyndham Lewis and Modernist Satire', in Morag Shiach (ed.), *The Cambridge Companion to the Modernist Novel* (Cambridge: Cambridge University Press, 2007), pp. 126–36: p. 128.
36. Tyrus Miller, *Late Modernism: Politics, Fiction, and the Arts between the World Wars* (Berkeley: University of California Press, 1999), p. 97.
37. Philip Thomson, *The Grotesque* (London: Methuen, 1972), p. 27, emphasis original.
38. Frances S. Connelly, 'Introduction', in Frances S. Connelly (ed.), *Modern Art and the Grotesque* (Cambridge: Cambridge University Press, 2003), pp. 1–19: p. 2 and p. 4.
39. For example, Ella Zohar Ophir, 'Toward a Pitiless Fiction: Abstraction, Comedy, and Modernist Anti-Humanism', *Modern Fiction Studies*, 52.1, 2006, pp. 92–120.
40. Mann quoted in Greenberg, *Modernism, Satire, and the Novel*, p. 14.
41 T. S. Eliot, 'The Love Song of J. Alfred Prufrock', *Poetry: A Magazine of Verse*, 6.3, June 1915, pp. 130–5: p. 135.
42. Marshall McLuhan, 'Lewis's Prose Style', in *MWL* pp. 64–7: p. 67.

Chapter 7

The Apes of God

David Bradshaw

The Apes of God is undoubtedly challenging and it is easy to challenge as diffuse and objectionable, but is it really 'virtually unreadable for any sustained period of time' (*JFA* p. 5), as Fredric Jameson has claimed so influentially? Is it really (to raise another persistent criticism) little more than a grotesque doorstop of a book in which sporadic passages of striking verbal bravura are well-nigh swamped by the un-channelled flood of Lewis's sundry revulsions and gargantuan verbiage? Is it just a 'massive and inscrutable volume buried in the plains of modernism as part of a kind of literary Stonehenge, a monolith admired from afar', as Scott W. Klein has memorably portrayed it, a satire that for all its bulky prominence in the literary landscape is seldom hugged with affection even by Lewis aficionados?[1] As our sense of what modernism might embrace grows ever more subtle and accommodating, Lewis's diverse and demanding output has come to seem increasingly 'congenial' over the past twenty years or so, but for many readers *The Apes* remains doggedly unwelcoming in spite of its spasmodic *élan*.[2] Replete with prejudice and polemical affront, no modernist novel (apart from Evelyn Waugh's *Black Mischief* (1932), perhaps) is likely to be more troubling for contemporary readers, but few, it could also be argued, are likely to prove so keenly and curiously engrossing for those prepared to see out its frequent *longeurs* and ride out its disturbing jolts. *The Apes* is almost pathologically odious in places, yet its abrasive monumentality can neither be sidestepped nor downsized by students of modernism. It looks and feels like *Ulysses* (1922), but it is *Ulysses* refitted for war.

Although a good deal of *The Apes* was written in 1929, it was begun much earlier in the decade and originated in Lewis's feuds with Roger Fry and, later, with Edith, Osbert, and Sacheverell Sitwell. After he'd published two short outriders to it ('Mr Zagreus and the Split-Man' and 'The Apes of God: Extract from the Encyclical Addressed to Daniel

Boleyn by Mr Zagreus') in *The Criterion* in 1924, T. S. Eliot wrote to express his delight with these pieces, telling Lewis in March that year:

> You have surpassed yourself and everything. It is worthwhile running the *Criterion* just to publish these. It is so immense that I have no words for it. I can only say that you have taken a weight off my mind, and off my chest, so that I breathe the better after it.[3]

Lewis's excerpts set up such a 'hue and cry', however, that Eliot asked him to make his targets less recognisable in his next extract.[4] Lewis did so, but nevertheless, in a portent of ructions to come, Eliot received a 'torrent of abuse' for publishing them, and a planned third excerpt, which was to have been taken from 'Lord Osmund's Lenten Party', thoroughly spooked Eliot and did not appear in the magazine.[5]

When *The Apes* was first published in its entirety in 1930 it was immediately apparent that, like so many other social satires of the inter-war period, such as Aldous Huxley's *Antic Hay* (1923) and Waugh's *Vile Bodies* (1930), Lewis's novel draws much of its edge and virulence from the devastation wreaked by the First World War and its traumatised aftermath: from one angle, it is Lewis's anatomy of a 'shell-shaken society'.[6] As such, it can be linked with other shell-shock-themed novels of the time, such as Rebecca West's *The Return of the Soldier* (1918) and Woolf's *Mrs Dalloway* (1925), though *The Apes* is never other than robustly subversive rather than tentatively reconstructive, reflecting Lewis's dissident compulsion to further churn up the cratered social and cultural landscape of post-war England. Its 'Prologue', in particular, contains some of the most pulverising satirical prose of the modernist era. Focused on the elaborate toilette of Lady Fredigonde Follett, her super-sized false teeth, *'scurfy'* head (*AG* p. 9), ear-trumpet, *'natty little high-born trotters'* (*AG* p. 20), and the *'spermy energy of her tongue'* (*AG* p. 9) are all noted in passing, but it is when Lady Fredigonde attempts to leave her capacious chair that Lewis unleashes his most devastating verbal weaponry against the vast bulk of her person:

> *A local briskness, of a muscular nature, was patent, in the depths of the chair. The massively-anchored person shook as if from the hidden hammering of a propeller, revolving at her stern, out of sight . . .*
>
> *As her body came away from the dense bolsters of its cyclopean cradle, out into space, the skimpy alpaca forearm of the priestly Bridget, a delicate splint, pressed in against the small of the four-square back. It was applied above the region where the mid-victorian [sic] wasp-waist lay buried in adipose.*
>
> *The unsteady solid rose a few inches, like the levitation of a narwhal. Seconded by alpenstock and body-servant (holding her humble breath), the escaping half began to move out from the deep vent . . . Something imperfectly animate had cast off from a portion of its self. It was departing, with a*

grim paralytic toddle, elsewhere. The socket of the enormous chair yawned just short of her hindparts. It was a sort of shell that had been, according to some natural law, suddenly vacated by its animal. But this occupant, who never went far, moved from trough to trough – another everywhere stood hollow and ready throughout the compartments of its elaborate animal dwelling. (*AG* pp. 22–3)

This passage and others like it in the novel (such as the account of the assembled chatterboxes at 'Chez Lionel Kein Esq.'):

> Most began by tuning-up the complicated round or sphenoid wind-instrument they had brought with them, that is their respective headpieces – in which the air trumpeted and vibrated in the darkness ... Soon all were working their bellows forcibly. When most in form, the hard palate could be heard producing its deafening vibrations in the buccal cavity (*AG* p. 272)

are of a piece with the notion of satire Lewis put forward beyond his text. '[N]o book has ever been written that has paid more attention to *the outside* of people', he writes of *The Apes* in his *Satire & Fiction*. 'In it their shells, or pelts, and the language of their bodily movements, comes first, not last' (*SF* p. 46). Had Lewis adhered more closely to his externalist principle and continued in the mordant manner of 'The Body Leaves the Chair' (*AG* pp. 21–4) and the 'Chez Lionel Kein Esq.' passage, it is likely that *The Apes* (for all its more rebarbative aspects) would by now have been long established as one of modernism's satirical masterworks.

Further showcase examples of the idiosyncratic boldness of Lewis's externalist satire might include the arrival of Admiral Benbow, Major Updick, Commander Perse, and General Walker-Trotter at Lord Osmund's Lenten Party:

> Commander Perse was first. His clean-shaven, salt-tanned, non-pareil senior-service face required no uniform to advertise his calling ... and everyone must have the conviction at the first glimpse of him – this royal-blue aquatint – that a topgallant was tattooed upon the stiff upstanding pillar of his back – that a mandril picked out in blue and scarlet swarmed up *one* of his sea-legs – that a rude specimen of what Jack Tar has one-each-of in every port bulged with her brawny limbs upon *the other* – that a Capstan Navy-cut british [sic] sheet-anchor was suspended upon his left breast almost certainly – that is in that portion alone not overstocked with a rank growth of male hair, above the beating-spot of his heart-of-oak. (*AG* p. 517)

Cast from the same briny mould is Mrs Bosun, Lord Osmund's maidservant and an 'egregious period-matron' who ogles Dan Boleyn (dressed as a woman)

with professional fish-eyed sex-banter born of a seafaring past . . . a digni-
fied red-white-and-blue domestic personage bluff and stout with blue and
steadfast eye, of best ocean-blue (as the waves used to be before Trafalgar but
especially prior to the Mutiny of the Nore). (*AG* p. 435)

As she helps Dan change his costume her 'fiendish sex-jollity – her
primitive prude-ragging proclivities' (*AG* p. 437) come to the fore and
Dan fears he will be picked 'dry of every stitch, as though he had been
a pre-war Pears-Soap-Baby' (*AG* p. 437). Unsurprisingly, he is terrified
that this

great mastodon of a matron from the brutalest of the British Past (and how
brutal the British Past was only an Irishman could guess) would come crashing out of her closet-within-a-closet, playfully lay hold of him possibly by a
leg, like a chicken to be plucked, and strip him in what she would of course
call two shakes yes of a Moke's tail or some such hearty horror of an expression. (*AG* p. 438)

Dan tries to escape but is foiled by Willie Service, Horace Zagreus's
flunkey, and he finds himself, once again, 'panting before the intoler-
ably cheerful personality of this period-nurse of gigantic tots, full of a
diabolical bustle of unmentionable preparation' (*AG* p. 440). Elsewhere,
the lesbian Miss Ansell, whose appearance creates the impression of 'a
bavarian [sic] youth-movement elderly enthusiast . . . She was wiry and
alert with hennaed hair bristling, enbrosse. In khaki-shorts, her hands
were in their pockets, and her bare sunburnt legs were all muscle and
no nonsense at all' (*AG* p. 222), is another figure who shows off Lewis's
satirical penmanship at its sharpest. Miss Ansell is bald and her

strawberry-pink pull-over was oddly surmounted by a stiff Radcliffe-Hall
[sic] collar, of antique masculine cut – suggestive of the masculine hey-day,
when men were men starched-up and stiff as pokers, in their tandems and
tilburys. The bare brown feet were strapped into spartan sandals. A cigarette-
holder half a foot long protruded from a firm-set jaw. (*AG* p. 222)

The trial (and eventual suppression) of Radclyffe Hall's *The Well of
Loneliness* had only recently concluded when Lewis began bringing *The
Apes* to completion, and Miss Ansell's inclusion in the novel is at once a
topical poke in the eye for the prudes while also being more than a little
one-eyed in its representation of a lesbian.

And while her treatment may displease some contemporary readers,
Miss Ansell might also be seen to personify the novel's liberating,
'prude-ragging proclivities'. On 25 October 1929 Lewis published an
article in *The Daily Express* entitled '***!!—...?***!!!' to protest about
the bowdlerisation of Richard Aldington's *The Death of a Hero*, and

at the end of his article he took yet another opportunity to state his opposition to what he called 'the militant feminine principle of a false and imbecile "niceness"', which he believed lay at the root of England's infantalising cult of prudery.[7] This dual position – a desire to write unhindered by Mrs Grundy and to spurn 'imbecile "niceness"' – offers a handy twin approach to *The Apes*. Within the novel's welter of words are buried such prude-provoking terms as 'bollocky' (*AG* p. 63) and 'pudenda' (*AG* p. 84); a passing reference to Zagreus's 'phallic hand' (*AG* p. 329); a quick peep at the 'scrotum-skin' of Ma Hollindrake's 'withered apple-of-Adam' (*AG* p. 208); a glimpse of a minor character named Cubbs, with his 'dreamy masturbatory eye of mild blue' (*AG* p. 185); a bird's-eye view of the frantic sexual preliminaries of Betty Bligh and Matthew Plunkett, which are only brought to a halt when they discover Dan Boleyn on Plunkett's bed (*AG* pp. 90–1); and the near ravishment of Dan (dressed as a woman) by an elderly roué at Lord Osmund's Lenten Party (*AG* pp. 461–9). The novel also contains such coinages as 'televisionally' (*AG* p. 152), and in many ways it foregrounds a teeming linguistic vitality and inventiveness that are only surpassed in the canon of modernist fiction by such works as *Ulysses*, *Finnegans Wake* (1939), and *Molloy* (1955).

Far too much of *The Apes*' verbal ingenuity, however, is conscripted into the service of its abject racial prejudice. On the front cover of the third issue of Lewis's *The Enemy* (1929), a statement in bold reads:

THE 'ENEMY' IS THE NOTORIOUS AUTHOR, PAINTER AND PUBLICIST, MR. WYNDHAM LEWIS. HE IS THE DIOGENES OF THE DAY: HE SITS LAUGHING IN THE MOUTH OF HIS TUB AND POURS FORTH HIS INVECTIVE UPON ALL PASSERS-BY, IRRESPECTIVE OF RACE, CREED, RANK OR PROFESSION, AND SEX. (*E3* front cover)

Yet although it is true that characters of both sexes and from across the social spectrum feel the heat of his pen, when Lewis, like Matthew Plunkett, 'drop[s] his *hates*, bomb by bomb' (*AG* p. 67) in this novel, it certainly does not appear as though he drops them '*irrespective* of race'. Despite the connections he was keen to draw between his novel and his impersonal theory of satire, a good deal of Lewis's writing in *The Apes* is not only corrosively personal but all too easily relatable to the racialist bigotry of his day. While he was not alone, for example, in adopting a pejorative attitude to jazz and the generally Black musicians who were associated with it between the wars – both Huxley and Waugh, for example, write dismissively of jazz and Black jazz musicians in *Those Barren Leaves* (1925) and *Decline and Fall* (1928) respectively – in no other social satires of the period do we encounter the sustained contempt, the repeated, ostracising emphasis on atavism and primitivism, that we find in *The Apes*. Soon after the beginning of the novel, Lady Fredigonde's toilette is interrupted, much to her displeasure, by an '*afro-american [sic], nigger-footed*' (*AG* p. 16) troupe of street musicians. This band is heard again at the end of the novel, and in the vast expanses of prose in between there are numerous jarring references to, among other things, 'idiot slaves, in cotton fields' (*AG* p. 43) and the 'nigger squabness' (*AG* p. 71) of Dan Boleyn's nose. And while it is one thing to characterise jazz as 'the folk-music of the metropolitan mass – slum-peasant, machine-minder – the hearty cry of the city-serf' (*AG* p. 404), it is quite another to vilify Black musicians with the gusto Lewis summons in the 'At the American Bar' section of the novel (*AG* pp. 442–55). Here the reader not only encounters 'the studied mass-energy of the [jazz] music, hurrying over precipices, swooping in switchbacks, rejoicing in gross proletarian nigger-bumps, and swanee-squeals shot through with caustic catcalls from the instrumentatlists' (*AG* p. 443), but an 'ex-cotton-helot' (*AG* p. 445) and a 'negro' who does not 'hide his teeth under a bushel' (*AG* p. 444), while further on in the novel another Black man is described as a 'savage' (*AG* p. 569). Indeed, the more Lewis's stock Black men roll their eyeballs and display their prominent white teeth, just as they do in the racist cartoons of this era, the harder it is to square their role in the novel (especially today) with anything that could be thought of as beneficially astringent, anything that might be regarded as a salutary or corrective. On the contrary, Lewis seems to lose all sense of satiric mission as his eye lingers obsessively on the limbs of the jazz musicians: 'The black hands were moving all the time, deft and black' (*AG* p. 570). The recurrence of the word 'black' in this sentence amplifies it beyond a repeated descriptor into something more morbid and disquieting. Nathan Waddell points out that in a later volume, *America and Cosmic Man* (1948), Lewis hails jazz as a '"splendid cultural instrument"', but such an apparent about-turn hardly compensates for his treatment of Black people in *The Apes*.[8]

But if this aspect of the novel is highly questionable, its treatment of Jews is extraordinary both in terms of its extensiveness and nastiness. Archie Margolin, for example, is described as a 'jew-boy [sic] from the slum' (*AG* p. 44), 'the militant slum-Jew in excelsis' (*AG* p. 46), a 'Sham-Yid' (*AG* p. 47), and an 'East End monkey-on-a-stick' (*AG* p. 507) with a 'mongol-yellow [sic] face' (*AG* p. 48) and obsession with money (*AG* p. 50). Julius Ratner, another East End Jew and a character who is obviously based on the Jewish writer John Rodker, is marginalised as 'a sort of ape-like hideous alien' (*AG* p. 154). He not only has a thick neck and a yellow complexion (*AG* p. 153), like

Margolin, but also 'fangs' (*AG* p. 155). As a writer he can do no more than muster an 'obscene diarrhoea of ill-assorted vocables' (*AG* p. 159), and when Lewis places him in front of a mirror, he is only capable of 'doctor[ing] the crater left by a blackhead and inspect[ing] a yellow fang, to rescue it from tartar' (*AG* p. 160). Ratner also smells (*AG* p. 169) and has 'a venereal disease' (*AG* p. 164), while his 'vulpine craft' (*AG* p. 543) and other attributes suggestive of a 'pogromed animal' (*AG* p. 596) are so pronounced that even the dull-witted Dan Boleyn believes that he '[s]hould be in the Zoo' (*AG* p. 173), where he would be exhibited, no doubt, alongside the likes of Lionel Kein, another Jew, with a 'shallow ranine muzzle' (*AG* p. 243), a 'batrachian muzzle' (*AG* p. 310), and his Jewish wife Isabel, the possessor of a 'long well-shaped piscine nose, like a metal fish' (*AG* p. 273). Lewis cannot leave Ratner alone for long, and his 'hooked nose' and 'asiatic [sic] profile' (*AG* p. 327) are again in focus at the beginning of Part XI, while he is described further on in the text as a 'bilious grease-spot' (*AG* p. 539). Taken as a whole, it is almost impossible to read *The Apes*' representations of Jews and Jewish life as anything other than straightforward vituperation. Commentators have been largely silent about the novel's rabid anti-Semitism, perhaps because it is so very hard to square with Lewis's doctrine of externalist, impersonal satire, but it cannot pass undocumented or unremarked.

In its polyglot plurality and omnium gatherum inclusiveness *Ulysses* resists the age-old alienation of Jews, whereas some passages in *The Apes* seem to have been knocked together from the worst excesses of anti-Semitic propaganda. 'Of all the inadequacies of literary and artistic London that people the pages of *The Apes of God*', Ian Patterson has observed, 'none is more extensively and more carefully anatomized than Julius Ratner ... He is in some ways the most creepily memorable of the book's many creations', while Andrea Freud Loewenstein has noted that even

> the notorious Protocols of the Elders of Zion come into play with heavy-handed references to 'a Lost Tribe' and to 'the elder [of] the Mediaeval Zion'. Ratner is also the Jew as moneylender, pornographer, pervert, masochist, communist, filthy disease-carrier, and child-killer.[9]

Patterson argues perceptively that despite the pervasiveness of Lewis's 'depressingly unoriginal' anti-Semitism, 'explosions of disgust and laughter co-exist in a high carnivalesque rhetoric in which Lewis's own psychological vulnerabilities are closer to the surface than is often recognized', yet while this is an astute analysis of the novel's complex and self-indicting satire as a whole, it hardly defuses the novel's hard-wired racism.[10] In November 1930 Lewis travelled to Berlin in pursuit of a German publisher for *The Apes* and while he was there he saw a Nazi rally, subsequently writing an appreciative book about Hitler, 'its jacket cheerfully festooned with swastikas'.[11] Despite the publication of both *The Hitler Cult* and *The Jews, Are they Human?* in 1939, in which he renounces his previous enthusiasm for the German leader and his politics, Lewis's reputation has been irrevocably damaged both by his treatment of Jews in *The Apes* (a novel, furthermore, in which Pierpoint's political-secretary, Starr-Smith, dresses as a blackshirt) and the openly laudatory *Hitler* (1931), which was published soon after *The Apes*. And as David Ayers has explained, the treatment of Jews as parasites in the novel is not only discordantly in tune with the emergent ideology of the Nazis but part and parcel of an anti-Semitic campaign that Lewis had been waging since 1924: 'Lewis develops a caricatural image of the Jew which expresses his own worst fears about the destruction of the artist, the individual and Western Man. The Jew is depicted as a self-obsessed and parasitic alien in Western society.'[12]

Homosexuality – and not least 'Proust's imposition of the pederastic motif upon post-war society' (*AG* p. 303) – is another of the novel's awkwardly discredited preoccupations, and Ratner is doubly indicted in that he is also gay (*AG* p. 148). *The Apes*' seam of homophobia, along with its other strident antipathies, will always present a major obstacle to readers of the novel, yet some critics have been at pains to complicate the text's obnoxiousness even if they can do nothing to reduce it. 'It should be pointed out', Paul Edwards has argued, 'that [Lewis's] analysis is ideological, and implies no disapproval or approval of actual women, homosexuals or others except insofar as particular people allow themselves to be uncritically socially determined by the ideological stereotypes Lewis identifies' (*AG* p. 632). Yet even as it seeks to explain Lewis's practice as a satirist, this line of argument still struggles to come to terms with the fact that Lewis's anti-Black, anti-Semitic, and homophobic diatribes are all too easy to align with the broader discourses of inter-war racial and homosexual intolerance. That Lewis told a correspondent in 1930 that *The Apes* comprised a 'quarter of a million of *carefully-written* and *often-corrected* words' (*L* p. 195, emphasis added) only compounds the book's problematic legacy. Yet the treatment of Margolin, Ratner, and others is at least consistent with the view of satire put forward by Zagreus in the novel. He tells Ratner: 'True satire must be vicious' (*AG* p. 450), and insists that 'it is impossible to devise anything sufficiently cruel for the rhinoceros hides grown by a civilised man and a civilised woman' (*AG* p. 255). Zagreus also believes that the 'air of being "scientific" and the paraphernalia of "detachment," used by the average literary workman, result in something the opposite of what you are led to anticipate. The Fiction produced in this manner becomes more *personal* than ever before' (*AG* p. 259).

In sharp contrast to its treatment of race, the novel's targeting of 'shabby Bloomsbury potentates' (*AG* p. 61), bogus Bohemians, and 'the canaille of the Ritzes and Rivieras' (*AG* p. 433) hardly raises an eyebrow nowadays. Matthew Plunkett has a 'big subaqueous Bloomsbury stare' (*AG* p. 79) and the painter Mélanie Blackwell is only capable of producing 'slick poster-landscapes of Riviera type, garish and geometric' (*AG* p. 94). As she speaks to Dan Boleyn, Mélanie's voice becomes 'more egregiously irish [sic], for she came from St. Louis of an immigrant galician [sic] family who were tailors, who had taken a fancy to the name of O'Konolly – becoming bigorras' (*AG* p. 95). As a hater of cliques and claqueurs Lewis was not alone, of course. 'London swarms with the dilettanti of letters', Arnold Bennett had declared in 1910: 'They do not belong to the criminal classes, but their good intentions, their culture, their judiciousness, and their infernal cheek amount perhaps to worse than arson or assault.'[13] Lewis, naturally, goes infinitely further than Bennett in his denunciation of London's dilettanti, and the broiling core of *The Apes* is the 'Extract from encyclical addressed to Mr. Zagreus' (*AG* pp. 118–25). Here, the eponymous Apes are identified as '*those prosperous mountebanks who alternately imitate and mock at and traduce those figures they at once admire and hate*' (*AG* p. 123):

> In England for a very long time this sort of *societification* of art has been in progress. It is even possible that the English were the first in the field with this *Ape* art-type. The notorious *amateurism* of the anglo-saxon [sic] mind makes this doubly likely. In *Bloomsbury* it takes the form of a select and snobbish club. Its foundation-members consisted of monied middleclass descendants of victorian [sic] literary splendour. Where they approximate to the citizens of this new cosmopolitan Bohemia is in their substitution of money for talent as a qualification for membership. (*AG* p. 123)

In *Time and Western Man* (1927), Lewis had indirectly attacked the Sitwells and openly named Gertrude Stein as pre-eminent exponents of the inter-war 'child-cult' (*TWM* p. 61), and in *The Apes*, barely disguised, the Sitwells are enshrined as 'God's own Peterpaniest family' (*AG* p. 498). Bloomsbury, too, is represented as a great *crèche* of babies, mewling, timid, and talentless. The painter Dick Whittingdon is marked by his 'towering bright-eyed juvenility' (*AG* p. 27), while Betty Bligh is a 'four-foot-ten adult-tot in toto' (*AG* p. 81), and whenever Matthew Plunkett becomes thoughtful his eyes go blank and his mouth pouts, 'since always in order to think he returned to the wet milky pout, the vacant stare, of the teething infant' (*AG* p. 77).

The rich efflorescence of the *roman à clef* between the wars is exemplified by such novels as Lawrence's *Women in Love* (1920) and Huxley's *Crome Yellow* (1921) and *Point Counter Point* (1928), but *The Apes* overshadows every other novel of this genre – and not just in terms of its size. Osmond Finnian Shaw is clearly based on Osbert Sitwell in *The Apes*, Phoebus is Sacheverell Sitwell, and their sister Harriet is heavily indebted to Edith Sitwell. Babs Kennson is drawn from Georgia Sitwell, Sacheverell's Canadian wife; Matthew Plunkett is recognisable as Lytton Strachey; Lionel Kein is a dead-ringer for Sydney Schiff; and Isabel Kein is based on his wife, Violet. Horace Zagreus is partly drawn from the prankster Horace de Vere Cole, while the nautically rendered Richard and Jenny are squarely derived from Edward and Fanny Wadsworth. Another painter, Richard Wyndham, is the original of *The Apes'* Dick Whittingdon; Zulu Blades borrows much from Roy Campbell; and Dan Boleyn may, to a very slight extent, have something of Stephen Spender about him. Betty Bligh owes much to Dora Carrington, Hedgepinshot Pickwort is Edgell Rickword, Arthur Wildsmith is Arthur Waley, while Kalman could not be more identifiable as the mathematician and Beethoven expert J. W. N. Sullivan.[14] And to this already lengthy roster of more or less see-through stand-ins and their originals many more contenders might be added (the 'well-worn London laughing-stock' (*AG* p. 392) Richard Wright, for example, is almost certainly based on the poet Robert Nichols (1893–1944)) to take their places alongside the inter-war artists, writers, and celebrities, such as James Joyce, George Moore, Pirandello, Mussolini, and Charlie Chaplin, who are mentioned by name in the novel. Sean Latham has argued persuasively that Lewis deliberately 'cultivated' the 'hostility' of those he incorporates into *The Apes* lightly disguised 'in order to expose what he believed to be the hypocrisy and petty snobbery of an aesthetic sphere that cloaked itself in the claims of radical autonomy only in order to preserve antiquated structures of social prestige.'[15] Unambiguously, Lewis's appropriation of the *roman à clef* was an act of aggression, a renunciation of the innocuous conviviality of the genre.

Ending his book amid the short-lived and unavailing General Strike of 1926, an event that marked the reaffirmation of Establishment power over the embryonic forces of industrialised mass labour, could not be more fitting in terms of Lewis's political vision in *The Apes*. As he put it in *Rude Assignment* (1950):

> All social Satire is political Satire. And in the case of my solitary book of Satire, that is the answer too. If anyone smarted because of it (and it seems that they did, for although the personal identification may have been

unfounded, the class identification was probably accurate) they smarted for a political reason. As a class, they had outstayed their usefulness and had grown to be preposterous parasites.

As once upon a time . . . it was the duty of any man, observing another rustling a horse, to apprehend him (if he could) and to hang him (if he had a rope) to the nearest tree (if there were one thereabouts): so it was incumbent upon all good citizens to turn satirists on the spot, at the sight of such as those exhibited in 'The Apes of God'. (*RA* p. 57)

Elsewhere in *Rude Assignment*, Lewis recalls that *The Art of Being Ruled* (1926) was an 'account, comprising many chapters, of the decadence occupying the trough between the two world-wars [that] introduces us to a moronic inferno of insipidity and decay (which is likewise the inferno of "The Apes of God")' (*RA* p. 183). A key task for the novel's reader, however, is to gauge the extent to which Lewis's prodigious animus drew him into a cauldron of his own making, consuming him in his own satirical holocaust. His contention that the art and fiction of his day had become little more than a chronicle of celebrity culture did not fall on deaf ears and many reviews of the novel were favourable. Similarly, Zagreus's claim that

the Reigning Order is the people with the pelf and the circle of those they patronize, and today it is the High Bohemia of the Ritzes and Rivieras. And the "great novels" of this time are *dramatised social news-sheets* of that particular Social World (*AG* p. 262)

spoke powerfully to the moment as far as many of Lewis's fellow writers were concerned. But does *The Apes* anatomise this culture or simply fall victim to it?

This question brings us to the most important consideration of all with regard to *The Apes*: the book's moral authority. It is a signal feature of the novel that all the characters who have apparently been blessed with Lewis's imprimatur end up so hopelessly compromised in that they acquire, or have always embodied, the very faults and failings they are supposed to be either exempt from or merely observing. Hugh Kenner described Dan Boleyn as 'an immense Irish moron with sore feet . . . fretting beneath the tutelage of the genius-specialist Horace Zagreus' (*KWL* p. 100), and in a novel that condemns infantilism, it is notable that Dan, the chief surveyor of so much puerile imbecility, is no more than 'a great simple irish [sic] schoolboy' (*AG* p. 98) himself. Dan follows Zagreus 'like a dog at successive lamp-posts' (*AG* p. 240), while Zagreus, for his part, only does what Pierpoint tells him to do. He shows no initiative of his own and he is also a homosexual, 'a bombastic faggot' (*AG* p. 321) as the novel has it, with an aggressive valet named Willie Service. At one level this secondary character's name is merely crudely comical, but at another it represents yet another way in which the novel's Olympian prejudices are intriguingly destabilised from within. So if unoriginality is the great crime of the would-be painters and writers condemned in the novel, it represents something of a problem that the hapless Boleyn is learning the ropes from Zagreus who receives his marching orders from 'that Great Absentee . . . the mighty Pierpoint' (*AG* p. 261), a 'painter turned philosopher' (*AG* p. 129) who tends to sound very much like Lewis himself. There is, indeed, one mention of 'our solitary high-brow pur-sang Lewis' (*AG* p. 401) in the text, but he does not appear in it and he is represented, instead, by a ghastly hierarchy of copycats who bring themselves into spectacular disrepute. Their ill-suitedness to their roles, in fact, renders the boundaries of imitation and fraudulence so indistinct in the novel as to become barely discernible. As Latham has remarked: 'Gossip, innuendo, and celebrity scandal drive *Apes of God* just as powerfully as they do the works Zagreus condemns, introducing into the text a bewildering hypocrisy that seems to undermine some of its most eloquent moments.'[16] 'If there is theology in *The Apes of God*', Edwards has added, 'it is not such as claims for its author transcendental exemption from the destructive satirical analysis he has perfected' (*AG* p. 638). By the end of the novel, the aging albino Zagreus, a '*raté*' (*AG* p. 291) or failure in more ways than one, a 'gimcrack sphinx-man' (*AG* p. 342) (in Ratner's words) who has been laid off by Pierpoint, appears to become engaged to the befuddled, nonagenarian, and already married Lady Fredigonde in order to leech her money, and the novel concludes with their hideous embrace. Zagreus's disgraceful conduct is no better than that of the frauds and time-wasters he has gone to such trouble to condemn and in many ways it is far more despicable.

Jameson sums up the challenge of *The Apes* when he notes that while it is

> in one sense little more than an episodic cage-by-cage exhibition of all the varieties of the Bloomsbury 'apes,' [it] nonetheless explicitly raises the structural issue of the vantage point from which they may reliably be observed and described: a privileged consciousness presumably itself immune to ridicule, which is however fatally drawn into its own exhibits after the now-familiar pattern of the 'satirist satirized'. (*JFA* p. 174)

At the end, Jameson says, the reader is left wondering

> whether the whole spectacle has not been somehow prearranged in advance by Zagreus, and through him, by the absent but all-powerful Pierpoint; whether these ostensible enemies of the unreal are not in fact themselves the

secret fomenters and promoters of such unreality for purposes known only to them. (*JFA* p. 175)

Overall, *The Apes* might be put forward as the most bloated symptom of the degeneration it sets out to expose; it becomes the fever chart of a cultural malaise rather than a detached and clinical dissection of it. In *The Mysterious Mr Bull* (1938), Lewis claimed that the satirist should approach his task 'with the equipment and the temperament of the surgeon . . . Where the pills and plasters of the physician cease to be effective, the surgeon steps in with his knife' (*MMB* p. 145). But *The Apes* comprises such a seething mass of material that Lewis's knife soon gets blunted, and Zagreus, the 'guide who brings us into the world of the "apes" . . . is himself revealed to be nothing more than a kind of empty, mechanical puppet who recites someone else's words':

> Even this mysterious off-stage voice, however, is deeply submerged in the same culture of gossip and celebrity it otherwise condemns, creating its own coterie that transforms Pierpoint into a media star. His incisive critiques are, therefore, less ironic than they are self-condemning, and the whole mass of *Apes of God* engages in this reflexive mode of satire that does not allow for a moral position outside of itself . . . Without a position to occupy outside of this system, author, reader, and characters alike all become the very apes the text condemns, left to wander the narrative warren in which fact and fiction are irremediably entangled.[17]

This assessment could not be more acute and it prompts us to ask this question: if inter-war culture in England was as much of a 'moronic inferno' as Lewis claimed, why was he so intent on logging its every flame? Why did he risk incineration? David Trotter, another critic who sees *The Apes* as 'imitative through and through', regards the book as 'among other things a reflection on [Lewis's] own satirical or "Enemy" persona, his own paranoia'.[18] Indeed, Trotter regards this profoundly conflicted and uncompromisingly experimental novel as the *locus classicus* of 'paranoid modernism', an *entre deux guerres* condition shot through with delusional anxieties about the burgeoning professionalisation of English society and culture.[19]

The Apes was self-published by Lewis (his usual publisher, Chatto and Windus, was too nervous to handle it) in a limited edition of 750 copies on 3 June 1930. It 'weighed three pounds and three ounces and, by a numerical coincidence, it retailed at three pounds and three shillings' (*SSG* p. 290), a huge, near-*Ulysses*-like price for a novel of near-*Ulysses*-like size. Given that these are 'the proportions of an artillery missile' (*KWL* p. 100), its critical reception was generally favourable. But when *The New Statesman* rejected Roy Campbell's very complimentary review of the novel, Campbell sent on to Lewis the letter of rejection (which he had torn to shreds in disgust) and his rejected review and Lewis included both items in *Satire & Fiction*, the pamphlet he wrote in response. This contained endorsements of the novel from, among others, H. G. Wells, W. B. Yeats, and Augustus John, with Lewis especially delighted with Yeats's comparison of his own satirical genius to that of Swift and grateful for his comment that with *The Apes* 'something absent from all literature for a generation was back again' (*SF* p. 29). Others, conversely, such as T. S. Eliot, thought that Lewis had been 'breaking butterflies upon a wheel' (*MTE* p. 182). This debate has continued off and on ever since, and Timothy Materer perhaps gets somewhere near to summarising the flawed achievement of the novel (while avoiding the issue of its racism) when he writes that although

> individual passages are unquestionably great, and its vast scope is masterly, too often it seems labored or even tedious ... [T]he brilliant style never gathers narrative momentum, nor does it create significant characters. Yet many passages and even entire sections at times give *The Apes* the power of a modern *Dunciad*.[20]

And, as with Pope, some of Lewis's 'malignities' (*AG* p. 121) can still be registered as bracing in their impact, whereas others continue to be experienced as simply malign.

Naturally enough, the voluble Lewis did not entirely discharge his loathings of Bloomsbury and bohemia in his infamously voluminous volume. As late as 1954, in *The Demon of Progress in the Arts*, he was still complaining that in the mid-1920s

> while the middle-class still had money, 'art' was very often chosen as a career by a young man who had nothing in particular he wanted to do ... It did not mean that any talent whatever was possessed by this young man; if he had told himself to start with that he had talent, he very soon found that he had been mistaken ... As the British Empire became a less and less attractive place to do nothing in ... such a 'profession' as this became an obvious refuge. (*DPA* p. 26)

'Extremism is symptomatic of a vacuum' (*DPA* p. 27) he says a little further on in this book, and we might be tempted to think of his own extremism in *The Apes* as at once counterbalancing the cultural imposture he despised, and, through the fanatical excess of his unrivalled, ambitious, and exasperating social satire, simply enlarging that cultural vacuum with another of the '*dramatised social news-sheets*' (*AG* p. 262) that Zagreus, allegedly, so deplores.

Notes

1. Scott W. Klein, *The Fictions of James Joyce and Wyndham Lewis: Monsters of Nature and Design* (Cambridge: Cambridge University Press, 1994), p. 22.
2. Rebecca Beasley, 'Wyndham Lewis and Modernist Satire', in Morag Shiach (ed.), *The Cambridge Companion to the Modernist Novel* (Cambridge: Cambridge University Press, 2007), pp. 126–36: p. 126.
3. T. S. Eliot, *The Letters of T. S. Eliot – Volume II: 1923–1925*, ed. Valerie Eliot and Hugh Haughton (London: Faber and Faber, 2009), p. 344. Lewis's outriders appeared in *The Criterion*, 2.6, February 1924, pp. 124–42, and 2.7, April 1924, pp. 300–10, respectively.
4. Eliot, *The Letters of T. S. Eliot – Volume II*, pp. 356, 364, and 364, n. 3.
5. Ibid., p. 392.
6. Wyndham Lewis, 'Introduction to the Twenty-Fifth Anniversary Edition', *The Apes of God* (London: Arco, 1955), n.p.
7. Wyndham Lewis, '***!!—...?***!!!', *Daily Express* (25 October 1929), p. 10.
8. Nathan Waddell, 'Wyndham Lewis's "Very Bad Thing": Jazz, Inter-War Culture, and *The Apes of God*', *Modernist Cultures*, 8.1, Spring 2013, pp. 61–81: p. 62.
9. Ian Patterson, 'John Rodker, Julius Ratner and Wyndham Lewis: The Split-Man Writes Back', in *WLC* pp. 95–107: p. 95; and Andrea Freud Loewenstein, *Loathsome Jews and Engulfing Women: Metaphors of Projection in the Works of Wyndham Lewis, Charles Williams and Graham Greene* (New York and London: New York University Press, 1993), p. 180.
10. Patterson, 'John Rodker', p. 100.
11. David Trotter, *Paranoid Modernism: Literary Experiment, Psychosis, and the Professionalization of English Society* (Oxford: Oxford University Press, 2001), p. 292.
12. David Ayers, *Wyndham Lewis and Western Man* (Basingstoke and London: Macmillan, 1992), p. 134.
13. Arnold Bennett, 'The British Academy of Letters' (1910), reprinted in Arnold Bennett, *Books and Persons: Being Comments on a Past Epoch 1908–1911* (London: Chatto and Windus, 1917), pp. 228–34: pp. 229–30.
14. I have borrowed some of these attributions from Edwards's 'Afterword' (*AG* pp. 635–6).
15. Sean Latham, *The Art of Scandal: Modernism, Libel Law, and the Roman à Clef* (New York and Oxford: Oxford University Press, 2009), p. 91.
16. Latham, *The Art of Scandal*, pp. 113–14.
17. Ibid., pp. 114–15.
18. Trotter, *Paranoid Modernism*, p. 324.
19. Ibid., p. 312.
20. Timothy Materer, *Wyndham Lewis the Novelist* (Detroit: Wayne State University Press, 1976), p. 83.

Chapter 8

Political Incorrectness Gone Sane: Lewis, Race, and Gender

Ivan Phillips

You should be human about EVERYTHING: inhuman about only a few things. (*B2* p. 82)

For my part, I have always felt it in my bones, I am afraid, that I had the makings of a heretic. (*LWE* p. 255)

Beyond Biography

There is, as I write, only one customer review of Paul O'Keeffe's biography of Wyndham Lewis on amazon.co.uk and it begins like this: 'Wyndham Lewis: "People are only friends in so much that they are of use to you." And that about says all you need to know about Wyndham Lewis.'[1] This might be read as a more critically precise and supported version of the general approach to knowledge of Lewis and his views, the one that enabled John Carey to write him off as being 'powered to a considerable degree by hatred and resentment' and James Fox, more recently, to describe him as having 'one of the most poisonous minds of the twentieth century'.[2] Lewis is well known to have been a nasty piece of work – 'a misogynist, fascist and anti-semite', as Fox reports – and William M. Chace's inventory of his prejudices, including women, Blacks, Jews, pacifists, feminists, and jazz lovers, has an air of breezy confidence that must surely have a basis in truth and that has rarely been challenged outside the eccentric realms of the Lewisite.[3] Lewis wrote a book in praise of Adolf Hitler, after all, and opposed the war against European fascism. He used words like 'nigger' and 'dago'. He belittled his long-suffering wife and said vicious things about homosexuals. It is small wonder that Jessica Burstein has felt compelled to write that '[b]eing Wyndham Lewis means never having to say you're sorry. Being a Lewis critic, on the other hand, means constantly apologizing.'[4]

Lewis styled himself 'the Enemy', of course, and it is perhaps hardly surprising that he has largely been taken at his word. The rampaging creature of spite and malice, deformed by a rebarbative illiberalism that is anathema to modern egalitarian sensibilities, is largely a monster of his own making and its footprints can be traced without difficulty through his forays into the realms of race and gender. It is alarmingly easy to discern signs of monstrosity in these territories, but it is even easier if second- or third-hand reports form the basis of the investigation, or if there is little or no attempt to study actual materials in the field. Alan Munton has charted the long-term impact of such relaxed critical practices:

> Lewis is so widely reviled that almost any claim about him, or his work, can be made. That he, or his work, is violent, fascist, misogynist and pathologically insane has become, not the end-point of argument, but the point of departure. For many practitioners, Lewis criticism is an act of sustained condemnation, the outcome of a network of sites infected by a hermeneutics of suspicion.[5]

Identifying 'a critical situation in which no good can be spoken', Munton cites David Trotter's description of Lewis's 'less than human nature' as a typical example of *ad hominem* excess. Even if the glib and cyclical dreariness of such a prefabricated non-critical attitude is set to one side, there remains the fundamental problem that there is far more to Lewis than the reputation that precedes him. The problem, as I hope to show, is also a possibility, and the reputation can act as a remarkable catalyst to appreciation.

In exploring Lewis's engagement with themes of race and gender, this chapter does not attempt to deny or evade the uncomfortable 'aggressivity' that Fredric Jameson has recognised in his work (*JFA* p. 136). Rather, it argues that this is a crucial – perhaps *the* crucial – component within a singularly restless and dangerously confrontational mode of cultural analysis. Lewis's treatment of sensitive issues is invariably provocative and uncompromising, often reckless, at times foolish, unpleasant, and culpably ill-considered (never more so than in his *Hitler* book of 1931). It is also, however, compellingly radical and can be surprisingly progressive in its sympathies and implications. The customary assumption of Lewis's racism and misogyny tends to reveal more about the preconceptions and methodologies of his critics than it does about his work, but it also indicates the clear and pressing need to subject that work to close and honest scrutiny.

The work, not the life. Lewis's detractors have inclined towards a biographical understanding of their quarry, with considerable emphasis being placed on his flaws, or perceived flaws, as a man. Carey is, as ever, a representative voice: 'Contempt for woman, or for a sexual stereotype that he identified as woman, was a key component in Lewis's thought about art and society. It seems probable that this derived from personal problems.'[6] Probable, possible, unprovable. Carey's selective use of Jeffrey Meyers's sensationalist and often inaccurate biography, *The Enemy* (1980), is unhelpful, even in the context of his own polemic. Whether access to O'Keeffe's *Some Sort of Genius* (2000) would have made any difference to either Carey's argument or his approach is doubtful, but it would at least have mitigated prolonged rhetorical travesty:

> He abandoned his first child and its mother in France in 1908, later giving it out, probably untruthfully, that he had dropped and killed the baby. Between 1911 and 1920 Olive Johnson and Iris Barry each bore him two illegitimate children, all of whom were quickly disposed of. When Iris returned from hospital with the second child, a daughter, Lewis was having sex with the shipping heiress and cultural groupie Nancy Cunard in his studio, and Iris had to wait on the steps until they had finished.[7]

Even leaving aside the shameful innuendo of 'were quickly disposed of' and '*probably* untruthfully', this shows the perils of a biographical engagement with Lewis's gender politics: the 'first' child, presumably that of Ida Vendler, was almost certainly not Lewis's, and the lurid tale of Cunardian copulation is demonstrably false (see *SSG* pp. 90–1 and p. 226).

It would be an act of brave revisionism to claim that the biographical Lewis was a model of the ideal husband or a prototype for the 'new man' – and there is really nothing that can be said in support of his behaviour as a parent – but it does not require an especially pronounced New Critical or Barthesian mutation in the analytical genes to sense that the life is a site of distraction rather than clarification. This holds true in relation to Lewis's outlook on race as well as to his lived attitudes to gender and gender relations. For Carey, the situation here is predictably straightforward – 'Several aspects of Hitler's public persona attracted [Lewis], not least his racism' – and a strategic (mis)reading of *Paleface: The Philosophy of the 'Melting-Pot'* (1929) presents a cultural critique driven by 'contempt for Negroes'.[8] This sits oddly, however, with – among other things – Lewis's dedicated and active support for the British Guyanan artist Denis Williams from 1949 onwards. Writing to Herbert Read in November 1950, Lewis expresses savage indignation at the effects of racial prejudice:

> Committeeman! the British Council has been helpful with regard to this young Negro, but if he is to survive he must be found a job. Because of colour this presents great difficulties. It is a pity that all this talent should be lost for

no better reason than that its possessors [sic] skin is controversial. I understand, for instance, that it is going to be exceedingly difficult to find a school prepared to engage a Negro teacher. (*L* p. 527)

A modern reader is likely to be uneasy with Lewis's language and tone here, but the sentiments are hardly those of a racist. Again, biography proves itself to be profoundly unreliable when we attempt to understand Lewis's ideas; it is in the work that their controversial intricacies can be tracked most powerfully and lucidly.

Lewis the Feminist

'I am a feminist, of course' (*H* p. 92). These six words, sitting at the heart of Lewis's most self-destructive publication, might strike even his most fervent advocate as surprising or perhaps delusional. It must be a strange definition of feminism indeed which can formulate such declarations as the following, from 'The Code of a Herdsman' (1917):

> As to women: wherever you can, substitute the society of men. = Treat them kindly, for they suffer from the herd, although of it, and have many of the same contempts as yourself. They are a sort of bastard mountain people. = There must be somewhere a female mountain, a sort of mirage-mountain. I should like to visit it. = But women, and the processes for which they exist, are the arch conjuring trick: and they have the cheap mystery, and a good deal of the slipperiness, of the conjuror.[9]

And in *Tarr*, first published a year later, the following remarkable rant – enhanced for the 1928 rewrite – can be found:

> How foul and wrong this haunting of women is! = They are everywhere! = Confusing, blurring, libelling, with their half-baked, gushing, tawdry presences! It is like a slop of children and the bawling machinery of the inside of life, always and all over our palaces. Their silly flood of cheap illusion comes in between friendships, stagnates complacently around a softened mind. (*T1* p. 32)

The obvious point to make here is that both of these statements are held in the tongs of a narrative voice, in the first case that of a Nietzschean pseudo-Zarathustra, in the latter that of the eponymous Tarr.[10] However, given that the Herdsman can be seen as an early version of the antagonist persona that Lewis was to adopt throughout his career and that Tarr has generally (and no doubt simplistically) been taken to be the author's 'spokesman' in the novel, the question of authorial distancing remains fraught. For the moment, though, it can be noted that Lewis's sexual politics, like his racial politics, like *all* aspects of his politics, are elaborately problematic.

The problems begin in the fierce eccentricities and contradictions of Lewis's approach, not least in its peculiarly gendered readings of social power relations. On the surface it seems clear enough that a text such as *The Art of Being Ruled* (1926) is concerned, in part at least, with a fundamental collapse of traditional gender roles in the West, an apparent erosion of masculine status and function being Lewis's principle anxiety:

> The economic incentive of the upkeep of a family circle, a wife and children, again, must affect a man's attitude to his dignity and duty in a great many ways. Relieved of that, he would care far less about his position in the world. (*ABR* p. 171)

Even this is less clear-cut than it might first appear, however, with Lewis's evident unease about the emancipation of women being in peculiar tension with his belief that the disintegration of the family unit is 'the central fact of our life' from which 'all the other revolutionary phases of our new society radiate'. The demise of the family is a trend that Lewis broadly approves of (and here again biography threatens to intrude), whereas the liberation of women from within its repressive structures is apparently a source of anxiety to him. This is a conflict that he recognises himself, describing his 'essay' as being *'against the family'* but 'not *against women'* (*ABR* p. 179). This might, in itself, indicate a kind of feminist stance – denying the essentialist conjunction of woman and family – although such an analysis is belied by other lines of argument within the book and elsewhere in Lewis's work of the inter-war years.

Always insistent that a sustained attack on 'the feminine' is not the same as a sustained attack on women, Lewis is at pains to assert a position of innocence in the 'sex-war':

> My entrance into it is effected without the accompaniment of set teeth and battle in the eye; a few elementary precautions are observed, but none of a slighting nature. I am able to observe very little difference between men and women, and my liking and interest are equally distributed. (*ABR* pp. 171–2)

The Enemy doth protest too much, we might think, and his subsequent suggestion that 'women represent . . . a higher spiritual average' (*ABR* p. 172) is likely to do more harm than good. The harm is critically useful, however, because it points towards a seemingly reductive categorisation in Lewis's approach to gender – or, perhaps more accurately, in his *uses* of gender. Predisposed to a binary model of understanding, Lewis's initial formulation of any problem is oppositional and this is where so many of the challenges of his work begin. Female and male, feminine and masculine, are not so much concrete social realities for Lewis as abstract philosophical concepts, with the former being associated with the soft, the fluid, the psychological, and the emotional, and the latter with the hard, the fixed, the intellectual, and the rational. 'The "feminine" values', he writes in *Doom of Youth* (1932), 'are all the lowest, poorest-blooded – the most featureless, boneless, softest, the most emotional' (*DY* p. 210). The inverted commas are an interesting attempt to hold the offence at arm's length, but Lewis's claim, following on from this, that 'any intelligent feminist would be with [him]' in his 'sensible' categorisation of the 'feminine' as 'low-grade, second-rate, child-minded, mesmerically-receptive, dependent, etc., etc., etc.' (*DY* p. 211) is as optimistic as it is objectionable.

The basic anatomy of power contained in Lewis's writings of the 1920s and 1930s is one in which the 'feminine' represents the principle of being ruled and the 'masculine' the principle of ruling. Within this paradigm, of course, most people – whether biologically men or women – are 'feminine'. This scarcely diminishes the surface chauvinism of the metaphor, founded as it is on a sense of women as more easily ruled, more childlike, credulous, and malleable than men, but it does expose an important instability in an ostensibly dogmatic worldview.

At its centre, Lewis's consideration of gender revolves around a dichotomous agitation – amounting at times to an intense anxiety – about the relationship between art and life. The messy preoccupations of sexual desire, procreation, marital love, and domestic responsibility are depicted as the mortal enemies of creativity. So, in the early story 'Cantleman's Spring-Mate', the protagonist's actions are governed by a conviction that 'all women were contaminated with Nature's hostile power and might be treated as spies or enemies' (*BB* p. 310). Tarr reflects in similar terms: 'Surrender to a woman was a sort of suicide for an artist' (*T2* p. 183). The animus behind this, caught sharply in Tarr's definition of art as '[L]ife with all the humbug of living taken out of it' (*T2* p. 264), is given a more measured articulation earlier in the novel:

> 'First of all, I am an artist. With most people, who are not artists, all the finer part of their vitality goes into sex if it goes anywhere: during their courtship they become third-rate poets, all their instincts of drama come out freshly with their wives. The artist is he in whom this emotionality normally absorbed by sex is so strong that it claims a newer and more exclusive field of deployment. Its first creation is *the Artist* himself.' (*T2* p. 16)

The cool narcissism which seems to sit behind this is intrinsically repulsive, or at least provoking, and it is a finely wrapped gift to those who see Lewis as a straightforward misogynist. But it should be noted that when Tarr delivers his slick definition of art to Anastasya in the 1928 version of the novel, her instant response – 'Very well: but what is life?' (*T2* p. 264) – is a genuinely persuasive unsettling of his position, and one that he can only bluster to recover from: 'Everything that is not yet purified so that it is art.' This cyclical rhetoric meets a flat 'No' (*T2* p. 264) from Anastasya, and she refuses to let him off the hook.

There is a suggestive paradox, a vital inconsistency, in the attempts by Lewis to celebrate the physical, classical, and masculine at the expense of the biological, romantic, and feminine. The systematic debasement of the biological human body that so appals Carey in Lewis's writing is impossible to avoid, and it points towards a misogyny – or, more precisely, a misanthropy – that is almost a mirror-image of that of one his great *bêtes noires*, D. H. Lawrence. Then again, the endeavour to depict life as an outrageous satirical sculpture, to turn it into something physical and active but not biological and emotional, is powered by discrepancies and, perhaps, in the end, by an awareness of its own impossibility. At the same time, the surface debate – and where else would we be expected to look, since an emphasis on the *surface*, the exterior, the outline is so much a part of Lewis's aesthetic agenda, both as an artist and a writer? – the binary quarrel is deeper, literally, than it appears at first glance. The resistance of Anastasya Vasek is powerfully emblematic of something that is easily missed in readings of Lewis: that not only do his female characters exceed the limitations of their grotesquely physical shells, but they also tend to outstrip the anti-feminine designs that seem to generate them. The context of satire is essential, but in blunt terms it can be stated that Lewis's female characters – in his paintings, in his novels – are stronger, more complex, and more affecting than his alleged aggressive misogyny would lead us to expect. Any examination that fixates on a few texts produced in a narrow but hectic band of time between *BLAST* in 1914 and *The Apes of God* in 1930 is likely to miss this.

In Lewis's early fiction, women are presented as parodic grotesques, characterised through descriptions of extreme and distorted physicality. In this respect, they are scarcely more ill-used than his male characters, but it is true that – like the 'bad' in *Hamlet* – they tend to end unhappily. This pattern continues beyond the stylistic and thematic transitions of *The Revenge for Love* in 1937. Valerie Parker has noted that the tragedy of Lewis's women is almost absolute: 'Bertha escapes, but other women in Lewis' novels never live happily.'[11] A character whose key phase of development is precipitated by the experience of being raped might seem a disturbingly unconvincing beacon of hope, and yet it is the capacity of the female characters in Lewis's novels to rise above their narrative circumstances and to transcend the taint of association with a widespread simplification of the sexual politics contained in *The Art of Being Ruled*, *Doom of Youth*, and elsewhere, which demonstrates a remarkable subtlety of achievement.

Parker notes that 'in his best three novels, *Tarr*, *The Revenge for Love* and *Self Condemned*, Lewis gives women central roles to play'.[12] Her discussion of Bertha Lunken, Anastasya Vasek, Margot Savage, and Hester Harding – and I would add April Mallow from *The Vulgar Streak* (1941) – allows for a development in Lewis's fictional depiction of women seemingly at odds with her contention that, in essence, he never really got beyond parodying women as 'time-bound, earthy, infinitely desirable yet destructive of creativity'.[13] In particular, the late novel *Self Condemned* (1954) is marked as a significant accomplishment, not only in its 'depiction of the ebb and flow of a long-term marriage' but in its resolution – via the impact of the death of 'Essie' on her anti-heroic husband – of tensions traced across a forty-year career in fiction:

> *Self Condemned* carries Lewis's discussion of the relationship between the sexes beyond the dandy aesthetics of *Tarr* and Victorian assumptions questioned in *Revenge for Love*, to show how destructive the creative ego can be, how it tempts the artist to be inhuman.[14]

Paul Edwards, more recently, has come to a similar conclusion:

> The dualism that had kept an absolute distinction between mind and body during Lewis's most extreme phase has broken down, and is replaced by a humanistic recognition that the mind is actually nourished by affection, sexual relationships, perhaps even parenthood. [*Self Condemned*] begins to acknowledge that there might be something pathological in a rejection of such things. (*EWL* p. 522)

Edwards stops short of accepting that 'the "self" condemned in the novel is a version of Lewis's own', but indicates unequivocally that a breakdown of any antagonism with the 'feminine' has been painfully, tragically enacted. It seems likely, as this chapter will go on to consider, that such a breakdown is implicit even in those texts where Lewis seems to be most obsessively and bloody-mindedly insisting on opposition. The plain fact, though – one so plain that it is easily missed – is that he wrote important, strong, articulate, and compelling women. These characters resist idealisation, are never marginal, have distinct and often complex motivation, and live on page after page, albeit not happily ever after.

Stirring the Pot

Lewis's treatment of race is, if anything, even more problematic than his treatment of gender and it has been represented, if anything, even more simplistically and with even less analysis. The key piece of evidence here is not, in fact, evidence at all: it is the widespread assumption of Lewis's fascism, which I have attempted to challenge elsewhere.[15] This leads to a repeated and invariably untested conclusion that he was – and that his work is – crudely and consistently anti-Semitic and racist: 'Lewis's resentment of Jews was even more forceful than his contempt for negroes'.[16] Additional evidence is found in Lewis's political and philosophical writings of the 1920s and 1930s, most notably in *Paleface: The Philosophy of the 'Melting-Pot'* and *The Jews: Are They Human?* (1939). Going beyond the titles of these publications has not seemed necessary for some of Lewis's most vociferous critics and it can hardly be denied that they are offspring with unfortunate faces and badly chosen names. The first has an intriguing but troubling cover illustration by Lewis, with an Aryan profile in ascendancy over – apparently *growing out of* – a black one that anticipates the physiognomic lampoons of the 'Censored Eleven' animations produced by Looney Tunes and Merrie Melodies between 1931 and 1944.[17] The latter, in turn, has lost any legitimising wit that its punning title might originally have had, referring as it does, with satirical but badly judged playfulness, to Gustaaf Renier's long-forgotten text *The English: Are They Human?* (1931). This was a humorous survey of English national stereotypes, whereas the subject of Lewis's book – the plight of Germany's Jews under the Nazis – was deadly serious. Not for the first time, Lewis's instinct to turn everything into satire led to a disastrous warping of his message.

There are grave difficulties, and severe discomforts, in Lewis's discussions of race, and not only in the painful contortions of his attempts to 'allow a little *Blutsgefühl* to have its way' in *Hitler* (*H* p. 42). He is prone to essentialist stereotyping and a mode of address that veers between condescension and hostile irritability, so a case against him would be easy to assemble. *Paleface*, the first half of which appeared originally in the inaugural issue of *The Enemy* in 1927, is a book which sets out to question romantic primitivism in the work of authors such as D. H. Lawrence and Sherwood Anderson, and, in doing so, to expose the growing 'inferiority complex' of white cultures. It is doubtful whether a discourse underpinned by totemic categorisations of 'the White Man' and 'the Black', and threaded through with an apparently unquestioning use of the word 'Nigger', could ever have survived its historical moment.

Even a cursory trawl through the text will discover incriminating evidence against its author:

> I find the average White European (such as Chekov depicted) often exceedingly ridiculous, no doubt, but much more interesting than the average Hopi, or the average Negro. I would rather have the least mind that *thinks*, than the average man that squats and drums and drums. (*P* p. 196)

Of course, a text such as this is precisely the kind that should receive more than a cursory trawl. This chapter is written out of a conviction that Lewis is one of the great alchemists of the English language, a unique and (in the truest sense) visionary prose stylist. But it is also written in the knowledge that he wrote too much, too often, and too fast, and that he was capable of lapsing into indolently offensive cliché and the lazy duplication of stock attitudes. Even so, the argument in *Paleface* is far more nuanced and progressive than its often repellent surface details would tend to indicate. As D. G. Bridson has recognised: 'There is nothing in *Paleface* or any other of Lewis's works to suggest that he was not fully in sympathy with the cause of Black emancipation.'[18] In sympathy, but not in full understanding. The argument of *Paleface* is complex, perverse, not always pleasant, and sometimes downright disagreeable. It needed refinement and shaping, and perhaps to be written by someone of a different ethnicity, class, generation, and temperament than Wyndham Lewis. But only Wyndham Lewis could have written it.

The problems that afflict *Paleface* also afflict *The Jews: Are They Human?* The book is thick with Semitic clichés – the Jews are depicted as intellectual, industrious, cliquish, arrogant, good in business, stoical, courageous, pacific, plain-spoken, uncompromising, effeminate, and so on – and is disfigured by a number of racist physiognomic caricatures: 'The dark mongoloid eye, the curled semitic [sic] lip' (*JAH* p. 17). When Lewis perpetrates lines such as this – 'like the Dago, the Jew is "oily" to Anglo-Saxon eyes' (*JAH* p. 40) – it becomes difficult to see how his argument might be redeemed from its inclination towards a cartoon scorn. 'The smell of the cheap cigar puts the final touch', he goes on, 'that acrid whiff of cheap self-satisfaction' (*JAH* p. 40). Can anything worth retaining really survive this kind of toxic banality? And yet, ugly as these expressions are, it would be a mistake to let the surface idiocies of Lewis's engagement with issues of race distract us from the basic tolerance, moderation, and farsighted multiculturalism of his enterprise.

If the substance and strength of Lewis's fictional women offer some redress for his transgressions within the discourse of gender, there is no such counterbalance available when it comes to his commentaries on race. Jewish characters such as Julius Ratner and Archie Margolin

in *The Apes of God* and Reuben Wallach in *The Revenge for Love* are
scarcely antidotes to grim generalisations in the political writings about,
for instance, 'the extremely bad manners and barbaric aggressiveness
of the eastern slum-Jew immigrant' (*H* p. 36). Black characters, on the
other hand, are most noticeable in the fiction by their absence. Lewis
clearly took the subject of race extremely seriously, however; it is a
theme that runs through his non-fiction writings, spanning *The Art of
Being Ruled* (1926), via *Filibusters in Barbary* (1932), to *America and
Cosmic Man* (1948). In itself, taking race seriously proves nothing about
outlook (Hitler took race seriously, after all), and Lewis's tendency to
mistake flippancy for satire, especially when arguing at speed, leads to
frequent ruinous lapses of judgement.

The central and constant problem in Lewis's approach to race is one
that goes beyond simple naivety and a tactless urge for plain talk. It is,
in broad terms, a category error in which complex, discrete, and sensitive issues are conflated within a single, unwieldy theoretical framework.
For Lewis in the first half of his career (which is where his problems
begin), an anxious hostility towards what he sees as 'group rhythms'
creates a model of social understanding in which race, sex, class, and
age become fused. This fusion is, for the most part, a *con*fusion, resulting in an implosion of controversies, with the same fretful anxiety about
collective social formations producing some of Lewis's most damaging oversimplifications. Geoffrey Wagner defines a group rhythm as 'a
coagulation of individuals into mass units'.[19] It is an obsessive dread of
such cultural coalescence – associated with flux, the 'feminine', and the
erosion of 'intellect' – which leads directly from the caustic aphorisms
of 'The Code of a Herdsman' to the misrepresentations of Lewis which
persist into the present day. There is an unintended irony, almost exqui-
site, in a suspicion of homogeneity within social groups which leads to
the homogenising of social groups in a way that promotes suspicion:
Lewis, troubled by the generalised individual, generalises about the individual. In the context of race, even more than in the context of gender,
this obscures the finer points of his discussion.

These finer points are fairly easily brought back into view and they
suggest an approach that is never less than humane even if, at times, it is
clumsily expressed, a hostage to haste, cheap jokes, and received opinions. In the final chapter of *Paleface* Lewis presents the case for cultural
mixing, arguing passionately against ideas of racial purity, exclusivity,
and nationalism, and in favour of miscegenation. 'I am heart and soul
upon the side of the Melting-pot, *not* upon that of the Barbed Wire'
(*P* p. 276), he writes, and he goes on to articulate a vision of what this
might mean:

If (to show my enthusiasm for fusion) I may allow myself a strikingly *mixed* metaphor, it is at the fountain-head that we should establish our Melting-pot – an example to all other Melting-pots. And it is here in Europe that we should start a movement at once for the miscegenation of Europeans – with *each other*, that is – Asia and Africa could be considered later, no doubt, for incorporation in our Model Melting-pot. (*P* p. 283)

This hardly describes a flawless project for multiculturalism and *Paleface* is far from being a taintless document. Even so, a book that argues in favour of cultural exchange and unity, whatever the archaic indelicacies of its language, can surely not be considered as, in any meaningful sense, racist.

As Lewis himself notes, the 'final proposal' of *Paleface* has precedents in his writing that can be traced back to *The Lion and the Fox* (1927) and that finds its ultimate expression in the utopianism of *America and Cosmic Man*. Here Lewis challenges assumptions about rootedness and celebrates the 'most pleasant disembodied sensation' of walking through the big cities of the United States, 'among all those herds of Italians, Germans, Jews, Irish, Negroes' (*ACM* p. 167). The use of that favourite word 'herds' – a few pages later 'the great polyglot herds' – is interesting, perhaps troubling, but the feeling for global synthesis that informs it is compelling: 'You at last are *in the world,* instead of just in a nation' (*ACM* p. 167).

America and Cosmic Man still makes casual, if speech-marked, use of words like 'Wop' and 'Chink', and its medium is often less progressive than its message – 'That dark lump *will* melt' (*ACM* p. 176) – but the desire for a 'hybrid' political ideal is both consistent with, and corrective of, Lewis's earlier writings: 'We lock ourselves up aggressively, or are locked up, in that antiquated group-pen the "nation," and pretend to be a "race," and a mighty fine one too, as did par excellence the National Socialists' (*ACM* p. 177). The desire is a logical development from the humane praxis of *The Jews: Are They Human?*, in which Lewis had reacted with vital determination to Hitler's planned expulsion of the Jews from Germany. This involved, as noted earlier, lapses into Semitic stereotyping and a feeble rhetoric of dissociation – 'I neither regard the person of Jewish race as a devil nor as a darling' (*JAH* p. 16) – but also an outright rejection of the superstitious racialism that had shaped Nazi ideology. Ultimately, the book amounted to a plea for active intercession:

We must make up for the doings of the so-called 'Christians' of yesterday – who degraded the Jew, and then mocked at him for being degraded. We must give all people of Jewish race a new deal among us. Let us for Heaven's sake make an end of this silly nightmare once and for all, and turn our backs upon this dark chapter of our history. (*JAH* p. 111)

Some might speculate that the expiation invoked here is rather more personal than historical, Lewis seeking atonement for the follies of his *Hitler* book. This misreads both Lewis (who never sought personal atonement for anything) and the circumstances in which the work was written. *The Jews: Are They Human?* constitutes an act of rapid journalistic engagement in the face of an immense humanitarian crisis. Lewis did not need to write the book, but it might be reasonable to suggest that the book needed to be written. Sadly, if it is remembered at all today, it is for its shoddy title and not for its embodiment of Lewis's stated belief that 'the artistic intelligence, however it may manifest itself, must always be tolerant' (*JAH* p. 41).

Breaking the Hush

Perhaps the greatest and most tragic irony about Lewis is that he has been categorised as an artist of frozen views and monolithic invention, almost completely lacking in subtlety and alteration, yet his career was long, his output prolific, and the development of his views unceasing. Even at its most outrageous, his writing is rarely as obstinately set or belligerently 'incorrect' as his reputation – and his own self-promotion – would suggest. It can be difficult, for instance, to locate the tolerant artistic intelligence espoused and enacted in *The Jews: Are They Human?* within his attitude to homosexuality. 'The "homo" is the legitimate child of the suffragette', he writes in *The Art of Being Ruled*, arguing that homosexuality is 'part of the feminist revolution' and essentially a lifestyle choice, part of the growing child-cult and general 'softening' of Western culture (*ABR* p. 218). Retreading the same dodgy ground in *Doom of Youth*, he further embroiders his views about '*the Pretty-Boy state of mind*' (*DY* p. 218), asserting that 'the homosexual is, of course, an imitation-woman' (*DY* p. 206). Indefensible as these views are, they nevertheless point, even in their own clumsy absurdity, towards an intriguingly unfixed concept of gender beyond the antediluvian categorisation of sexualities. Men, he claims, 'are made, not born':

> Men were only made into 'men' with great difficulty even in primitive society; the male is not naturally 'a man' any more than the woman. He has to be propped into that position with some ingenuity, and is always likely to collapse. (*ABR* p. 247)

It is in this kind of teasing, paradoxical utterance that both the challenges and the possibilities of Lewis's work begin. Casting himself in the role of an illiberal extremist, a man of hard-line and unassailable opinions, he can often be caught in the act of frustrating the very binary oppositions that he has set up: 'So "a man" is an entirely artificial thing, like everything else that is the object of our grudging "admiration"' (*ABR* p. 248). At points like this, the iron enemy of flux begins to resemble an exemplary poststructuralist, relishing the ironic collapse of categories and the mythic potentialities of the anomalous zone.

The surprising spirit of unsettlement within Lewis's style and approach is implied at the outset of his career. 'You must talk with two tongues, if you do not wish to cause confusion', he writes in the second issue of *BLAST* (*B2* p. 91), and in 'The Code of a Herdsman': 'Contradict yourself. In order to live, you must remain broken up.'[20] The same view is expressed towards the end of his life, in *Rude Assignment*: 'To think is to be split up' (*RA* p. 76). This deep strategic instability – missed by so many of Lewis's critics, who have tended to take him at face value – aligns his work with the procedures of 'double encoding' identified by Linda Hutcheon as one of the key features of postmodernism.[21] Similarly, it positions him as an arch exponent of the kind of Menippean or carnivalesque discourse celebrated by Julia Kristeva as 'politically and socially disturbing', a 'scandalous and eccentric' mode associated with parody, 'cynical frankness', and a 'desecration of the sacred'.[22] This is close to what Jameson has in mind when he claims that Lewis's

> artistic integrity is to be conceived, not as something distinct from his regrettable ideological lapses (as when we admire his art, *in spite of* his opinions), but rather in the very intransigence with which he makes himself the impersonal registering apparatus for forces which he means to record, beyond any whitewashing and liberal revisionism, in all their primal ugliness. (*JFA* p. 21)

Close to, but not quite.

In *The Mysterious Mr Bull* (1938), Lewis's forgotten exploration of Englishness, he characterises himself as 'a man of the *tabula rasa* both in art and politics' (*MMB* p. 230), essentially anarchistic in his motivations: 'I was born, if ever a man was, for utopias, built upon a dazzlingly white and abstract ground. I was cut out to erect visionary residences, for the "free spirit"' (*MMB* pp. 229–30). Lewis's writings are often acts of provocation, heretical performances intended – as he reflected in *Rude Assignment* – to adopt a 'note of solitary defiance' and break 'the hush' in a culture which he saw as increasingly consensual and lacking in dissent (*RA* pp. 211–12). The free spirit will inevitably offend and the performance of the satirist – described in *Men without Art* as 'a sort of Cain among craftsmen' (*MWA* p. 12) – can easily be mistaken for life. Stan Smith has described Lewis as 'the model of the artist engaged in a continual guerilla war with the hegemonic culture', and Andrzej Gąsiorek has written of his ability 'to go beyond ossified categories of thought' (*GWL* p. 8).[23] Ultimately, in relation to gender, race, and many other aspects of social being, it might be argued that it is the sheer savagery of Lewis's idiom – its tendency to inflict indiscriminate damage, not least on its own author – that makes it so devastating, giving it a strength that is often beyond reason.

Notes

1. Bruce Oksol, 'A Squandered Life', review of Paul O'Keeffe, *Some Sort of Genius: A Life of Wyndham Lewis* (London: Jonathan Cape, 2000) – available at http://www.amazon.co.uk/Some-Sort-Of-Genius-Wyndham/ dp/0712673393 (accessed 24 November 2014).
2. John Carey, *The Intellectuals and the Masses: Pride and Prejudice among the Literary Intelligentsia, 1880–1939* (London: Faber and Faber, 1992), p. 182; James Fox, *British Masters*, Episode 1, BBC4, July 2011.
3. William M. Chace, 'On Lewis's Politics: The Polemics Polemically Answered', in *MWL* pp. 149–65: p. 150.
4. Jessica Burstein, review of Vincent Sherry, *Wyndham Lewis, Ezra Pound, and Radical Modernism*, and Toby Avard Foshay, *Wyndham Lewis and the Avant-Garde: The Politics of the Intellect*, in *Modernism/modernity*, 1.2, 1994, pp. 172–4: p. 172.
5. Alan Munton, '"Imputing Noxiousness": Aggression and Mutilation in Recent Lewis Criticism', *Wyndham Lewis Annual*, 4, 1997, pp. 5–20: p. 5.
6. Carey, *The Intellectuals and the Masses*, p. 183.
7. Ibid., p. 183.
8. Ibid., pp. 194–5.
9. Julian Symons (ed.), *The Essential Wyndham Lewis* (London: Vintage, 1991), p. 28.
10. The 'rules' are, we are told, included in a letter from one Benjamin Richard Wing to his friend Philip Seddon, although it is not stated whether Wing actually wrote them or simply discovered them. See Symons (ed.), *The Essential Wyndham Lewis*, p. 25.
11. Valerie Parker, 'Lewis, Art and Women', in *MWL* pp. 211–25: p. 216.
12. Ibid., p. 212.
13. Ibid., p. 215.
14. Ibid., p. 225.
15. Ivan Phillips, 'In His Bad Books: Wyndham Lewis and Fascism', *The Journal of Wyndham Lewis Studies*, 2, 2011, pp. 105–34.
16. Carey, *The Intellectuals and the Masses*, p. 195.
17. The 'Censored Eleven' is a series of cartoons made by Tex Avery, Chuck Jones, and other classic animators that was withheld from syndication by United Artists in 1968 because of the cartoons' insulting depictions of black

and other ethnic minority characters. Although still officially 'banned', the cartoons are now in the public domain.

18. D. G. Bridson, *The Filibuster: A Study of the Political Ideas of Wyndham Lewis* (London: Cassell, 1972), p. 75.
19. Geoffrey Wagner, *Wyndham Lewis: A Portrait of the Artist as the Enemy* (New Haven, CT: Yale University Press, 1957), p. 44.
20. Symons (ed.), *The Essential Wyndham Lewis*, p. 29.
21. Linda Hutcheon, *The Politics of Postmodernism* (London and New York: Routledge, 2001).
22. Julia Kristeva, 'Word, Dialogue and Novel' (1980, English trans.), in Toril Moi (ed.), *The Kristeva Reader* (Oxford: Basil Blackwell, 1986), pp. 34–61: pp. 51–4.
23. Stan Smith, 'Re-Righting Lefty: Wyndham and Wystan in the Thirties', *Wyndham Lewis Annual*, 9–10, 2002–3, pp. 34–45: p. 40.

Chapter 9

Lewis and Politics

Nathan Waddell

Lewis's politics were provocative but considered. They were also polemical, demanding, and contradictory. Sometimes they were abhorrent. It can also be shown that they were humane and peaceable. The difficulty, as is so often the case with Lewis, lies in deciding how best to evaluate a man whose opinions were so complex and on what grounds to characterise a career that had so many twists and turns. He was, as he wrote in *The Mysterious Mr Bull* (1938), 'a man of the *tabula rasa* both in art and in politics' (*MMB* p. 230), but this back-to-square-one approach arguably served him better when it came to evaluating and creating works of art than when it came to judging human lives en masse. He approached political questions from an artist's perspective (a tendency that helps to explain some of his lapses in political judgement), and he insisted that art should not be subordinated to political imperatives and that artistic freedom depends upon 'non-practical, non-partisan passion' (*E3* p. 29). He saw such disinterestedness as a prerequisite not only for genuine artistic creativity but also for a realistic assessment of society and its possible futures. Furthermore, in all of these endeavours Lewis was unashamedly bookish. His impressive grasp of political history mainly came from reading works of political philosophy rather than from direct administrative experience, and this lack of practical expertise at times led him to generalise about human affairs with a disquieting insouciance. But for all his idealism, and in spite of the deplorable views that mark his writings of the late 1920s and early to mid-1930s in particular (among them misogyny, homophobia, racism, and anti-Semitism), Lewis's deeply cultured, perceptive outlook on political matters remains distinctive.

However, much of Lewis's writing about politics has acquired a peculiar distinction in the wrong sense. Critics have been too willing to read parts for the whole and in general have assumed that Lewis's political commitments were fixed. Close readings of Lewis's views on politics are

certainly less numerous than close readings of the politics of his modernist peers.[1] Moreover, the significant shifts in outlook that characterise
his thoughts about politics during the 1930s tend to get lost in many
accounts of his work, and one of Lewis's books in particular – *Hitler*
(1931) – has come to stand, with only partial justification, for everything
in Lewis that allegedly is mad and bad. Part of the problem here is that
he wrote so much about political matters, about ideology and its effect
on subjectivity, about culture and its social implications, and about
the utopian premises upon which civilisation might be changed. Of
the numerous books Lewis published, approximately twenty could be
considered sustained works of political analysis. All of Lewis's journals
(*BLAST*, *The Tyro*, and *The Enemy*) contain political essays, and many
of his novels, especially *The Human Age* sequence and *The Revenge for
Love* (1937), can be deemed political literature. Sheer volume of material, in other words, means that in dealing with Lewis's politics it can be
hard to see the trees for the wood.

The continuities in Lewis's *oeuvre* coalesce around several issues.
Inevitably his thoughts on any given topic evolved across so large an
output as his, but he more or less consistently rejected the politics of
nationalism, imperialism, and militarism; lamented class difference, capitalist iniquity, and socio-cultural standardisation; ridiculed the 'child
cults' of the 1920s and 1930s; dismissed Simple Life philosophies and
socialist austerity; and queried rhetorics of progress and perfectibility.
He increasingly accepted the necessity of political governance, devoting
significant proportions of his work to discussions of European political
history and of the paths he thought Britain's political scene in particular
should have followed in his lifetime. He also defended the necessity,
if not the desirability, of politicians. As he wrote in *Rude Assignment*
(1950):

> without *something* there, where politicians are, there would be no great
> books, no Venus of Cyrene, no insulin, penicillin, no ether, no pasteurisation,
> there would be no Raphaels or Titians, no great actors, no great philosophers
> or musicians or mathematicians. We do not owe all this to the politicians –
> we owe them nothing – but *without* them it could not exist. (*RA* p. 64)

Lewis was sympathetic to different kinds of government throughout his
career, his qualified attraction to fascism during the inter-war period
being his most notorious stamp of approval.[2] Yet by the end of his life
he became more judgemental of government per se, and in particular
of the all-pervading influence of wealth from which the leaderships of
capitalist societies are inseparable. Assessing the workings of capitalist modernity, he criticised the trap of 'loan-slavery' (*CYD* p. 276) and

'the grip of the moneyspider' (*CYD* p. 354), finding in both the signs of indifferent overlords 'upon whose prodigious web we are convulsed like helpless flies' (*RA* p. 180).

Such metaphors reveal Lewis's populist, progressivist credentials. This side of Lewis has often been underplayed. He supported the careers of many important women modernists (including Jessica Dismorr, Helen Saunders, and Rebecca West), and he promoted the idea that gender is a performative construct. In spite of that, Lewis frequently wrote about society using gendered, essentialist terminology; his political writings are often marked by dubious assumptions, intellectual disdain, and simple reductiveness. His work challenges us to weigh the authority and power of his political assessments against the hurt and harm of his prejudices, both operating in his books in surprising combinations. *The Jews: Are They Human?* (1939), a pro-Semitic book with a poorly chosen title (about which I have more to say below), is the obvious case. It is also problematic that in Lewis's *Hitler*, the book most commonly used to prove his reactionary credentials, he should describe himself as a feminist (*H* p. 92), insist that Black people 'should not be discriminated against' (*H* p. 96), and point out that 'the Hitlerist's arch-enemy, the Jew, can make rings round him in all that universe that is not war, or mechanical technique' (*H* p. 137). The remark about skin colour, for instance, contradicts statements Lewis made elsewhere at the start of the 1930s, and links with the progressive viewpoints advanced in *America and Cosmic Man* (1948) and *Rude Assignment*. We should argue about why Lewis foregrounded certain forms of tolerance in *Hitler* in particular, but the fact that he foregrounded them at all at the very least forces us to query how simplistically his political views should be classified.

However we characterise Lewis's position, he himself tended to be wary of the notion of fixed political identities. He ridiculed party politics, suggesting that party lines merely strengthen the very antagonisms that the political process is meant to solve, and consequently he reserved the right to be ideologically chameleonic, changing his attitudes as needed in response to a changing world. Thus he stated at the end of the 1920s, only half-jokingly, that his politics were 'partly communist and partly fascist, with a distinct streak of monarchism in [his] marxism [sic], but at bottom anarchist with a healthy passion for order' (*E3* p. 70). This statement contains a serious anxiety about the viability of political identity itself in the modern age. Lewis was troubled by a growing sense that the question of political allegiance in Western societies, and in parliamentary democracies especially, amounted to a false dichotomy. As he put it in 1929:

if you do not thrill at the thought of the modern Capitalist State and all that it entails, then you must be a Communist . . . And there is no margin in which the individual can exist, *effectively*, outside these gigantic organisations. (*E3* pp. 79–80)

For Lewis, the languages of inter-war politics not only sustained an illusion of choice while simplifying 'mercurial and diverse realit[ies]' (*LWE* p. 42), but more bleakly restricted choice in the act of celebrating it: align oneself with a traditional political emphasis and its reductive stratagems, or abandon accepted political categories and forsake intelligibility.

Given how deeply sceptical he was about the political process, it is not surprising that Lewis often insisted that his abilities did not lie 'in the economic or the political field at all, but in that of the arts of expression, the library and the theatre' (*P* pp. 82–3). Nevertheless, he was preoccupied with politics throughout his life, and his extensive writings on the subject demonstrate his first-rate political mind. He regularly stated that he was 'awakened' politically during the First World War. In his second autobiography, *Rude Assignment*, he insisted that his political sense 'manifested itself first as reactions to being a soldier and to the war generally' (*RA* p. 148), and in his first, *Blasting and Bombardiering* (1937), he recalled reading one of his key intellectual influences, the anarchist philosopher Pierre-Joseph Proudhon, in the trenches (*BB* p. 144). This is not to say that Lewis was naive about politics before 1914. He was a thirty-two-year-old man by the start of the First World War, after all, and we know that in 1905 he attended a meeting in Paris to help get the Russian novelist and political activist Maxim Gorky out of prison (see *L* p. 17). *Tarr* (1918), the novel Lewis began writing around 1908, is also clearly sensitive to national differences and shows that he was politically literate well before he put on khaki. However, his retrospective sense of the war as a watershed in his political development shows how far he felt that the conflict determined everything he wrote in its wake. Indeed, not only do substantial tomes like *The Art of Being Ruled* (1926), *Time and Western Man* (1927), and *Men without Art* (1934) continually return to the effects the war had upon culture and society, but they also indicate Lewis's need to explain to a general audience how such a calamitous war could have transpired and how it might be stopped from happening again.

Among the many quirks of fate with which Lewis grappled during the inter-war period, perhaps the bitterest was his sense that the First World War, a war by many accounts fought to make the world safe for democracy, had in fact finally snuffed out a discredited democratic ideal. Hence his allegation that Britain and its American allies entered the First World War 'to make the world *safe*', but in the event made it 'safe for something that never existed, and whose very possibility the War finally destroyed' (*LWE* pp. 283–4).[3] This brickbat was one among many Lewisian criticisms of the ways governments justify wars fought to preserve economic interests; of the idea that violence might counteract violence; and of the flaws of parliamentary politics in an age of revolutionary impulses, economic slump, global tensions, and emerging dictatorships. In Lewis's view these pressures had been exacerbated by the terms of the Treaty of Versailles and by the efforts of the League of Nations, leading him to diagnose a 'fatal progression' that would result 'within a shorter or longer period, [in] a situation in which a general war, all over the world, will take place – Great War No. 2, in short' (*LWE* p. 93). Indeed, the increasing likelihood of a Second World War bolstered Lewis's sense that the First had inflicted a 'terrible blow to all hopes of civilization and a humaner, happier life' (*ABR* p. 80), and at least initially confirmed his view that democracy incubated rather than curtailed man's belligerent tendencies.

Lewis later wrote that his days as a soldier made him 'more pacific than most confirmed civilians' (*HC* p. 42). His wartime experiences also turned him into a self-styled guru, a figure who hoped, through the educational remit of his non-fictional writings, to give his readers ideological 'keys' with which they might expose hidden social and cultural logics. The objective was to lead his predominantly Western audience onto a 'path of political discovery' (*LWE* p. 23). Thus during the inter-war period he wrote books designed to help people think critically about capitalist and democratic culture, society, and history; to reveal the trends by which democracy repressed its citizens even as it celebrated their 'liberties', on the one hand, and to help swell the ranks of enlightened selves who might eradicate socio-political injustice, on the other. Lewis's concept of 'justice' changed over time, initially being geared towards the preservation of artistic and intellectual autonomy at the expense of the general social mass. But his elitist preferences consistently brushed up against a very different drive to help interested ordinary people escape from political oppression of every kind. Among Lewis's core targets were the mystifying effects of apparently transparent political language – the problem, as he called it, 'of the survival of words, after the fact they symbolize has long vanished' (*P* p. 71) – and culture's 'ideologic or philosophic basis', the place 'where so many false ideas change hands or change heads' (*P* p. 109). He was, in this sense, a radical critic of false consciousness who tried to dismantle 'the very terms in which existing political positions were articulated in order to try to break out of the realm of ideology altogether' (*GWL* p. 3).

Lewis's assaults on language, culture, and society in this period earned him numerous admirers. However, the bulk of his devotees belonged, as he himself recognised, to the wrong audience. In writing long, complicated books of sociological and political critique he hoped, through a sort of 'self-help' technique, to rally round common citizens and assist their escape from ideological and material enslavement. He was not in the first instance interested in speaking to fellow intellectuals, even though it was the intelligentsia who took most notice of his writing in newspapers, journals, and letters. He thought that mostly it is 'the wealthy, intelligent, or educated' – namely, those who have benefited from privilege – 'who are revolutionary or combative' (*ABR* p. 17), and asserted that many people do not have the time, desire, or even capacity to be politically minded. Hence the fluctuations in his work between a view of society populated by oppressed individuals who might pull themselves 'like a mammal growing wings' (*ABR* p. 106) into a more enlightened, unfettered existence, versus a deterministic world split into puppets and puppet-masters, the former doomed to blind subservience to the latter (see, for instance, Part V of *The Art of Being Ruled*, '"Natures" and "Puppets"'). But even if we grant Lewis the benefit of the doubt here, nevertheless the form of his arguments bordered on a paradox. His goal was to help people become independently minded by forcing them to grapple with political history and theory, yet his writing assumed a significant degree of readerly knowledge and interpretative fluency, and certainly more competence than someone uninterested in, or ignorant of, the inner workings of the political sphere could reasonably be expected to possess.

There is evidence that Lewis was unsettled by these problems. He introduced *The Art of Being Ruled* by saying that its intended audience would have to bring itself into being through self-directed effort, a point he reiterated in *Time and Western Man*:

> There is no way . . . of making this study so attractively simple that the most breathlessly busy of Plain Men can be induced to engage upon it with the guarantee that its essentials will be economically garaged in his head under half an hour. It is quite impossible to 'pot' the thought that makes the world go round in such a way that anybody, after a fortnight's application for half an hour a day, will, for the rest of his life, recognize at a glance the true nature of any ideology that is sprung upon him. That cannot be done. (*TWM* pp. xii–xiii)

Lewis made much the same claim in *Men without Art*, in which, discussing the ideological content of literature, he reminded his readers that one 'must be prepared to work a little bit, to look an abstract idea in the face and mildly cudgel your brains, if you are going to understand much about books and other products of the artistic intelligence' (*MWA* p. 11). And by the late 1930s, during a period of increasing sympathy for 'the ordinary person', he noted that his socio-political tomes addressed a reader-type who already 'has some knowledge of the world' and who is aware that it is 'singularly wicked' (*JAH* p. 69).

Lewis's discussions of such expectations reveal his compassion for ordinary suffering and lack of social advantage. While it is true that much of Lewis's work 'stakes a claim for the superior intellect that can recognize the ideological game and transcend it for the sake of something more enlightened', Lewis also repeatedly drew attention to those who, in their varying circumstances, face a disabling upwards social struggle.[4] He insisted that democratic societies are more likely to produce '[u]seful and docile citizens' than those 'trained to think for themselves' (*ABR* p. 360) because in his view the educational systems through which many people have to pass reinforce, rather than challenge, the status quo. He suggested, too, that even highly educated people have 'very little leisure for reading' (*TWM* p. 247), thus disclosing the problem with his particular brand of cultural criticism, which to be digested effectively depended on an audience of unhurried, engaged readers. Lewis knew, moreover, the ironies caused by his books' exorbitant price tags. In a related vein, he contended that the operations of capitalist society rooted most people into functions, their destinies being little more than those of 'salaried slaves' (*ABR* p. 182) or the 'servants of some big trust' (*ABR* p. 142). Passages such as these show a pessimistic Lewis convinced that most people will never benefit from his advice, or, even if they are remotely interested in it, will be unable change their lot in life. And the optimistic Lewis hopeful of social transformation acknowledged that his identity as an intellectual risked making his commentaries unpalatable. He mocked the 'experts' who claimed that his writings were difficult to follow, even though he was well aware that capitalism marginalises society's 'most intellectually energetic and imaginative individuals' (*RA* 23), that certain forces construct intellectual discourse as 'aloof' and 'remote', in order more effectively to maintain Establishment power.[5]

Lewis's political writings were never quite free from this fundamental tension: on the one hand, an insistence on the need for a stagnant social 'mass' against which artists and intellectuals necessarily should define their existence; on the other, a desire for 'intellectually energetic and imaginative individuals' to transform society and its citizens. Vorticism focalised the problem at an early point in Lewis's career. The opening pages of *BLAST*, for instance, herald 'an art of Individuals' (*B1* p. 7) whose good works depend on the crowd's 'stupidity, animalism and dreams' (*B1* p. 7). Thus the problem of exactly who qualifies as an 'individual' is foregrounded in the magazine from the outset, reproducing the dilemma at the level of form by using journalistic marketing strategies to present a movement of abstruse, seemingly self-contradictory slogans and artworks. Lewis later insisted that Vorticism portended a new civilisation and that it was meant to provide 'fresh eyes for people, and fresh souls to go with the eyes' (*RA* p. 135). In retrospect, however, it can be difficult to know how seriously to take these claims. Lewis was committed to the idea that Vorticism would 'not appeal to any particular class, but to the fundamental and popular instincts in every class and description of people' (*B1* p. 7), yet his dismissal of the 'Man in the Street and the Gentleman' (*B1* p. 7) seems to contradict this all-embracing bombast.

Was Vorticism an elitist enterprise aimed at a coterie of already like-minded fellow practitioners? Or was its highbrow avant-gardism part of a campaign to transform society more generally, a crusade that would have flourished but for the disaster of the First World War? Both accounts contain grains of truth. We can be sure that Lewis's forcible removal from the avant-garde circles of pre-war London, his experiences as an artillery officer during the war, his short-lived attempt to revive Vorticism after his return from France, and his subsequent disillusionment with what he deemed an 'especially diseased and directionless' (*WLA* p. 207) post-war culture left their mark on him. Lewis did not abandon art in the 1920s, but he did become increasingly convinced that democracy was the wrong framework within which high-quality artisanship and genuine selfhood could be fostered. Taking art as his guide in all matters, he questioned democracy and its 'more primitive relative', communism, both producing, as he saw it, societies of 'emotionally-excited, closely-packed, heavily-standardized mass-units, acting in a blind, ecstatic unison, as though in response to the throbbing of some unseen music' (*E1* p. 49). Lewis opposed this predicament to harmoniously proportioned cultures within which subjectivity and creativity might flourish. *The Art of Being Ruled* includes an extended defence of this point. In this key book Lewis assaulted democracy's levelling tendencies; derided parliamentarianism as a farcical sham; highlighted the supposed naivety of liberalism; sought a social model that would privilege the right of artists simply to work by accepting people's supposedly 'natural' limitations; and proposed an alternative to democracy inspired by the examples of Soviet Russia and fascist Italy.[6]

Much of the difficulty of *The Art of Being Ruled*, a book filled with fragmentary, sometimes ambiguous reasoning, comes from its mix of 'common sense' deduction and often repugnant hard-heartedness. The added fact that it is one of the most brilliant works of political analysis produced in the 1920s, and arguably the most intelligent of modernism's sociological treatises, is a significant complicating factor for historians of the period. It is also a problematic text whose failings should be stressed no less so than its triumphs. Lewis later stated that he approached the question of 'the state-beautiful' from 'the standpoint of [his] trade' (*MWA* p. 191) – that of an artist. This method allowed him to consider political problems from the seemingly detached perspective of an external, cultured observer. Yet that detachment often blinded him to lived social complexities and to the human costs that can accompany efforts to simplify them. In this guise, Lewis traced with unparalleled insight the crushing of the modern subject by corporate structures and by widespread myths of easily achieved social equalities, even though it also led him to make highly questionable political recommendations. He was convinced that apart from periodic gestures to individual liberty in the form of elections, parliamentary democracy was little more than despotic rule masquerading as representative government. *The Art of Being Ruled* builds on these theories point by point, interpreting Western civilisation as a sham that continually hovers on the brink of war, that uses insidious techniques of suggestion to pacify its citizens, and that makes its voters bloodthirsty by encouraging a combative media, aggressive popular entertainments, and a ruthless world of business.

In the 1920s Lewis thought that the hidden operations of democracy made it more than worthy of being abandoned. Thus he suggested that parliaments might be dissolved and representation discarded in favour of a system truer to his conception of social realities. Fascism appealed to Lewis largely because it seemed to solve this problem. Fascism's authoritarian processes 'respected' citizens by ruling them openly and hierarchically. Its caste structures enabled people to occupy self-contained, distinctive subject positions with clear *raisons d'être*, rather than the indistinctness of 'democratic abstraction[s]' (*ABR* p. 324). Lewis acknowledged that the historical traditions of European liberty and law should not be jettisoned lightly (see *ABR* p. 323), but so vitriolic was he at the workings of parliamentary democracy that he was willing to abandon those traditions and to welcome systems centred on recognised, purposeful authority. This side of his thought persisted well into the 1930s, as an ambiguous text like *Left Wings over Europe* (1936) shows all too clearly. It was also the departure point for *Hitler*, a book Lewis wrote to explain the dictator's policies and the character of post-war Germany, and to apply some of the abstract theorising of *The Art of Being Ruled* to a controversial post-war scenario.

The low point of Lewis's political writings undoubtedly lies here. He rightly insisted that *The Art of Being Ruled* does not contain blueprints for social planning, thus making it hard to reject it as a fascist 'mani-festo'. Yet *The Art of Being Ruled* nevertheless outlines authoritarian tendencies that influenced the regrettable statements Lewis made in the book itself and in those that followed it during the next decade or so. *Paleface* (1929) is a superbly nuanced critique of morality, race identity, and ethnicity. It also contains extremely dubious assumptions about personhood in the context of race relations and human rights. *Hitler*, likewise, is more perceptive than it seems. Yet the book is also filled with statements that were either ill-advised at the time or which sorely seem so in retrospect. Lewis acquitted Hitler and his followers of being uniquely anti-Semitic, suggesting that all nationalisms are xenophobic, and he disagreed with those who argued that the Hitlerists intended cynically to use 'this handy weapon of race-antagonism for their own ends' (*H* p. 37). Lewis could not have known about the atrocities lying in wait for Jewish people in Nazi Europe, atrocities he unequivocally condemned in *Rude Assignment* and *The Writer and the Absolute* (1952). However, when we read Lewis referring to 'drastic proposals directed against the Jews' in early 1930s Germany as a 'preliminary snag' (*H* p. 35), it is hard not to feel that he had put his critical faculties on hold.

How we deal with the Lewis of such books as *The Art of Being Ruled* and *Hitler* is open to debate. For some, *Hitler* is the terminal point of a career that was fascistic from the outset, the damning evidence of a diseased mind whose work should be forgotten or lastingly viewed in a negative light.[7] For others, Lewis's qualified sympathy for fascism rep-resents the nadir of a political trajectory that moved from left to right and back to left, and which became more tolerant and open-minded as time wore on.[8] Both perspectives criticise *Hitler* and the phase of Lewis's career in which it was written. However, only the second viewpoint permits the idea that his sympathy for fascism had an afterlife in which he abandoned authoritarianism and more or less became an egalitarian. The key switch happened in and around 1937, after Lewis wrote a series of books – *Left Wings over Europe* and *Count Your Dead: They are Alive!* (1937) among them – designed to help the cause of appeasement in the face of an increasingly militaristic Germany. These texts are some of the critical books Lewis later acknowledged he had not written care-fully (see *RA* p. 237), though they do contain valuable discussions of the media's role in swaying international opinion, national sovereignty, war-to-end-wars thinking, and the financial imperatives lurking beneath pugnacious speechifying. They also indicate that Lewis's politics were still unsettled. Having written approvingly of centralised power in *The Art of Being Ruled* he reversed his position in *Left Wings over Europe*, in which he described centralisation as 'the greatest evil it is possible to imagine' (*LWE* p. 16). Yet *Count Your Dead* complicates matters, with Lewis nailing his colours to a pyramidal view of 'democracy' (see *CYD* p. 6) and, through the Lewisian character Ned, praising fascism as the nearest thing to democracy (see *CYD* pp. 275–6) on the modern stage.

Other aspects of Lewis's inter-war writings reveal the multi-sided nature of his politics. Although he was critical of communism, he insisted that this did not make him a simplistic British flag-waver or capitalist lackey. Lewis disliked in communism 'what is mechanical and what, as the name "communism" alone suggests, threatens to regularize too much the individual's duties to his neighbour' (*E3* p. 18). He later argued that communism 'started from a great principle of social justice, and was planned as a great feat of social engineering', though by 1930 it seemed to him that it had become 'a racket' (*HC* p. 44). However, Lewis's anti-communism did not send him running uncritically towards fascism, either. He made it clear in *The Art of Being Ruled* that he strove to avoid 'all violence as an article of faith' (*ABR* p. 359) and that he condemned 'the stupid violence of physical force' (*ABR* p. 19). Thus he criticised Italian fascism for its thuggishness and lampooned Mussolini's personality cult for its rabble-rousing melodrama. 'The fascists have the word *action* on their lips from morning till night', Lewis wrote: 'It is their magic word, recurring in all their speeches or incantations; Violence is their god' (*E1* p. 164). Fascism seemed to Lewis to be the only source from which society could expect 'any really uncompromising criticism of so-called democratic institutions' (*LWE* p. 53), but he refused to accept that having sympathy for fascism meant that he was *ipso facto* in favour of violence or that his aims were 'identical with those of the militant "right"-winger' (*LWE* p. 54).

After 1937, and following condemnation of Italian fascism in *Blasting and Bombardiering*, Lewis changed his tune. He still sympathised with the revolutionary rather than gradualist positions that had characterised his thought since the days of Vorticism, but in such texts as *The Mysterious Mr Bull*, *The Jews: Are They Human?*, *The Hitler Cult* (1939), *America, I Presume* (1940), and *Anglosaxony: A League that Works* (1941) he showed a new awareness of the human sacrifices occasioned by politics based on blueprint planning, models of human perfectibility, and 'year zero' radicalism. Evoking the example of the rebuilt, re-ordered London explored in *The Caliph's Design* (1919), Lewis maintained that politically he tended to seek 'a clean slate, upon which to construct something perfectly new and entirely untried' (*MMB* 225). Yet the way Lewis clarified this statement reveals how far he had come from his earlier sympathies, and especially from his provisional backing of an authoritarianism with which to transcend democracy.

In *The Art of Being Ruled* he presented fascism as a way to break 'the humbug of a democratic suffrage' (*ABR* p. 321) and to create a new social system that would be ruled openly and policed judiciously. In *The Mysterious Mr Bull*, by contrast, Lewis queried such notions. Whereas in *The Art of Being Ruled* he had been confident that revolutionary political change could be realised with minimal blending between the old and the new, in *The Mysterious Mr Bull* he claimed that all societies contain vested interests that cannot be expunged. Any attempt to do so necessarily means brushing up against 'sentiment, bigger than houses, with foundations far deeper down' (*MMB* p. 260) and ignoring lived human realities. Reflecting on the vocabularies habitually used to discuss such matters, Lewis emphasised that human individuals 'are not bricks and mortar, or ferro-concrete' (*MMB* p. 231). Thus he revealed a heightened awareness of the problems caused by using such metaphors to hypothesise social change, and a shift from the Lewis who in *The Art of Being Ruled* had conjectured about utopianism in a more detached manner.

Lewis's discussions of politics in *The Mysterious Mr Bull* compassionately accept the complexities of 'the semi-animal, irrational, basis of human life' (*MMB* p. 232). *The Jews: Are They Human?*, *The Hitler Cult*, *America, I Presume*, and *Anglosaxony: A League that Works* show this side of Lewis even more plainly. The first book was not meant to cast doubt on Jewish selfhood. Its title was a taunt aimed at G. J. Renier's *The English: Are They Human?* (1931), though Lewis might have anticipated the inevitable loss of context here more shrewdly. This point aside, *The Jews: Are They Human?* continues Lewis's assaults on capitalism, social standardisation, British imperialism, and nationalism, and bemoans the conditions of a Europe still plagued by the socio-economic consequences of the First World War. At its core the book rejects the 'ugly nonsense of the diatribes of the antisemite [sic]' (*JAH* p. 99), and in this regard it should be read alongside *The Hitler Cult*, in which Lewis withdrew many of the arguments of *The Art of Being Ruled* and of *Hitler* in particular. By 1939 he was ready to dismiss Nazism as a 'pernicious racket' (*HC* p. 23) and to admit that his earlier, 'rather contemptuous tolerance' (*HC* p. 40) of Hitler had been woefully short-sighted. Lewis urged this position in book after book, his scorn for 'that barbarous little mountebank, Hitler' (*AIP* p. 59), whom he now finally saw as 'a mass-murderer' (*AIP* p. 171), burning through his prose.

Anglosaxony: A League that Works (1941) united these emphases. A pamphlet written to extol the virtues of the English-speaking world, it marks a volte-face in Lewis's output. Democracy had long functioned for him as a sign of everything that was politically bad about the Anglo-American West. Now, faced by Hitler's expansionism and in a flush of enthusiasm for parliamentary government, Lewis urged that people do enjoy 'a system, in democratic countries, which as such things go is pretty good' (*ALW* p. 13); that democracy is predicated upon 'the desire for human freedom' (*ALW* p. 68), and should consequently be protected from dangers; and that in contrast to the League of Nations, which Lewis mauled throughout the inter-war period, Anglo-Saxony represented a successful confederacy, its parliaments 'in full working order' (*ALW* p. 75). He particularly stressed the continuities between fascist politics and the Futurist rhetorics he had lampooned since before the First World War (*ALW* p. 48). Lewis also went further than he had previously by equating fascism and nationalism, and by insisting on the need for modern communities to adopt a 'truly international state of mind' (*ALW* p. 67). In earlier texts Lewis had dwelled on the congealing effects of nationalist language. Now he condemned nationalism as little more than the search for 'an ideal excuse for breaking somebody else's head' (*ALW* p. 32), a view which eventually led him to the interlocking claims that nationalism simply meant xenophobia and warmongering, and that therefore nations themselves should expire (*RA* p. 237).

Lewis's politics had, in other words, changed significantly by the beginning of the Second World War. Whereas in the 1920s he arguably had been modernism's arch-anti-democrat, by the 1940s he had become one of democracy's staunchest defenders. He still had problems with democracy, which in his view was not sufficiently internationalist and was marked by socio-economic injustices, but he was ready to embrace it over fascism for its comparative egalitarianism. His plea for the benefits of democracy hinged on a renewed denunciation of utopian and particularly messianic, perfectibilistic, and totalitarian thought. Lewis was not ready to abandon *tabula rasa*-style philosophies even in 1941 (*ALW* p. 13), though he did point out that gradualism is the humane alternative to ideologies which deny 'that a community, tribe, or nation, grows like a tree' (*ALW* p. 72). He had long championed the idea that all forms of politics take their cue from some utopian principle, irrespective of the nature of the anticipated goal (see *P* p. 258). Yet Lewis was never convinced that a 'perfect' society is possible and he resisted ideas of communal living 'founded upon a notion of the "common good" which [attempt] to weigh out to everybody an equal amount *and* kind of "good"' (*P* p. 88). *Anglosaxony* took Lewis's rhetoric up a notch. In this text he maintained that totalitarianism throws human beings 'back into the era of the jungles' (*ALW* p. 17), and claimed that theorists 'who impose something ready-made – some brilliant generalization of the intellect – upon recalcitrant organic bodies' (*ALW* p. 29) will not only bring suffering to mankind but also undo themselves by sowing the seeds of future rebellions.

Lewis's reference to 'some brilliant generalization of the intellect' is telling. In *The Art of Being Ruled* he insisted that only by rooting politics in the theoretical workings of the intellect, but without letting the intellect be corrupted by politics, would 'the terrestrial paradise' (*ABR* p. 81) be attained. A decade or so later he had moved away from this position. As if writing about himself, Lewis reminded his readers that approaching the reorganisation of societies in the way a mechanic approaches a machine was impossible, not only because the world does not cleave together machinically, but also because intellectuals cannot occupy an Olympian viewpoint from which to theorise about social structures (*MMB* p. 265). *The Art of Being Ruled* is a complicated text that cannot be summarised easily, but even if it shied away from offering a blueprint of an authoritarian future nevertheless it made several theoretical recommendations for how Lewis's world could be re-constituted. Lewis's objective here was to jettison class-based, capitalistic, and nationalistic democracies in favour of a fascist 'world-state and a recognized central world-control' (*ABR* p. 367), one that would unify humanity and thus prevent world wars. By the mid-1930s he had altered his stance, aligning himself with the politics of national sovereignty, and by the late 1930s he had switched positions yet again, ultimately seeking to persuade people of 'the great disadvantage of competitive nationalist emotions, and of the desirability of cosmopolis' (*RA* p. 192).

Lewis wrote in *The Art of Being Ruled* that in the 1920s 'original' individuals were being forced more and more out of the 'rigid system of clans, societies, clubs, syndics, and classes' (*ABR* p. 364). Eventually, when enough originals had been marginalised into an outside space from which to evaluate the world, the 'moment of the renascence of our race' (*ABR* p. 364) would have been reached. In 1926 this was very much an elitist position that placed philosopher-types at the summit of an intellectual aristocracy. A revolution of the intellectuals portended an authoritarian future, however nuanced. Lewis in the 1940s and 1950s still believed in social hierarchies (see *RA* p. 200), but he now viewed such hierarchies as compatible with the democratic impulse. Having previously attacked Europe's libertarian traditions, Lewis now defended them. In 1948 Cecil Gray wrote that Lewis's 'masterly and devastating critical analyses of art, politics, sociology and philosophy' in the 1920s and 1930s suggested that 'he might be the guide for whom the world was waiting, to whom all were looking'.[9] Looking back on Lewis's career almost sixty years after his death, it now seems obvious that Gray was overly sympathetic to a writer whose politics remain in many

particulars deeply objectionable. But in tracing Lewis's gradual enchant-
ment with democracy, and in examining his increasingly hospitable,
yet always fiercely analytical, attitude towards representative government, we can more accurately reconstruct his unique perspective on the
destructive and seductive politics of his time.

Notes

1. For overviews of Lewis's politics see D. G. Bridson, *The Filibuster: A Study
   of the Political Ideas of Wyndham Lewis* (London: Cassell, 1972); Alan
   Munton, 'The Politics of Wyndham Lewis', *PN Review*, 1, March 1976,
   pp. 34–9; William M. Chace, 'On Lewis's Politics: The Polemics Polemically
   Answered', in *MWL* pp. 149–65; Andrzej Gąsiorek, '"Jujitsu for the
   Governed"? Wyndham Lewis and the Problem of Power', *Wyndham Lewis
   Annual*, 8, 2001, pp. 30–49; David A. Wragg, *Wyndham Lewis and the
   Philosophy of Art in Early Modernist Britain: Creating a Political Aesthetic*
   (Lampeter: Edwin Mellen, 2005); and Ivan Phillips, 'In His Bad Books:
   Wyndham Lewis and Fascism', *The Journal of Wyndham Lewis Studies*, 2,
   2011, pp. 105–34. See also Michael Valdez Moses's and Munton's chap-
   ters in Peter Brooker et al. (eds), *The Oxford Handbook of Modernisms*
   (Oxford: Oxford University Press, 2010), pp. 139–55 and pp. 477–500.
2. See also my chapter 'Lewis and Fascism', in Tyrus Miller (ed.), *The Cambridge
   Companion to Wyndham Lewis* (Cambridge: Cambridge University Press,
   forthcoming).
3. For more on this subject, see my chapter 'Providing Ridicule: Wyndham
   Lewis and Satire in the Postwar-to-end-war World', in Alice Reeve-Tucker
   and Nathan Waddell (eds), *Utopianism, Modernism, and Literature in the
   Twentieth Century* (Basingstoke: Palgrave Macmillan, 2013), pp. 56–73.
4. David A. Wragg, 'More Matter, Less Art?: Occam's Razor, "Philosophy",
   and Wyndham Lewis's Modernism', *The Journal of Wyndham Lewis
   Studies*, 4, 2013, pp. 104–26: p. 120.
5. See Wyndham Lewis, *The Old Gang and the New Gang* (London: Desmond
   Harmsworth, 1933), p. 18.
6. For more on this point see Moses, 'Modernists as Critics'.
7. John Carey's account of Lewis in *The Intellectuals and the Masses: Pride and
   Prejudice among the Literary Intelligentsia, 1880-1939* (London: Faber and
   Faber, 1992) remains the *locus classicus* for this view. Ivan Phillips notes
   that 'Lewis was far from isolated in his (relatively brief) attraction to the far
   right, but only he, it often seems, has been judged on this point alone'. See
   Ivan Phillips, 'Enemy Lines: Form, Politics and Identity in Wyndham Lewis's
   One-Way Song', *Wyndham Lewis Annual*, 12, 2005, pp. 59–79: p. 65.
8. See Alan Munton, 'Wyndham Lewis: From Proudhon to Hitler (and back):
   The Strange Political Journey of Wyndham Lewis', in Jennifer Birkett and Stan
   Smith (eds), *Right / Left / Right: Revolving Commitments: France and Britain
   1929–1950* (Newcastle: Cambridge Scholars Publishing, 2008), pp. 47–60.
9. Cecil Gray, *Musical Chairs, or Between Two Stools* [1948] (London: The
   Hogarth Press, 1985), p. 272 and p. 273.

Chapter 10

The Revenge for Love
Ian Patterson

A tear is an intellectual thing. (William Blake, *Jerusalem*)[1]

Wyndham Lewis was distrustful of all ideologies, or at least he was distrustful of all the ideologies he was aware of. Powerfully convinced that he, almost alone, was able to see the true state of affairs, his determination to open the eyes of his readers, and the many who were not his readers, to 'the paths that lead from the metaphysical principle to the *event*' and reveal 'the true nature of any ideology' (*TWM* p. xiii) informs pretty much all his writing at one level or another. As he puts it a couple of pages later in *Time and Western Man* (1927), the discussion of 'art, novels and pictures' needs to tempt 'the lazier or busier of my audience into taking *the critical step* over into the abstract region, there where ideas, and not people or events, have to be encountered' (*TWM* p. xv). The 'abstract region' is the realm of art as well as ideas, but in novels it is harder to separate thought from people, and *The Revenge for Love* (1937) is a novel, though rather an odd one; it also stages what is unmistakeably an 'event' as the culmination of its anatomy of deception, self-deception, and manipulation. When we first encounter Margot she is thinking, 'What could love do against events? . . . *love*: which made everything worse, not better' (*RL* p. 69). As the free indirect monologue continues we start to feel that this is a bit melodramatic, a bit self-dramatising, purposely designed by Lewis to reveal Margot's sentimental naivety. And there is indeed a pervasive note of mockery in Lewis's narrative style, indeed in all his writing, which works to construct that 'critical step' into the realm of ideas, and subject the characters (and through the novel, its readers) to ruthless critique.

In his 1934 essay '"Detachment" and the Fictionist', Lewis asserts that

demonstrations of uneasiness are required of all who handle words; ceaseless uneasiness not regarding the words themselves (for the dogma of the *mot juste* is a thing of the past), but regarding the assumptions on which so much of language is based. (*CHC* pp. 214–15)

And ceaseless uneasiness is exactly what readers of his prose experience. It is the price of detachment, of independence from 'bogus' value systems like communism and fascism. Lewis's readers must submit to his 'personality', because fiction writers

> cannot afford to treat contemporary society as though it were *dead* ... In order to get the maximum of drama out of it you must 'in the destructive element immerse'; allow it to bring into play your personality ... Do not be intimidated ... by the propaganda of the *nuance* – the prevarication – the half-light – the *pseudo*-statement and the *pseudo*-truth. (*CHC* pp. 228–9)

It is always the case in a Wyndham Lewis novel that everything is filtered through the author's managerial voice; there is not much space for the illusion of actuality or the seductions of free and independent life. This is because he is all the time telling us that there is no free and independent life; even the most powerful, the manipulators, the puppet-masters, are responding to circumstances they cannot in the end control. And since Lewis never misses an opportunity to involve his own (subjective) values in acts of description, he creates an unusually densely-layered moral integument around each character. The condescension we feel in the evocation of Margot's 'ecstasy of lovesickness' is matched by the 'dizzy gloating' (*RL* p. 70) in her eyes. Having been patronised, she is then infantilised by the term 'rocked' (*RL* p. 70) – though the implicit pun also opens the way to 'steady' (*RL* p. 70) – and thus freighted we move into free indirect discourse for a closer experience of her impotence in the face of Victor's evasiveness, his macho indifference, her inability to make him acknowledge her, and her still lingering doubt that he might really be avoiding her. Even the tear that 'slid down her cheek' (*RL* p. 70) does not warrant a less clichéd verb.

All this works to detach us from the emotional involvement with character and narrative that novels normally encourage, and to prod us (and sometimes push or kick us) into thought and judgement. Or at any rate into recognising Lewis's thought and judgement. As a method it is essentially satirical, and so for the most part is *The Revenge for Love*. But what makes the experience of reading it so unusual is the way in which Lewis uses something close to sentimentality to counterbalance the satire and give it the illusion of pain and emotional depth. This gives us as readers a troubling access to a sense of human vulnerability underlying the bluff or scathing or mocking authorial tone.[2]

When Fredric Jameson describes the function of different elements in Lewis's style as 'to interfere with each other, to clash visibly within the sentence itself in such a way that . . . [it becomes] an amalgam of hetero-geneous forces which must not be allowed to congeal' (*JFA* p. 33), he points to something important in the larger scale too. But his belief that this is a visual process, related to his work as a painter and so mitigated in the works of his blindness, is not quite right. The 'almost eighteenth-century sobriety' (*JFA* p. 34) Jameson detects in Lewis's late narratives is increasingly present in the writing of the 1930s, including *The Revenge for Love*, a product of the urgent need Lewis felt to campaign against polarising politics and the threat of another world war.

A world where the ground of value is deceptive and uncertain (and where reproduction antique furniture like Agnes Irons's desk enjoys full legitimacy) is a breeding ground for 'fakers': counterfeits, forgeries, pre-tence, fronts, manipulation, and ordinary lies abound in the social world as they do in *The Revenge for Love*. Similarly, Reed Way Dasenbrock notes that '[a]cting, disguises, false appearances, conspiracies . . . are the materials out of which Lewis constructs many of his narratives. His plots are made of plots' (*RL* p. 391), but Dasenbrock fails to draw out the full implications of his observation. Lewis certainly relies heavily on these elements, and he draws on the props and plots of popular fiction, whether parodically or seriously, and on the many forms of pretence and counterfeit to be encountered in social, artistic, and political life – but he also sees actual plots all around him, with people plotting against him, conspiring against him as a professional artist, and conspiring to obfus-cate the true nature and aims of political interests.

It is the way in which Lewis combines this overview of what he thinks everybody else is thinking (and the paranoid outlook that underlies it) with his jovial, slightly confidential, somewhat disingenuous authorial persona, that gives his 1930s writing its characteristic tone and leads him to occupy so many politically wrong or tonally misjudged posi-tions in his polemic interventions; yet that collocation is also what gives this novel its power. For all his tonal layers of defensive self-protection and his 'Enemy' persona, the insistence on unmasking everybody else sometimes leaves his own viewpoint curiously vulnerable. Lewis's self-designation as 'The Enemy' is as odd, when you think about it, as the idea of a revenge for love. To think of oneself as the pugnacious enemy of other people is already to take up a dialectical position in relation to one's own self, to come at oneself and one's agency through the eyes of hostile or vulnerable others, a procedure which leaves the artist open to being hurt as well as violent and extreme in his pursuit of his point of view. In the same way, the naive and sentimental exercise of love is shown to be simultaneously anachronistic and necessary, in the same way that it operates in the novel to provide humanity and to demonstrate its irrelevance and require its own defeat. Love needs some kind of liberty (though it may be paradoxical, as Don Alvaro claims on the novel's opening page),

> [b]ut of course, 'Liberty' is, in fact, quite the last thing that any of us are talking about today; or, rather, those of us who pretend to be doing so are merely trying to fool the others. The sooner, therefore, we see through each other, and get down to brass tacks, the better. For what we are talking about is not 'liberty', but Power.[3]

No absolute freedom, then, just brass tacks, red in tooth and claw.

Published in 1937, though completed two years earlier, *The Revenge for Love* is not really a novel about politics, or about art, or about gun-running, let alone a novel about the struggle between right and left in Spain. All those things figure in the narrative, but at its centre the novel is, as the title suggests, about love and revenge, and about role playing, and the extreme difficulty of knowing, finding, or even imagining what is real.[4] It is here that the ideas implicit in the novel's original title, *False Bottoms*, come together with the semi-tragic melodrama of Margot's love for Victor and shape the novel which Lewis in 1936 called 'probably the best complete work of fiction I have written' (*L* p. 242). Fredric Jameson sees it as 'more openly political' than Lewis's other novels, drawing its 'unaccustomed emotional resonance' (*JFA* p. 145) from the choice to enable us 'to witness the deadly onslaught of the aggressive impulse' (*JFA* p. 146) this time 'from the woman's, from the victim's, point of view' (*JFA* p. 145). This is right, but it is complicated by the way it is done: victimhood is problematised both by the unsettling of the sources of certainty, and by the carefully constructed layers of ideological attitude that make up the presentation of Margot in particular, but that also pervade the gender politics of the novel. It is not just that in Lewis's fantasy world 'the Marxists are out to destroy "individuality"', as Jameson argues, and that the concomitant 'transfer of guilt' for aggressivity enables the novel to express 'for the first and last time genuine emotion, a real sympathy and feeling for the victims' (*JFA* p. 148). This is special pleading. The laughter that overcomes Margot at the end of the novel as she clear-sightedly contemplates the 'patent car, built for pawky racketeers' (*RL* p. 331), converts all the many 'false bottoms' of the novel into a single great absurdity. One murderous event reveals to her the bottomless fantasy world on which her love was based. But the tear that Percy Hardcaster sheds in the final sentence of the novel can only be read in the context of all the tears that precede it.

If the novel had been published in the spring of 1936, as it should have been, it would not have been mistakenly regarded as a novel about the

Spanish Civil War, but as a novel about people in situations and places where all basic values had gone seriously awry and lost their bearings. Europe between 1933 to 1936 was a place of increasing political uncertainty, volatility, and crises of authority, and Spain since the late 1920s had been more volatile than most countries, providing a paradigmatic illustration of political disorder, with its many and frequent changes of government, widespread strikes, armed uprisings by anarchists and socialists, and counter-attacks by the police, army, and Guarda Civil. In his reports, the Madrid correspondent of *The Times* regularly described 'revolts against authority'. Discussing the (communist and left-wing) 'roots of the revolt' at the end of 1933 (and demonstrating a characteristically right-wing point of view), he asked:

> Is Spain to be at the mercy of an organisation capable of periodically defying the forces of law and order, plunging whole cities into the chaos of general strikes, imperilling the lives of citizens and smirching the name of Spanish civilisation?[5]

Spain had the additional advantage of possessing a heroic past with which its present could, implicitly at least, be contrasted (as Lewis did in paintings like *Siege of Barcelona* (later *The Surrender of Barcelona*)). It was dangerous, romantic, a country of extremes.

Spain, therefore, represented a genuine crisis of authority, a crisis of state power, a crisis of monarchy, republicanism, religion, and legitimacy. As such, it drew Lewis's interested attention. Since his 1920s works of political theory, *The Art of Being Ruled* (1926) and *The Lion and the Fox* (1927), he had been constantly involved in political commentary, mostly motivated by anti-communism and his passionate wish to avert a repetition of the First World War. He was also a voracious reader of (and contributor to) newspapers, weeklies, and literary and political magazines; his first appearance of the new decade was a 1930 interview in *Everyman*, significantly titled 'Our Sham Society'. In the years that followed Lewis published a sequence of hasty, eccentric books in which he attempted to outline an interpretation of international politics that might help avert another world war, books marked by ill-judged chattiness, by disastrous failures of tone, and by a powerful conviction that, as Ned puts it in *Count Your Dead* (1937),

> the present system of government in England is *a fake antique* ... A full parliamentary cast performs for our benefit, with people playing 'P.M.' and all the rest of it, possessing as little political power as screen-stars in a *House of Rothschild* film. A disarming façade of 'democracy' conceals what is in fact a Money Trust, which runs us like a national waxworks, but for whom we are a side-line, not their main concern. (CYD p. 79)

In this last claim, of course, he was far from alone. Many on both right and left, for a variety of reasons, shared 'the dawning recognition of the fact that the Democratic façade has today worn thin.'[6]

So although it is not a Spanish Civil War novel, *The Revenge for Love* is partly set in Spain in the period of unrest preceding the Falangist rebellion. Lewis knew Spain fairly well. He spent two months there in 1902 and visited again in 1908, providing experience which found its way into the stories in *The Wild Body* (see *SSG* pp. 45–7). ('Spain is an overflow of sombreness', he observed; *CWB* p. 17.) In 1934 he took a holiday in the border region where the final scenes of *The Revenge for Love* are set, and he wrote to Roy Campbell beforehand to ask for advice (*L* p. 219). Spain was evidently much on his mind, and continued to be throughout the decade.

The novel opens in Spain, in a Spanish prison, and it ends in the Spanish Pyrenees and in another Spanish gaol. Like his Spanish history paintings, the opening section of the novel, entitled 'The Civil Guard', is a genre piece, including a quasi-operatic presentation of that brutal and disciplined body of men.[7] It begins, dramatically, and ironically enough for a novel in which opacity is pervasive almost to the end, with the word 'Claro' (*RL* p. 13). The opening paragraph, a conversation between Don Alvaro, seemingly incorruptible prison warder and former civil guard, and British communist organiser Percy Hardcaster, is highly stylised, dominated by Lewis's idiosyncratic tone. A relatively simple debate between warder and prisoner about the nature of freedom is elevated by a quasi-parodic irony to the level of a 'great logician' (*RL* p. 13) through a pattern of overlapping and exaggerated repetition. The effect is to make Don Alvaro's instancing of the one moment of freedom in our lives into a melodramatic overstatement, inviting the reader's disagreement: '[It] is when at last we gaze into the bottom of the heart of our beloved and find that it is false – like everything else in the world' (*RL* p. 13). The 'brilliant operatic light' (*RL* p. 13) of the Andalusian evening illuminates the defeated political prisoners and the victorious political guards alike, as if the narrator's moral detachment were complete, despite the personal tone of the narration. Spain is operatic, it is implied, with its exaggerated code of honour, the arrogance of the 'incorruptible' (*RL* p. 17) ex-Civil Guard, Don Alvaro, its 'wife-killers and bullfighters' (*RL* p. 21), but operatic, too, in its artificiality, Don Alvaro's 'back as stiff as pasteboard' (*RL* p. 21), the peasant girl with her 'sultry swirl of the skirt' (*RL* p. 21), even a 'CHORUS OF TERRORISTS' (*RL* p. 29) simultaneously greeting Percy. The theatricality is further emphasised by the way Lewis describes the encounters between Percy and Don Alvaro: the 'socratic turnkey' (*RL* p. 37) acts different parts – when he is angry he displays 'a capital imitation of an angry warder', his eyes blaze up, but with 'a false flame' (*RL* p. 37) – and by the insistent and repeated play on the literal and metaphorical idea of 'false bottoms', of the basket, of motives and behaviour, and even of objective appearance.[8]

Against the melodrama of this backdrop, Lewis's occasionally intrusive, directive style assumes a degree of dispassionate altruism. Percy is neither as swaggering nor as confident as he at first appears, and his prison persona as revolutionary gunman is a bluff. He 'was not a *front-fighter* or anything of that nature, but rather a careerist of the propaganda section: wielding the pen, not the pistol' (*RL* p. 45) and 'bluff was the tactical basis of the latterday revolutionary personality ... *The bogus* ... made it a game' (*RL* p. 53). But however honest Percy is in his adoption of his persona, the fact of playing a part necessarily changes him: 'neither bluff nor belief remained quite the same as they were in their natural state', Lewis tells his readers, referencing 'the comic element in the Shakespearean tragic technique' (*RL* p. 53). Even for Hardcaster 'the dogma of Spanish revolt' is a 'stock Aunt Sally' (*RL* p. 53), the wrong object of his genuine anger. When later, acclaimed as a heroic communist martyr, he reveals to Gillian the extent to which his story is necessary propaganda for the cause, because 'Lies are the manure in which truth grows' (*RL* p. 190), as Lewis rather savagely has him say, Gillian rejects him, and has Jack beat him up, because he has failed to conform to the fantasy of masculinity, sex, and politics she needs to sustain her privileged parlour-pink world. After the attack, which almost kills Percy, Jack nervously claims he is 'only shamming' (*RL* p. 199). But the account of sheer violent brutality is perhaps the most relentlessly authentic moment of the novel: Jack

> delivered a pile-driving kick at his fallen rival's weak spot, the mutilated stump. As the boot struck him, where the Spanish surgeon's knife had cut in, Percy Hardcaster turned over, with a bellowing groan, against the wall, and Jack sent another one, after the first, to the same spot, with a surgical precision in the violent application of his shoe leather. Then he followed it with a third, for luck. (*RL* p. 199)

The combination of sexual *ressentiment* and masculine aggression ('The interests of *all* his glands were engaged in this transaction'; *RL* p. 198) works to make the incident a touchstone to measure the novel's other 'transactions' against.

Almost everything is transactional: from Percy's failed escape to Victor's fatal drive, money is at the root of things. In the figures of Sean O'Hara, Abershaw, and Freddie Salmon, Lewis attacks the phariseeism of the Communist Party, and the link between power and *ressentiment*, clear-eyed about the form it takes – cynical exploitation for money. Both class warfare and art are fair game here, and even Percy Hardcaster is drawn in by the prospect of financial gain or 'business' and the assurance that 'there is no organization behind' (*RL* p. 256) the gun-running. If we are to take the evidence of Lewis's political tracts of the mid-thirties, this is all part of his ardent but unbalanced view of democratic and international politics. But however accurate his observation of parliamentary and extra-parliamentary politics may have been, the machinery of power was and is too complex to be discursively represented by reductive arguments about façades and Trusts or Jewish–Bolshevik plots. Surprisingly, though, Lewis's emphasis on the relative parts played by political Machiavellianism, naivety, Comintern manipulation, and 'the will to action' animates his fiction in an unpredictably sophisticated way, and allows for the curious perceptiveness and even truthfulness of *The Revenge for Love*. For all his inability to see the true motivations of political movements and their leaders, Lewis was acutely aware of the shady purposes to which talk of war and peace could be put in international politics, and his 'enemy' pose was as apt there as in the art world. His targets, as ever, were amateurishness, gullibility, and self-interest; his satire primarily directed at those who encouraged and exploited them, though not excluding those (like Victor) pliable enough to want 'action', or parlour-communists looking for adventure and 'reality'. The 'bogus' rhetorics of class war, he believed, were dangerously imbricated with the logics of world war and the drift towards war. As he observes in *The Revenge for Love*,

> an intelligent man picks up a newspaper and addresses himself to the absorption of the thick dope that is poured out, in the orderly ducts of its political columns – endeavouring, perhaps, to discover (if it is his business to discover such things) what motive the words conceal: not at all what facts, of course, it has been sought to convey, but what facts it has been intended to reduce to a deliquium. (*RL* pp. 125–6)

Like Joseph Conrad and Ford Madox Ford, or Graham Greene, Lewis borrowed the structure of popular or genre fiction to explore matters of more profound and serious concern. But even though the narrative style of *The Revenge for Love* is less alienating than most of his fiction up to that point, it is still decidedly eccentric, and the different strands that make up the seven sections of the narrative – Percy Hardcaster and the Spanish prison, Margot and Victor and the art-fakers, communism, gun-running – are self-consciously exemplary: their existence is overtly controlled by Lewis, or so the novel's style appears to proclaim. The sheer fact of Lewis's deep involvement in the issues the novel raises, however, and the pressure of the contradictions of the political moment at which he was writing, make a deeper impression on his subject matter than he knows. His close involvement is present, most pertinently, in the sheer density, vivacity, and lexical unpredictability of the prose, but, as Jameson has noted, one of the strengths of his position – his inability to set ideology within 'the total social process of which [it] is a part' (*JFA* p. 135), which leads him to conspiracy theories and his 'enemy' persona – is also in this novel given its most radical form 'as Lewis denounces himself in the person of the Marxist enemy, lending him ... his own (discarded) name (Percy)' (*JFA* p. 176). Or rather, he denounces some aspects of himself. Others he explores more sympathetically. Margot is usually adduced at this point, as if she were in some sense the embodiment of some form of truth in the novel, but I would rather look at her in relation to Lewis's investigation of femininity.

By the time we encounter Agnes Irons, we have been introduced to a considerable variety of women. First, in the opening chapters, Josefa de la Asunción, with her false-bottomed basket, detected by Don Alvaro and forced to deliver the smuggled letter to Percy ('Large tears detached themselves and crashed down her cheeks'; *RL* p. 25); then Margot, of course; Jack Cruze's floozies ('He had plunged into London headfirst as if into a dense forest of women'; *RL* p. 95); Eileen O'Hara, 'a peregrine romantic' who had 'wandered so far from her illusion that she might have been mistaken for a daughter of the grim universe of cause-and-effect' (*RL* p. 130); Ellen Mulliner, who knows that Sean O'Hara is a double-crossing betrayer of every cause he professes but comes to his party because Percy wants her to; and Gillian Phipps ('Gillian flung herself down and, with the deliberation of someone turning on a bathroom tap, wept into her hands. A couple of ounces of water, perhaps, were discharged by her tear-ducts, and flowed through her fingers. She felt better'; *RL* p. 203). Part VI, 'The Fakers', begins with a meditation by Margot, as she looks out of the window of Agnes Irons's 'posh little service-flatlet' (*RL* p. 214) at the secret 'garden-lagoon' (*RL* p. 213) behind the house fronts. What attracts her is the fantasy generated by the elms, legacy of a past grandeur, of her own sensitive, solitary fragility, and of the 'listless contemplation' (*RL* p. 213) of a lost world of Victorian aesthetics and Woolfian feminism. It is factitious, as Lewis makes clear, and his presentation bears closer scrutiny.

Margot is self-made, self-fashioned, in 'voice, coiffure, and carriage', having started life as the daughter of 'a tradesman ... in a factory-city' (*RL* p. 214). As such, she belongs neither to the working class of Hardcaster (or the fantasy working class of people like Gillian Phipps, who snobbishly despises her) nor to the rentier class of her bohemian friends. *A Room of One's Own* (1929) ('that militant little treatise') had been her '*livre de chevet*' when she was 'still painfully in the making' (*RL* p. 213). Margot is situated as a believer in the fancies of Woolf's '"highbrow" feminist fairyland': 'delicately dipping-in, hovering above the delicious pages' (*RL* p. 214), she is captivated by Woolf's speaking lines from Tennyson's *Maud* so that the 'phantom of sound' intensifies the dream of devotion embodied in the 'words, so diaphanously winged' (*RL* p. 215), amplifying in her impressionable imagination the redemptive, transfiguring power of monogamous love, a love instantiated in her love for Victor: descended from the writings of 'those splendid Victorian monogamists – flowering, as great-hearted passion flowers, hyperpetalous and crimson red, upon the spoils of the Angloindies and of the Dark Continent' (*RL* p. 215). Even as he mocks Margot for her susceptibility and the inauthenticity of her new self, Lewis is also stripping away the veil of sentimental aesthetics and reminding us of the imperial exploitation that provides the conditions for Tennyson's civilisation and Woolf's rescension of it. But before that, Woolf's ideas themselves have been presented as definitively dated, even dead; spiritualist emanations taking in gullible seekers at a séance: '[T]his seductive train of images – which had contrived by the medium of Margot, to quicken themselves to quite a respectable degree, if not exactly to achieve the status of protoplasm – these were all rudely dissolved' (*RL* p. 215). Similarly, and more explicitly, she rises from her chair at Agnes's entrance 'with the movement . . . of an entranced medium' (*RL* p. 216). The world Woolf portrays is already a lost world, and Margot's adoption of it is somnambulistic, and prevents her from seeing the true nature of the world she inhabits and the values it operates by. Lewis further complicates his exposition of this 'seductive train of images' by a glancingly allusive prose figure: the secret garden is described as a 'well of beautiful loneliness', suggesting the exclusion of men from this '*Park of One's Own*' (*RL* p. 213) through a suggestive echo of Radclyffe Hall.

Margot's attenuated fantasy of privileged femininity is soon dispelled by the arrival of the mannish, golf-playing Agnes, who provides a complete contrast in scale and loudness and confidence and philistine jollity. Where a moment before she was floating in a self-created fantasy, her imaginary world is momentarily suppressed by the 'dynamic intrusion' of Agnes, which turns her briefly into a pastiche of a Victorian portrait, almost entirely 'suppressed' (*RL* p. 215), almost not there, replaced by an imaginary nineteenth-century version of herself. Agnes Irons is one of Lewis's caricatures, bluff, sporty, philistine, literal-minded, good-hearted, intellectually unsophisticated, and too loud. When she greets

Margot, she 'hail[s] her, at very close range' (*RL* p. 216): the relation of sound to scale and perspective here creates a sort of free indirect perception of Margot's relative fragility. It is a technique Lewis uses quite a lot, often on a micro-scale: too loud, too near, too bad, too loving, too trusting, too hopeful, too deluded – all these are questions of *scale*, and they feed critique as they feed satire. But the satire, as Paul Edwards has pointed out (*EWL* p. 447), is directed at the simplistic notion of gender for which Lewis criticised Woolf in *Men without Art* (1934). Agnes, 'Empire girl' and 'jingo' (*RL* p. 223), 'open golf champion of the Straits Settlements' who swims 'in a homeric ocean of thunderous laughter' (*RL* p. 218), thinks (slowly) about Victor's new job faking pictures, and gradually suspects it may be rather less acceptable than fabricating reproduction antique desks like the one she has just bought for herself. '"Is it *honest* – you know what I mean, could one get into trouble? – to fake these pictures? Especially by *living persons*, Margot – even if they *are* foreigners!"' (*RL* p. 223). Underneath the comedy of her exchanges with Margot, there is an intellectual struggle, of sorts, which mirrors the moral questions foregrounded by the forgery narrative: how to gauge the balance between the law, ethical responsibility, and the need to make money. The 'business woman' in Agnes thinks it 'very *irregular*', but knows that 'artists are a funny lot', and concedes that 'it *is* regular work' (*RL* p. 224). Drawlingly dismissing Margot's crowd as absurd, she 'straddled in front of the window, her hands in her skirt pockets' in a parodic echo of Margot at the opening of the chapter. '"These mangy trees give me the hump," she said' (*RL* p. 225) in symmetrical and anti-romantic contrast to Margot's response to them.

Although this is only one of many scenes in which Margot's outlook is tested and contrasted with others, it is an instructive one. The delicate presentation of her sense of social inferiority in Chapter Two of 'Sean O'Hara', and her desire to think that the moth-eaten but alarming gentlemen and their snobbish 'grinning, donnish highbrow Molls' are not real, is balanced by her thought that 'if she *really* came to believe that they were not, she would feel afraid. Who would not?' (*RL* p. 162), and this in turns leads into a brief comment about Victor's sense of reality, seen from Margot's point of view, and her recognition that they 'made Victor believe that he was not "real"'. Lewis continues her thinking:

> It was *their* reality, that of Victor and herself, that was marked down to be discouraged and abolished, and it was *they* that the others were trying to turn into phantoms and so to suppress. It was a mad notion, but it was just as if they had engaged in a battle of wills, to decide who should possess most *reality* – just as men had fought each other for money, or fought each other for food. (*RL* p. 163)

In this battle of wills, neither Margot nor Victor has the capacity to win, Margot because she cannot impose her sense of reality, Victor because he only sees what is in front of his nose. The upshot is that reality can be manipulated by those who have power, money, and ulterior designs.

Toby Foshay writes allusively that 'Margot is that point of the novel where interior and exterior, thought and action, art and politics, coalesce.'[9] But rather than coalesce, they might be thought to intersect and be refracted. Margot is the most developed of the various presentations of femininity in the novel, and the only one through whom we can think about love, but Lewis deliberately makes her an artificial construct, with so little purchase on the actual world that her emotional life as it comes to us through Lewis's prose is a purely intellectual critique. It is a function of Lewis's ventriloquial use of free indirect discourse that her voice is 'a little hollow' and that when Victor's arms release her 'there was a vacuum, a chasm, where there had before been a plenum' (*RL* p. 71). Imagination is crucial to her existence. As she is jerked back to the present from her 'self-consecrated' (*RL* p. 215) Bloomsbury daydream by the entrance of Agnes, '[s]he became sorted out from all those shapes which were susceptible to extinction at the mere vibration of a human voice, and resumed the narrower mould which was contingent upon the mortal give and take of objective experience' (*RL* pp. 215–16). But that narrower mould, pressing ever closer on her as it does, is always felt and seen through all the ideological, desired, and fantasy structures of her imagination. Only when Victor discovers that the car they have been driving so recklessly contains nothing but bricks, and that its false bottom is itself false, does she see reality for what it is. And then she laughs.

The novel prepares us for this in that brief pastoral interlude when Margot lies by a mountain stream, encountering the boisterousness of nature at first hand with some puzzlement and trying to take stock of her response to it as it 'jazzed around her breaking heart, so that she was astonished, if not scandalized' (*RL* p. 276). It is just another stage for the action she is involved in, 'obsessed with the actors, for whom these pastoral sets were the incongruous backgrounds' and 'part of this agony of men' (*RL* p. 276). Even here, Lewis encourages a level of detachment through the theatrical metaphor, so that Margot's sense of the pathos of disharmony is unsettled from any real emotional basis. It is a real struggle she is facing: 'Did her quarrel with nature involve everything upon which her personality had been grounded?' (*RL* p. 276). Yet it is also Lewis's struggle as a novelist, filtered through Margot's struggle with Ruskin (she is rereading his *Sesame and Lilies*), to find the ground of independence in a hero, whether man or woman. Margot considers Victor through the eyes of Ruskin, but recognises that he is 'not a hero in a book – she only wished that he were! They were hemmed in by a chaotic reality against which "heroism" (book-heroism) would be of little avail' (*RL* p. 278). It is Ruskin's depiction of Ophelia as the one weak woman in Shakespeare that stiffens her resolve to save '*her* Prince of Denmark' (*RL* p. 279) and, abandoning her copy of the book, and rejecting the 'empty box of tricks' that nature had rattled in her face, she takes on a new purposefulness, one which could be read as a rejection of political ideology as well. 'Without looking to left or right she started back, at a rapid walk, in the direction of the village' (*RL* p. 279).

This is the point at which she tries to take matters into her own hands, despite Victor's patronising attempt to cajole her objections into insignificance, as he was wont to do when he needed to 'rout the wicked dwarfs and cantankerous Duchesses that infested her Unconscious' (*RL* p. 288). But this time, to the surprise of Hardcaster as well, it does not work. Both are unable to take seriously her realisation that Sean O'Hara has duped them with the signature forged by Abershaw, as they are unable to take seriously any move to equality on her part. For Victor, simple-hearted, bovine, intuitive, only able to make a halfway-good painting by chance, Margot is just there to adore him, support him, and make him tea. Any other manifestations are regarded as intrusive. So her intervention, her decision to write to Sean, seems to both of them as inappropriate as if she were wearing her nightgown in public; the internal plane brutally invading the external plane, an 'advanced sort of nonsense' rather like surrealism 'for which Victor felt no sympathy' (*RL* p. 288). Victor can only cope with Margot as reassuring internality; she is forced by circumstance, by the forged signature, in fact, to assert herself in terms of her love for him. As she argues with Percy, it is obviously hard for her to abandon her usual role and speak so plainly and decisively 'and to come out', as Lewis puts it, 'as the opposite number to this masterful male' (*RL* p. 293). But for all Margot's plain-speaking, Victor is unmoved, taking it as a gamble or a dare, 'for nothing' (*RL* p. 296), and denying the riskiness of the operation, he goes ahead with it.

Margot's unrestrained laughter at the 'false bottom on wheels' (*RL* p. 331) would be less convincing if it were not for the conversation between Mateu and Percy in that penultimate sequence. Through the argument they have in the wake of Margot's decision to take the train across the frontier in an attempt to stop Victor, Mateu just about succeeds in persuading Percy that Margot really loves Victor, 'with every cell of her little shrimp of a flat-chested anatomy' (*RL* p. 305). At the same time, it gradually dawns on Percy that Victor has been calculatedly set up, made expendable in pursuit of profit, and that he is unwittingly complicit in the whole affair. Conscience trumping class struggle at this point – Mateu accuses him of being 'an Englishman, and at bottom an individualist' (*RL* p. 305) – he hurries off in Margot's footsteps, to warn Victor (though he is arrested before he is able to do this). All through these chapters in the 'Honey-Angel' section there has been occasional play on the idea of nothingness, on any conviction being better than none, on artists having no place in the world, on Victor not existing, being a nobody; so Percy's recognition that there is actually something where in each case he had seen nothing shifts our emotional perspective. Just before the culminating event of the encounter with the Civil Guards, Margot persuades herself that Victor is not a nobody because he is a symbol, and therefore stands for something. Unfortunately, by this point he is a hunted symbol of something he is not, an arms smuggler. In the end, faced with the negation of his symbolic existence, she perceives the nothingness the whole plot has been built round, sees the car 'all full of nothing at all, except packing-paper and bricks!' (*RL* p. 331). Her laughter, when it comes, swallows up her earlier tears, her soundless weeping, her sense of acting out of character, possessed by 'some evil spirit of that foreign place' (*RL* p. 327), and dispels her fear of '*scale*' (*RL* p. 328).

Scale is a curiously significant presence in the novel. This is surprising in some ways, as the melodramatic sublime pits the (small) individual against the (large) forces of politics, chance, and human malevolence; but Lewis uses the idea of scale throughout the book as part of his battery of satiric effects.[10] One instance is the parodic use he makes of Cecil Day Lewis's very mockable sonnet, 'The Road These Times Must Take' ('Yes, why do we all, seeing a communist, feel small?').[11] In Gillian Phipps's dealings with Percy Hardcaster, for instance, his making her feel small is the spur to her anger at his propaganda lies, which in turn reduces him in her eyes. 'She gazed at him in amazement. He was turning into something else definitely – beneath her eyes. Into a stupid fat little man' (*RL* p. 191). Scale has already been mentioned in relation to Agnes Irons and her larger-than-life bonhomie. Percy tries to explain to Tristram Phipps that what seemed to him (and probably to us as readers) extreme violence when he was attacked by Jack Cruze was 'perfectly normal' (*RL* p. 248). 'Tristy blinked . . . He had not changed enough. This was after all a frontfighter he had in front of him, and he "felt small", in the words of the poet' (*RL* 249). Then there is the dwarf in the Plaza Cabrinetty at Puigmoro, that 'uncanny parasite upon the normal world' (*RL* p. 267) with his ear-splitting mimicry of an abandoned child (which makes Margot's eyes water, like tears, and later makes her cry in earnest), and Margot's distressed muttering that he is frightening her by making too much noise. The towering Pyrenean landscape, by contrast, seemed like 'unfriendly giants' to her (*RL* p. 270), malign and occult presences that remind her of the dwarf, terrible mountains that seemed alive and breathing. 'Their mere size made them feel *alive*. Was that possible, that *scale* should take with it *life*?' (*RL* p. 328).

Scale also figures as a measure of authenticity, so ties the question of false bottoms, forgery, and ideology into the intellectual narrative, along with violence and tears. The intellectual work done by the formulations of Lewis's prose has been well analysed by Jameson, who argues that Lewis 'tirelessly produc[es] amalgams of words whose function is no longer to re-produce the real, but rather, as it were, to testify to our powerlessness to do so and to the inescapable contamination of the collective mind and of language itself.' He goes on to suggest that '*to articulate such a motivation and such an intent would be to reveal the whole epistemological dimension of Lewis' work*'.[12] It is beyond the scope of this essay to do that, but before we take Percy Hardcaster's final tear as any kind of guarantee of tragedy or authenticity, we might think of all the tears that have preceded it. In that final paragraph, Percy hears in his imagination 'a strained and hollow voice, part of a sham-culture outfit, but tender and halting', reproaching and denouncing him for causing not her death but the death of Victor ('the young man, Absalom'), the man 'whose life he had had in his keeping and who had somehow, unaccountably, been lost, out of the world and out of Time!' (*RL* p. 336). At this he is hard put to retain his 'INJURED PARTY' mask (which is also a Communist Party mask 'for militant agents in distress' (*RL* p. 336) and thus another false front). But the imploring voice he hears conjures up a precipice. In his mind's eye, a sublime image of sudden fathomless death, and 'a sudden tear' of self-pity rolled 'down the front of the mask' (*RL* p. 336). It is a tear that reveals a sentimental side to the hitherto decidedly unsentimental Hardcaster, and shows him to be human as well as part of the Comintern machine. But its function is not emotional; it is part of the critique of sentimentality that runs throughout the novel, from the moment when Don Alvaro tells Josefa that 'Tears are nothing!' (*RL* p. 25). Tyrus Miller has described polemical moments (especially in relation to Woolfian lyricism) when 'Lewis's prose becomes a curious mélange of mimicry and violent rejection', and the use of tears in this novel is a small example of this process at work.[13] They are very consciously, indeed strategically, placed, demonstrating various degrees of bogus and real powerlessness or sorrow, but they have less power to communicate sorrow and despair than laughter does. This tear, like many other small events in Wyndham Lewis's fiction, far from communicating tragic sentiment, is very much an intellectual thing.

Notes

1. William Blake, 'The Grey Monk' (stanza 8), a poem from the Pickering Manuscript (Pickering Ms, 7). See http://www.themorgan.org/collection/William-Blakes-World/169 (accessed 24 November 2014).
2. For a more developed argument about this aspect of the text, see my 'Beneath the Surface: Apes, Bodies and Readers', in Paul Edwards (ed.), *Volcanic Heaven. Essays on Wyndham Lewis's Painting & Writing* (Santa Rosa: Black Sparrow, 1996), pp. 123–34.
3. Wyndham Lewis, 'Notes on the Way', *Time and Tide*, 16.9, 2 March 1935, pp. 304–6.
4. The most intelligent and informed discussion of Lewis's criterion of 'reality' in *The Revenge for Love* is Paul Edwards, 'False Bottoms: Wyndham Lewis's *The Revenge for Love* and the Incredible Real', in John Attridge and Rod Rosenquest (eds), *Incredible Modernism: Literature, Trust and Deception* (Farnham: Ashgate, 2013), pp. 99–114.
5. 'Outlook in Spain. Roots of the Revolt', *The Times*, 30 December 1933, p. 9.
6. Cecil F. Melville, *The Truth About the New Party, and Much Else Besides Concerning Sir Oswald Mosley's Political Aims, the 'Nazis' movement of Herr Adolph Hitler, and the Adventures in Political Philosophy of Mr. Wyndham Lewis* (London: Wishart & Co., 1931), p. 45.
7. For a typical illustration of the way the Civil Guard tended to be romanticised in the British press, see 'The Civil Guard of Spain. Men Who Checked the Revolt', *The Times*, 7 January 1931, p. 11.
8. This theatrical and operatic presentation recurs in the final pages, as Margot pieces together the realisation that she and Victor have killed a Civil Guard. 'She admitted, a fragment at a time, the components of the scenery for this new Act . . . [A]ll the facts that went to make the complete event she allowed to pass inside. She even assisted in the setting-up of this sinister backcloth' (*RL* pp. 325–6).
9. Toby Avard Foshay, *Wyndham Lewis and the Avant-Garde: The Politics of the Intellect* (Montreal: McGill Queen's University Press, 1992), p. 119.
10. For a discussion of melodrama and the political sublime in the 1930s, see my 'Wild Geese Over the Mountains: Melodrama and the Sublime in the English Imaginary 1933–9', *Tate Papers*, 13, Spring 2010, n.p. Available at http://www.tate.org.uk/research/publications/tate-papers/issue-13 (accessed 24 November 2014).
11. Cecil Day Lewis, *A Time to Dance* (London: Hogarth Press, 1935), pp. 58–9.
12. Fredric Jameson, 'Wyndham Lewis as Futurist', *The Hudson Review*, 26.2, Summer 1973, pp. 295–329: p. 325.
13. Tyrus Miller, *Late Modernism: Politics, Fiction, and the Arts between the World Wars* (Berkeley: University of California Press, 1999), p. 76.

Chapter 11

Lewis and Technology
Andrzej Gąsiorek

A recent essay on modernism and technology makes no mention of Wyndham Lewis and Filippo Tommaso Marinetti, and no mention of the two movements with which the two men were so closely associated: Vorticism and Italian Futurism. Christopher Green ends his chapter on the subject on an up-beat note, suggesting that:

> If machine Modernism succeeded, it was not because it actually restored collective use-value above the seduction of the image . . . but because it spoke clearly and passionately for a sharply defined cluster of values associated with reason and progress. By doing so in traumatized societies rebuilding after war and revolution, it made the machine something that could satisfy at deep levels, something that offered hope, at least for those who wanted not just the excitement of the unprecedented, but also the seeming safety of control.[1]

This is to offer a utopian-functionalist conception of the machine, which posits a rationalist and progressivist modernism. Technology is presented as a source of beauty and is seen as a viable means of bringing about significant socio-political change. Such an account belongs to the context of post-World War One reconstruction. Green's touchstones are clear: communal use-value, reason, progress, hope, control.

This description of the relationship between modernism and technology is valuable only up to a point. It concentrates to the exclusion of all else on individuals, movements, and trends that viewed the machine age in almost entirely positive terms. Missing from this rosy picture is any suggestion that the machine also was a source of anxiety (even dread) to many early twentieth-century observers. Its implications, moreover, were thought to be wide-ranging but uncertain. As early as 1880, Nietzsche maintained that '[t]he press, the machine, the railway, the telegraph are premises whose thousand-year conclusion no one has yet dared to draw'.[2] Much of D. H. Lawrence's writing is preoccupied with technology's deleterious impact on human life, the sculptor Henri

Gaudier-Brzeska feared that it was overmastering social existence, and Humphrey Jennings, in the posthumously published *Pandaemonium* (1985), collected a massive range of texts that demonstrated conclusively how troubling it was to numerous commentators.

Italian Futurism, in contrast, embraced the coming of the machine age. A radiant vision of technology shines through everything that Marinetti wrote on the subject. At once a showman and a provocateur, Marinetti used the relatively new form of the avant-garde manifesto to declare his unalloyed passion for technology and the gleaming new world it was to inaugurate. 'The Founding and Manifesto of Futurism' (1909) presents the modern city as the site upon which a much needed renewal would take place because its embrace of industry manifested a sublime fusion of the human with the mechanical. Hence Futurism's exaltation of velocity, which led Marinetti to discover 'a new beauty' in the thrilling sensation of speed and to depict the modern individual as a techno-human hybrid.[3] It is by means of technology that Marinetti's ennui-ridden protagonist is energised in his manifesto, for he comes alive when his automobile's engine is switched on and he can race through the city like a bright avatar of the coming age. 'Time and Space died yesterday', Marinetti announced, explaining this necessary death in the following terms: 'We already live in the absolute, because we have created eternal, omnipresent speed.'[4] Futurism, moreover, challenged the idea of the human. Burning with a promethean fire, Marinetti imagined 'an incalculable number of human transformations' and proclaimed 'that wings are asleep in the flesh of man', a belief to which he gave imaginative expression in his novel *Mafarka the Futurist* (1910).[5] For Marinetti, in short, technology was not only altering every facet of modern life but also offering human beings the chance to become supercharged overlords of creation.

Futurism's influence on Vorticism is visible throughout *BLAST*. Futurism's primitivism, for example, informs the rhetoric of Lewis's manifestos and proclamations. The assertion that 'WE ONLY WANT THE WORLD TO LIVE, and to feel it's [sic] crude energy flowing through us' (*B1* p. 7) might have been made by Marinetti, and Lewis's passion for 'vivid and violent ideas' (*B1* p. 7) expresses a distinctly Futurist mood. But as is well known, Lewis also sought to distance Vorticism from Futurism in a number of ways. He argued in *BLAST* that technology and nature (life) had the power to subjugate individuals. Determinism was the nightmare from which Lewis was trying to escape. The world of blind nature, if accepted uncritically, did people's 'thinking and seeing for them' (*B1* p. 130), he maintained, and this passivity needed to be contrasted with 'something very abstruse and splendid, in no way directly dependent on "Life." It is no EQUIVALENT for Life, but ANOTHER Life, as NECESSARY to existence as the former' (*B1* p. 130). This alternative life is that of the creative mind and the autonomous agent. It is a way of being for individuals who seek to understand the social forces to which they are subject and who endeavour to act with as much independence as it is possible to achieve under the circumstances.

In contrast to Futurism, Lewis offered a sober assessment of technology, arguing that because it was transforming the modern world it should be treated with scepticism and subjected to critique. Vorticism 'sought out machine-forms' (*WLA* p. 340) and aimed to create pictures that were 'a sort of *machines* [sic]' (*WLA* p. 340) in order to demonstrate that an art which sought to be 'organic with its Time' (*B1* p. 34) needed to engage with a technologised reality, one that manifested itself 'in the forms of machinery, Factories, new and vaster buildings, bridges and works' (*B1* p. 40). This interest in technology did not disclose a belief in its utopian potential so much as a desire to register its social significance. As Lewis later put it, Vorticism accepted the machine world 'in a stoical embrace, though of course without propagandist fuss'; the movement 'did not identify the artist with the machine' but '*observed* the machine, from the outside'.[6] Ford Madox Ford grasped what was at stake when he noted that the 'ocular and phonetic break between today and the historic ages is incredible' and suggested that 'the business of the young artist of today is to render those glooms, those clamours, those iron boxes, those explosions, those voices from the metal horns of talking-machines and hooters.'[7] In Vorticist terms, this meant that different forms of representation were required, since a transformed physical and mental world demanded an alternative vision and type of art. 'All revolutionary painting to-day', Lewis declared, 'has in common the rigid reflections of steel and stone in the spirit of the artist', and it followed from this perception that the public was being invited 'into a transposed universe as abstract as, though different from, the musicians [sic]' (*WLA* p. 57).

Lewis's emphasis on transposition is instructive. It indicates that the task at hand is not only to engage with the machine world but also to translate it into forms that function not as mimetic representations but as suggestive analogues of it. This is significant because it makes clear that the Vorticist artist is to intervene imaginatively in modernity rather than to register it passively. If technology was to serve human purposes, not direct them, then the artist's transposition of the raw data of the modern age into constructed art objects signalled this order of priorities. Pound stressed the point when he described the Vorticist 'as DIRECTING a certain fluid force against circumstance, as CONCEIVING instead of merely observing and reflecting' (*B1* p. 153). Lewis's ambivalence about technology stems from his recognition that it was altering people's experience of their own subjectivity by creating a world in which, as individuals, they were becoming less and less significant. For Lewis, the subject was being diminished as an autonomous agent, and this meant that 'the old form of egotism is no longer fit for such conditions as now prevail' and 'the isolated human figure of most ancient Art is an anachronism' (*B1* p. 141).[8]

What role did technology play in this process? A consideration of texts like BLAST, *The Caliph's Design* (1919), *The Art of Being Ruled* (1926), *Time and Western Man* (1927), *The Apes of God* (1930), *Snooty Baronet* (1932), and *Men without Art* (1934) suggests that Lewis was disturbed by the power of technology to subordinate the individual to its inner imperatives, enabling mechanisation, in Sigfried Giedion's fine phrase, to take command.[9] This anxiety is vividly articulated in Lewis's war story 'The Crowd Master', a tale in which people are shown to be plugged into networks that manufacture their identities for them. Describing the feverish atmosphere generated by newspapers, Lewis presents the crowd that responds to the declaration of the war as a manipulable organism that is brought into being by the crashing headlines of the papers they are reading. The crowd threatens to overwhelm the detached observer as it 'surge[s] into him from these sheets of inconceivable news. Tons of it a minute gushed out and flooded the streets with excitement. You seemed to swim in it outside' (*B2* p. 99). 'The Crowd Master' suggests that this abandonment of the self to ideology can be read as a desire to accept one's death as a conscious individual: 'A fine dust of extinction', Lewis writes, 'a grain or two for each man, is scattered in any crowd like these black London war-crowds. Their pace is so mournful. Wars begin with this huge indefinite Interment in the cities' (*B2* p. 94).

'The Crowd Master' describes a form of thought control, or hypnosis. It connects this process to technology (the mass produced newspaper) and in doing so suggests that the people who read the newspaper become its products (by being interpellated into a certain kind of subjectivity) just as the artefact itself is a literal product of particular mechanical processes. Lewis made a related point in the second issue of *BLAST* in the short piece 'The European War and Great Communities'. Focusing on the troubling relationship between technology and the armaments industry, he satirically suggested that human reproduction exists solely for the purpose of manufacturing 'little human cartridges', which henceforth should be regarded as nothing more than 'War Material' (*B2* p. 16). His irony communicates his disgust:

Women's function, the manufacturing of children (even more important than cartridges and khaki suits) is only important from this point of view, and they evidently realize this thoroughly. It takes the deft women we employ anything from twelve to sixteen years to fill and polish these little human cartridges, and they of course get fond of them in the process. However, all this is not our fault, and is absolutely necessary. We only begin decaying like goods kept too long, if we are not killed or otherwise disposed of. Is not this a proof of our function? Only latterly, our War Material has become so much more expensive to make, and takes so much longer, that we have to avoid causing a belief in peoples' minds that we are wasting it! (*B2* p. 16)

Predicting sardonically that in future matters 'will be arranged for the best convenience of War', Lewis suggested that technology (in the form of the armaments industry) was remaking human life to such an extent that henceforth it would be driven entirely by the requirements of what Eisenhower, forty years hence, would call the military-industrial complex: 'For the good of War, yes, of endless unabating murder and misery, then, I think the great communities will have to go' (*B2* p. 16). This bleak view expressed Lewis's conviction that human existence was in danger of slowly but inexorably being turned into an industrial process that was in thrall to violence.[10]

The Caliph's Design: Architects! Where is Your Vortex? is an important document for any discussion of Lewis's developing thought about technology. It was in this fairly short, but powerfully argued, pamphlet that he elaborated on the Vorticist position initially laid out in the two issues of *BLAST*. He did so by suggesting that for Vorticism to play a role in the nation's social life it was necessary for it to escape the confines of the artist's atelier and the art market's monopoly of his or her creative efforts. Vorticism, in short, had to emerge from the studio and be released into public life. Lewis thus demanded a complete overhaul of painting, design, architecture, and engineering on the grounds that were this to happen 'a new form-content for our everyday vision' (*CD* p. 34) would be created and would contribute to the transformation of communal life.

What role was technology to play in this optimistic scenario? *The Caliph's Design* did not depart from the position articulated in *BLAST*, since it maintained that technology was a resource to be interpreted and adapted, but not accepted on its own terms. 'If the world *would only build temples to Machinery* in the abstract', Lewis argued, 'then everything would be perfect' (*CD* p. 58). For Lewis, it was not the machine itself but its conceptual significance that mattered, and this significance, in turn, needed to be established through a process of sustained reflection. In keeping with his rejection of Futurism's exalted view of technology, he suggested that machinery was not a good in itself but should be treated as 'a new resource, as though it were a new mineral or oil, to be used and put to different uses than those for which it was originally intended' (*CD* p. 57). Separated from its mundane function as a complex tool, its meaning and purpose had to be 'transformed' by the agency of 'the aesthetic consciousness' (*CD* p. 57). In *BLAST* Lewis had claimed that art was not of direct social utility but imaginatively interpreted and re-envisaged modern life. *The Caliph's Design* goes a step further, suggesting that art – and Vorticist art, specifically – had the capacity to remake the urban environment by taking its point of departure from technology but forcing it to serve consciously chosen human purposes.

Once again, it is important to stress how different this conception of technology is from the Futurist view of it. Noting that each 'living form is a miraculous mechanism', Lewis insisted that Marinetti's unbounded faith in technology was 'at bottom, adulation for the universe of beings, and especially the world of insects' (*CD* p. 77), an observation that can be related to his critique of nature in *BLAST*. This unreflective attitude stranded the human species in 'the indiscriminate, mechanical and unprogressive world' (*CD* p. 77) that needed to be transformed rather than accepted on its own terms. For Lewis, votaries of the machine age like the Futurists were simply too willing to abandon themselves to a technological system that would swiftly render them nugatory. Evelyn Waugh made the point in a finely judged image when he suggested that cars – the Futurists' most adored love objects – had 'become masters of men' and should be seen as anthropomorphic 'creations of metal who exist solely for their own propulsion through space, for whom their drivers, clinging precariously at the steering-wheel, are as important as his stenographer to a stock-broker'.[11] Lewis put it in different terms, but the sentiment was the same:

> Let us substitute ourselves everywhere for the animal world; replace the tiger and the cormorant with some invention of our mind, so that we can control this new Creation. The danger, as it would appear at present, and in our first flight of substitution and remounting, is evidently that we should become overpowered by our creation, and become as mechanical as a tremendous insect world, all our awakened reason entirely disappeared. (*CD* p. 76)

This vision of a society so mechanised that it resembles a vast hive has clear implications for Lewis's theory of satire. *The Caliph's Design* imagines the urban environment being transformed by deliberate acts of individual creativity; in doing so it upholds a specific conception of subjectivity. The pamphlet's emphasis on order, design, and beauty in daily life derives from Lewis's conviction that human beings can resist their mechanisation by technology only if they engage in cultural practices that require autonomous thought and independent creative work. The artist should 'desire equity, mansuetude, in human relations, fight against violence, and work for formal beauty, significance and so forth, in the arrangement and aspect of life' (*CD* p. 25).

Lewis, however, always doubted that the majority of people had the capacity to participate in this kind of work, and *BLAST*'s claim that it wanted to 'make individuals, wherever found' (*B1* p. 8) has to be set against its assertion that the Vorticist required 'THE UNCONSCIOUSNESS OF HUMANITY – their stupidity, animalism and dreams' (*B1* p. 7). In fact, Lewis feared that most people preferred to subordinate themselves either to an external power or to an interiorised fetish because such self-subjection provided them with a sense of security. In his essay 'Inferior Religions', he described figures who latch onto beliefs or habits that then take over their lives. Worked by forces that are hidden from their self-perceptions, they are 'only shadows of energy, not living beings', since their 'mechanism is a logical structure and they are nothing but that' (*CWB* p. 150). For Lewis, such machinic caricatures of human beings are legitimate targets of the satirist's puncturing laughter.

Two texts make this aspect of Lewis's thought especially clear: *The Apes of God* and *Snooty Baronet*. It should be noted, furthermore, that whereas *BLAST* and *The Caliph's Design* intimated that avant-garde art could have a positive effect on public life, these later books offered a pessimistic diagnosis of inter-war culture and society, which is why they are so beholden to the satiric mode. It is no accident that *The Apes of God* begins with a senescent Victorian world and concludes with the impasse of the General Strike, since both textual moments suggest that cultural stasis is the order of the day. A would-be revolutionary considers that the Folletts' culture is a 'carcass' that 'would take a hundred years to melt' (*AG* p. 43), but his 'marxist-fierceness [sic]' (*AG* p. 43) is countered by the claim that 'bolshevism [sic]' will not emancipate the populace but will drive them further into servitude because it will mechanise them (*AG* pp. 284–6). 'The General Strike' section of the novel, in turn, functions as a coda that both parodies the Strike and implies that no revolution could be successful in a land peopled by the imbeciles Lewis has traduced for over 600 pages. *The Apes* thus offers a bleak response to *BLAST*'s optimism, as expressed in its suggestion that 'a movement towards art and imagination could burst up here, from this lump of compressed life, with more force than anywhere else' (*B1* p. 32).

The Apes of God targets individuals and groups who have cultural power but are unable to grasp, let alone resist, what Lewis saw as the enucleation of public life in the post-war period. The novel depicts a topsy-turvy world in which those who should be opposing cultural decline are slaves to the rhythm of contemporary social life. Their servitude takes two major forms: they are either the benighted victims of a machine age that turns them into its robotic avatars or the foolish purveyors of ideologies to which they are in thrall. *The Apes of God* is thus filled with characters who are not so much affectless ciphers as naive vessels filled to bursting with the wrong kind of energy – in short, more up-to-date versions of the electrified war crowds in 'The Crowd Master'.

After the scarcely animate Fredigonde completes her morning toilet, a thirty-year old 'firework – marked "boyish high spirits"' (*AG* p. 27) explodes into her room. This outsize juvenile, all 'jolly sprawling fragments' (*AG* p. 27), can offer no serious alternative to Fredigonde's fusty Victoriana. He is simply an overcharged machine whose legs keep 'turning to the massed gramophoning of his slowly revolving eardrums, like the disks of records' (*AG* p. 33). Or he is a strange organo-mechanic hybrid that has not escaped infancy: 'a jerky and unwilling toy dragged forward by a ghostly umbilical cord' (*AG* p. 38). This depiction of a sputtering automaton is accompanied by its obverse in *The Apes of God*: the attribution of life to machines that have more life than the people around them:

> That van again! Like a bad penny, cracking off as it went, the thing had turned up. It had rushed past him with its bomb. SHELL IS SO DIFFERENT! He grinned after it, it was a thing that was a music-hall turn, the clown-van. He and the clown-van played peep-bo in Bloomsbury, each had a distinct rôle who could doubt. The thing had recognized him immediately: it went petarding into the next street, tail up. (*AG* p. 80)

In contrast to the fizzing van, the human character in this scene is a puppet who welcomes his nullification. Faced with the possibility that he has been 'manufactured like the – Hoffman doll', he 'blushe[s] with pleasure' at the thought that he is another's 'plaything' (*AG* p. 205).

Society in *The Apes of God* is a dead zone characterised by cultural standardisation, the etiolation of purposive subjectivity, and the destruction of the public sphere. Above all, it is a world from which the utopian promise of pre-war avant-gardism has been expunged. *The Apes of God* depicts a culture mired in mediocrity and riddled with *ressentiment*. But the novel's criticisms are aimed also at post-war politics. Its defining note is pessimism; there is no optimism of the will here. 'For my part', Lewis wrote in *Men without Art*, 'I am unable to imagine any human system of law and government that would not be bad' (*MWA* p. 213). On the one hand, revolutionary politics hover in the background in *The Apes of God*, but on the other hand they pervade it. Like the aged matriarch with which the text begins, they are half in life and half out of it, existing in an unrealisable dream-world.

The theme is sounded early on when Fredigonde slips into a reverie – a *'prophetic photo-play'* (*AG* p. 19) – that dramatises her fear of revolution. The scene is parodic. A bunch of boy scouts led by a *'Red Scout-Master'* (*AG* p. 19) steal her lace-caps and try them on for size while she watches helplessly. This *'robot-youth'*, with their *'Communist skull-caps of orphanage-cut'*, are *'little jumping bolsheviks'* (*AG* p. 19). The reader is subjected to Fredigonde's *'private photo-play'*, and as she wakes from her nightmare she *'passes into a sequence of solider facts'* (*AG* p. 21). Lewis depicts Fredigonde's muddled inner life as a cinema show; her mind is a screen upon which moving images flicker. Thus when she closes her eyes and withdraws into her deepest self she enters the realm of filmic make-believe:

> *The day and night cinema that exists immediately within was encouraged to operate. The brain on its own initiative from its projector was flashing lace-caps upon the screen. All her collection was idly called forth, in startling close-ups, for her inspection.* (*AG* p. 23)

Lewis viewed cinema as a complex technology with multiple effects, but he was critical of what he saw as Hollywood's dumbed down view of human life, which he described as 'the saccharine travesty of art' (*BB* p. 259). Well aware that cinema could be used as a propaganda tool that shaped viewers' minds, he sometimes blamed people for their apparent willingness to be duped, while at other moments he viewed them as victims of forces that it was hard for them to resist.[12] *The Apes of God* portrays cinema as a key factor in the cultural levelling down it deprecates, suggesting that analysis of post-war society must begin with film because it was preparing the way for acceptance of a mass culture that sought to sedate the public rather than to stimulate it to think. People have become 'accustomed to watching animated photographs of plays written for children', the novel's impresario suggests, before he goes on to argue that they have been 'broken in by the Film to unrelieved stupidity' (*AG* p. 403) as a result. On this view, the relatively new technology of cinema (like the newspapers in 'The Crowd Master'), contributes to the creation of a culture in which citizens can be controlled more easily because they are encouraged to adopt infantile ways of thinking.

Lewis argued in *Men without Art* that the purpose of satire was to mock human beings when they reduce themselves to 'machines, governed by routine' (*MWA* p. 93). By giving up on their capacity for independent reflection such figures accept their mechanisation and turn themselves into the playthings of external forces. Above all, they become the dupes of powerful ideologies, which they no longer have the ability to decode or resist. For Lewis, the thinking subject was the only place from which a philosophical, political, or artistic critique of modernity could emerge. His despair at a cultural situation in which the capacity for sustained and independent thought appeared to be being eroded led him on the one hand to lambast those who accepted their mental subjugation and on the other hand to urge them to fight against it. He sometimes maintained that people desire to live according to fixed norms (ideally established for them from elsewhere) because the effort required to be self-directed individuals is beyond them:

> People ask nothing better than to be *types* – occupational types, social types, functional types of any sort. If you force them not to be, they are miserable . . . For in the mass people wish to be *automata* . . . they wish to be obedient, hard-working machines, as near dead as possible. (*ABR* p. 151)

But this pessimistic view was contradicted by Lewis's yearning to educate people about their condition and to encourage them to stand up to their rulers. The modern citizen, he declared,

> has this alternative. Either he must be prepared to sink to the level of chronic tutelage and slavery, dependent for all he is to live by upon a world of ideas, and its manipulators, about which he knows nothing: or he must get hold as best he can of the abstract principles involved in the very 'intellectual' machinery set up to control and change him. (*TWM* p. xi)

The recently developed theory of behaviourism was a particular Lewisian *bête noire*, precisely because it denied consciousness, treating human beings as little more than Pavlovian dogs. Behaviourism, Lewis argued, represented 'the extreme gospel of the Machine Age' (*P* p. 161) and was to be vilified 'not because it *leads*, but because it *follows* the little average "goose-stepping, superstitious, sentimental" unit of the mass-democracy, and makes a mechanical imitation of this robot in the philosophic field' (*P* p. 162). In short, according to behaviourist logic the individual is not a deliberative agent but a programmable unit. In John Broadus Watson's chilling words: 'The time seems to have come when psychology must discard all reference to consciousness.'[13] And Lewis, we must remember, was aware that behaviourism originally was developed in a military context (*TWM* p. 299). A clear intellectual line runs from his critique of the behaviourist position in *Time and Western Man* and *Snooty Baronet* back to his satire on the armaments industry in the 'War Number' of *BLAST*.

A scene in *Snooty Baronet* is pertinent here. The novel's narrator finds himself among a crowd of onlookers who are all struck by the life-like nature of a hatter's doll in a shop window. He goes for a closer look and is disturbed by what he sees:

> There was something abstruse and unfathomable in this automaton. Beside me a new arrival smiled back at the bowing Hatter's doll. I turned towards him in alarm. Was not perhaps this fellow who had come up beside me a puppet too? I could not swear that he was not! I turned my eyes away from him, back to the smiling phantom in the window, with intense uneasiness. For I thought to myself as I caught sight of him in the glass, smiling away in response to our mechanical friend, *certainly he is a puppet too!* Of course he was, but dogging that was the brother-thought, *but equally so am I!*[14]

This moment of recognition takes us into the realm of the uncanny. Confronted by the fact that the puppet before him cannot be distinguished from a human being, the troubled observer is led to question his ontological status. Could it be that, unbeknown to himself, he may be a mechanical toy and not a person? For Lewis, this ontological confusion lies at the heart of behaviourist doctrine because it treats individuals as though they were mechanical entities when in fact they are (or have the capacity to be) ratiocinative beings. It follows from this reduction of the human to the mechanical that behaviourism provides the perfect intellectual rationale for ideologies that seek to mould people to their own purposes, for if they are simply programmable machines then they can be directed and controlled. As 'One-Way Song' (1933) put it: 'The philosophy of a full-blown automaton / Is cooked up for you: and then one by one / All pleasant things removed from out your reach / They show you hunger. Nonentity they teach' (*CPP* p. 85).[15]

Behaviourism's disastrous consequences for any notion of independent agency hardly require spelling out. Lewis's assault on this particular technology of the self runs in tandem with his critique of vitalist philosophies that undermined the idea of purposive subjectivity by privileging intuition and voluntarism over intellection and deliberation. Like Lukács (with whom he shares a good deal of intellectual ground, even if their politics are very different), he was hostile to psychologically inclined versions of modernism, especially those associated with writers like Joyce, Stein, and Woolf, on the grounds that the inward turn resulted in artistic formlessness, dissolved the subject, and eroded any shared understanding of the external world.[16] For both Lewis and Lukács, subjectivity in such modernist writing becomes associated with random thought processes (the 'stream of consciousness') that gradually destroy the public sense of a reality held in common. Lewis's particular target here was Bergsonian philosophy, which, he argued, demanded 'a rendering back to LIFE, magiscular abstraction of a feverish chaos, all that the mind had taken from her to build into forms and concepts'

(*ABR* pp. 336–7). His derisive view of this retrogression features prominently in 'One-Way Song', which depicts Bergson's followers as 'Poor ostriches of Temporality! – / Occulted backwards', a process that leaves them 'neck-deep in Nothing' (*CPP* p. 72). For Lewis, Bergsonism needed to be seen as the philosophical counterpart of Futurist technophilia and Lawrentian naturalism, for these romantic tendencies denied humanity its hard-won (and necessary) gains of vision and intellection. *Time and Western Man* was explicit about this issue:

> My standpoint is that we are creatures of a certain kind, with no indication that a radical change is imminent; and that the most pretentious of our present prophets is unable to do more than promise 'an eternity of intoxication' to those who follow him into less physical, more 'cosmic,' regions; proposals made with at least equal eloquence by the contemporaries of Plato. (*TWM* p. 110)

In the 1910s Lewis objected to Futurism's modernolatry and its worship of the machine, which he later (rightly) connected with far-right politics: 'Marinetti was the first prophet of the Machine: he was the theorist, Mussolini the politician, and man-of-action, of the Fascist ideal' (*CHC* p. 192). In the 1930s Lewis was equally unimpressed by the Marxist adulation of technology, arguing that this new form of technophilia, like that of its Futurist predecessor, amounted to nothing more than a crude valorisation of power. The obsession with force, in turn, implied a diminished regard for the fragile and imperfect individual. Thus we return again to Lewis's concern with the value and dignity of human beings. 'The machine', he argued, 'can do all the donkey-work of the world with a djinn-like efficiency', but 'its productions are not ... however elaborate, art' (*CHC* p. 260). They are not art because despite their technical slickness they lack the very qualities that are required for serious human creativity: thought, intention, discipline, effort, and above all the risk of failure and the acceptance of (inevitable) imperfection.

Throughout his life, and even during his most optimistic phase, Lewis consistently argued that technology had to be adapted to conscious human purposes and should be seen neither as inherently evil nor as an unqualified good. But throughout his life he abjured all those who sought to subordinate human beings to technology and warned against the dangers of seeing them as inferior to it. Unlike technology – however mechanically perfect its products might be – people had the invaluable capacity to be self-directed, conscious agents even if the price they paid for this capacity was their imperfection and therefore their proneness to the most horrendous errors. Indeed, the conjunction of the human and the flawed lay at the heart of Lewis's understanding of significant creativity and, by implication, of meaningful life:

> The art impulse reposes upon a conviction that the state of limitation of the human being is more desirable than the state of the automaton; or a feeling of the gain and significance residing in this human fallibility for us. To feel that our consciousness is bound up with this non-mechanical phenomen [sic] of life; that, although helpless in face of the material world, we are in some way superior to and independent of it; and that our mechanical imperfection is the symbol of that. (*WLA* p. 204)

Notes

1. Christopher Green, 'The Machine', in Christopher Wilk (ed.), *Modernism 1914–1939: Designing a New World* (London: V & A Publications, 2006), pp. 71–111: p. 89.
2. Friedrich Nietzsche, *Human, All Too Human*, trans. R. J. Hollingdale (Cambridge: Cambridge University Press, 1996), p. 378.
3. F. T. Marinetti, 'The Founding and Manifesto of Futurism', in Umbro Apollonio (ed.), *Futurist Manifestos* [1909] (London: Thames and Hudson, 1973), pp. 19–24: p. 21.
4. Ibid., p. 22.
5. F. T. Marinetti, *Selected Writings*, ed. R. W. Flint and trans. R. W. Flint and Arthur A. Coppotelli (London: Secker & Warburg, 1972), p. 91.
6. Wyndham Lewis, *Wyndham Lewis the Artist: From 'Blast' to Burlington House* (London: Laidlaw & Laidlaw, 1939), p. 79.
7. Ford Madox Ford, *Critical Essays*, ed. Max Saunders and Richard Stang (Manchester: Carcanet, 2002), pp. 183–4.
8. For more on this point, see Alan Munton, 'Abstraction, Archaism and the Future: T. E. Hulme, Jacob Epstein and Wyndham Lewis', in Edward P. Comentale and Andrzej Gąsiorek (eds), *T. E. Hulme and the Question of Modernism* (Aldershot: Ashgate, 2006), pp. 73–92.
9. Sigfried Giedion, *Mechanisation Takes Command: A Contribution to Anonymous History* (Oxford: Oxford University Press, 1948).
10. For some acerbic remarks about this aspect of the First World War, see *BB* pp. 259–60.
11. Evelyn Waugh, *Vile Bodies* (1930), ed. Richard Jacobs (Harmondsworth: Penguin, 2000), p. 136. For a comparable presentation of the automobile, see *RL* Part VII, Chapters VI and VII.
12. For these tensions in Lewis's thought, see especially *ABR* pp. 105–7 and 125–9, and *MWA* p. 201.
13. Quoted in Jon Agar, *Science in the Twentieth Century and Beyond* (Cambridge: Polity, 2012), p. 77. The 'theoretical goal' of psychology, Watson claimed, 'is the prediction and control of behavior. Introspection forms no essential part of its methods ... The behaviorist, in his efforts to get a unitary scheme of animal response, recognizes no dividing line between man and brute' (p. 77).

14. Wyndham Lewis, *Snooty Baronet* (1932), ed. Bernard Lafourcade (Santa Barbara: Black Sparrow Press, 1984), pp. 135–6.
15. For more on this point, see *TWM* pp. 298–9.
16. Lukács made similar arguments in *The Meaning of Contemporary Realism*, trans. John and Necke Mander (London: Merlin Press, 1972) and *The Destruction of Reason*, trans. Peter Palmer (London: Merlin, 1980).

Chapter 12

Lewis and Modernism

Michael Nath

I

What I would insist upon is that at the bottom of the chemistry of my sense of humour is some philosopher's stone. A primitive unity is there, to which, with my laughter, I am appealing. Freud explains everything by *sex*: I explain everything by *laughter*. (*CWB* p. 18)

As it is sometimes understood, modernism is the art of the lost horizon and groundless present, of a world disenchanted by rationalism; knowing that all authority concerning the meaning of things is question-able, it nevertheless aspires to it.[1] The doctrine of Lewis's 'showman' exemplifies such aspiration. I will try to argue here that Lewis's concep-tion of laughter presents the most persuasive claim to authority of his *oeuvre*; but I will also indicate some areas in which doctrinal habits have obscured that *oeuvre*'s depth.

A stimulus is specified by the showman: 'my eye sparkles at once if I catch sight of some stylistic anomaly that will provide me with a new pattern for my grotesque realism' (*CWB* p. 18). The reference to 'anomaly' and 'pattern' reveals something about Lewis's own style, which will occupy us as his primary means of 'explaining'. 'Pattern' hints also at the complex relationship between painting and writing in Lewis, recurring in the account of the 'crisis' in his development caused by Dostoyevsky: 'since I was not interested in problems of good and evil, I did not read these books so much as sinister homilies as monstrous character patterns, often of miraculous insight' (*RA* p. 158). This will accord with the experience of many readers of Lewis, in whose creative scheme character often signifies by means of visual presentation. The association of pattern with the miraculous hints at the figuration of reli-gious painting ('monstrous' has the obsolete sense of 'miraculous', so the point is made with some force).[2]

These remarks raise the question of the genealogy of Lewis's modernism, which Paul Edwards's influential book has formulated as 'a continuation of Romanticism by other means' (*EWL* p. 4), along two vectors: one 'theologico-metaphysical', the other directed towards a 'zestful' interpretation of modernity (*EWL* p. 7). The first of these terms may have the effect of obscuring the evidence of Lewis's apprenticeship to the Renaissance.

Thus we might infer a pre-Russian source of both visual figuration and literary characterisation in Lewis from work by Philip Head. Head reminds us of Michael Baxandall's conception of fifteenth-century Italy as practised (in both art and commerce) 'in reducing the most diverse sort of information to a form of geometric proportion', issuing in a culture 'apt to interpret various kinds of visual interest in moral and spiritual terms'.[3] T. S. Eliot's opinion that Lewis was 'the greatest prose master of style of [his] generation', gains interest when contextualised within, and limited by, Eliot's special estimation of seventeenth-century sensibility, and of Shakespearean prose (see *EWL* p. 1).[4] That the only full-length monograph dedicated by a modernist to Shakespeare reveals something of Lewis's own creative patterns – and that he began his literary career with imitation of Shakespeare's sonnets (produced with uncanny facility) (*RA* pp. 123–4) – are facts that so far have seemed too large for specialist criticism.[5]

To indicate such a background, however, leaves much to account for in Lewis's development in his own time. This may be broadly associated with the phenomenological task of 'relearning to look at the world'. In the words of Maurice Merleau-Ponty:

> If phenomenology was a movement before becoming a doctrine or a philo-sophical system, this was attributable neither to accident, nor to fraudulent intent. It is as painstaking as the works of Balzac, Proust, Valéry, or Cézanne – by reason of the same kind of attentiveness and wonder, the same demand for awareness, the same will to seize the meaning of the world or of history as that meaning comes into being. In this way it merges into the general effort of modern thought.[6]

Lewis might join Merleau-Ponty's list of artists, since he illuminates the latter's discussion of an arduous undertaking, namely, the recovering of perception and direct experience from both empiricism and rational-ism: 'Nothing is more difficult than to know precisely *what we see*.'[7] Merleau-Ponty's project requires the re-insertion of the individual and his/her immediate situation into the act of perception; Lewis's fiction represents instances of this.

We may also discern in Lewis's fiction at least a provision of those 'preparatory studies' which Edmund Husserl had sought 'in vain in world literature', in his elaboration of the theme of the 'life-world' (permanently primitive, intuitive and practical, and opposed to the world as represented by scientific rationalism).[8] Husserl's goal was to consider the life-world as given to us 'at first in straightforward experience', so that we could 'comprehend precisely this style, precisely this whole merely subjective and apparently incomprehensible "Heraclitean flux"'.[9] The idea that Lewis was an enemy of 'flux' has attained the status of dogma.[10] It needs to be modified by consideration of a statement such as the following, with its pointed transition from subjunctive to indicative: 'If the material world were not empirical and matter simply for science, but were organized as in the imagination, we should live as though we were dreaming. Art's business is to show how, then, life would be' (*B2* p. 45; see also *B1* p. 138). To dream is regularly to confront anomaly.

II

Lewis had in fact been publishing and revising the stories collected in *The Wild Body* (1927) since about 1909. The span suggests something about Lewis's creative practice (notably, *Tarr* also exists in two distinct editions, of 1918 and 1928). Indeed he later declared: 'What I started to do in Brittany, I have been developing ever since' (*RA* p. 121). Lewis's practice might be considered in the light of some remarks of Paul Valéry, where it is suggested that by means of revision '*literature enters the domain of ethics*'. It does so through '*resistance to the facile*', and by converting the reader to the value of difficulty.[11]

The stories deal with encounters between the narrating showman, Ker-Orr and Breton peasants. María Hernáez has indicated their difference from much modernist fiction in the short-story form, in which minor-key effects of tact, arrested significance, empathy, mood, and 'muffled tragedy', have defined the genre. Against the objection that Lewis's short fiction effects a breach with decorum (being stylistically abundant and humorous), Hernáez argues that the canonised short story has been critically invested with a false therapeutic function.[12] Her suggestion that Lewis's stories work according to a model of 'incongruence held in suspension' points to their presentations of the world as on the verge of being comprehensible, provided that certain conventions be set aside. In another formulation of Merleau-Ponty, they study the '*advent of being to consciousness, instead of presuming its possibility as given in advance*'.[13]

Their reader is apt to be reminded of how much is ready to hand stylistically in the fiction of Lewis's contemporaries. We may take as example James Joyce's 'An Encounter' (1914). Here, the narrator's observation of an old man crossing a field is marked by a sullen facility or decorum; the story depends on morally provocative content (the old man's speech) as confirmation of its modernity.[14] By contrast, Lewis's showman tends to marvel at a character's corporeality:

> On reaching the door into which he had sunk, plump and slick as into a stage trap, there he was inside – this greasebred old mammifer – his tufted vertex charging about the plank ceiling – generally ricochetting like a dripping sturgeon in a boat's bottom – arms warm brown, ju-jitsu of his guts, tan canvas shoes and trousers rippling in ribbed planes as he darted about – with a filthy snicker for the scuttling female, and a stark cock of the eye for an unknown figure miles to his right: he filled this short tunnel with clever parabolas and vortices, little neat stutterings of triumph, goggle-eyed hypnotisms, in retrospect, for his hearers. (*CWB* p. 79)

From such a cinematic impasto of anomaly, it is difficult to achieve a synthesis. The presence of another body casts a spell upon perception itself. Such a style combines the archaic principle of 'pneumatic physiology' with a form of organic Futurism, projecting character as 'magic' in its very movements.[15]

Something similar to the structure of the showman's experience was to be suggested by Merleau-Ponty's account of bodily subjectivity:

> No sooner has my gaze fallen upon a living body in process of acting than the objects surrounding it immediately take on a fresh layer of significance: they are no longer simply what I myself could make of them, they are what this other pattern of behaviour is about to make of them. Round about the perceived body a vortex forms, towards which my world is drawn and, so to speak, sucked in: to this extent, it is no longer merely mine, and no longer merely present, it is present to X, to that other manifestation of behaviour which begins to take shape in it. Already the other body has ceased to be a mere fragment of the world, and become the theatre of a certain process of elaboration, and, as it were, a certain 'view' of the world ... [N]ow, it is precisely my body which perceives the body of another, and discovers in that other body a miraculous prolongation of my own intentions.[16]

The reflexive mystery of the other is represented by both Lewis and Merleau-Ponty in terms of 'vortex' and 'theatre'. The showman pats and handles the 'brown-coated ducts and muscles' (*CWB* p. 80) of Bestre, as if a spectator were unable to resist stroking an actor, so as to acknowledge *himself* in the role played on stage. An ethical dimension of this is that because detachment gets absorbed into identification, the other cannot be completely represented, known, or mastered as body-subject.[17]

The opening of this dimension depends on a dissolution of the subject–object understanding of experience that has deep roots in

Western culture, and of which Lewis's 'dualist' perspective is habitually supposed to form a strong instance.[18] The dissolution occurs not
just between people, but with respect to person and space. Thus, when
Ker-Orr first sees Bestre he feels that the latter's 'odiously grinning
face' is peering in at his window. The opposite is the case: 'in fact, it
was I myself who was guilty of peering into [Bestre's] window' (*CWB*
p. 77). Subject and object, inside and out, the illusion of being housed,
are converted to flux. Such dreamlike confrontation undergoes extreme
development in 'The Death of the Ankou', when the narrator's reverie,
induced by reading, is penetrated by a figure confused with the mythic
subject of his book (*CWB* pp. 109–10). The following repetition is peculiarly uncanny: 'Low houses faced the small vasey [muddy] port. It was
there I saw Bestre. / This is how I became aware of Bestre' (*CWB* p. 77).

No modern novel attaches more significance to laughter than *Tarr*.
The challenge that Tarr sets himself, 'to swear off humour for a year'
(*T2* p. 30), has something of the fantastic quality of a folk-tale. To effect
a split with his fiancée, Bertha Lunken, Tarr announces a doctrine of
humour: humour is the national trait of the English and paralyses the
'sense for Reality' (*T2* p. 30), causing us to live as if in a dream. Reality
should be the artist's priority, not dreaming – or romantic involvement.
Tarr's decision to forego humour and to practise 'indifference' may
remind us of Rupert Birkin in D. H. Lawrence's *Women in Love* (1920).
In both characters, relationships, and their difficulties, occasion insistent
theorising whose tone may verge on the preposterous.[19] Part of the fascination of these novels is that the life-world is not obedient to doctrinal
men. Thus, when he visits Bertha to break off their engagement:

> Tarr examined the room as you do a doctor's waiting room.
>   It was really quite necessary for him to learn to turn his back upon this
> convenience, things had gone too far, he had ceased even, he realized, to see
> it objectively. To turn the back, that appeared at first sight a very easy matter:
> that is why so far he had not succeeded in doing so . . . But would this little
> room ever appear worth turning his back on? It was really more serious than
> it looked: he must not underestimate it. It was the purest distillation of the
> commonplace: he had become bewitched by its strangeness. It was the far-
> thest flight of the humdrum unreal: Bertha was like a fairy visited by him, and
> to whom he 'became engaged' in another world, not the real one. So much
> was it the real ordinary world that for him with his out-of-the-way experi-
> ence it was a phantasmagoria. Then what he had described as his disease of
> sport was perpetually fed: sex even, with him, according to his analysis, being
> a sort of ghost, was at home in this gross and bouffonic illusion. Something
> had filled up a blank and become saturated with the blankness.
>   But Bertha, though unreal, was undeniably a good kind fairy and her feel-
> ings must be taken into consideration. (*T2* pp. 42–3)

The elastic, and curiously tenacious, use of terms relating to the ordinary and the phantasmagoric appears here because Tarr is testing Lewis's intuition (of which I shall have more to say below) that perception itself may be intrinsically uncanny. Since it has been looked at, Bertha's room looks back, casting a spell that undoes the control of the character who arrived with a theory, thinking to control the situation. If you look at something a lot, it becomes familiar; if you look at it still more, it may become strange. In the artist's experience, this commonplace may condense. To complete the picture, Bertha appears as a fairy. In a variation on the usual order of magic, it is the room and its objects that turn Bertha into a fairy, not she who casts the spell. Beginning with space, everything becomes subjective. The process is inseparable from laughter, because Tarr has described it as a form of dreaming (the actions coalesce in the phrase, 'bouffonic illusion'). The attempt to break the dream by swearing off humour issues only in more laughter:

> As the earliest Science wondered what was at the core of the world, basing its speculations on what deepest things occasionally emerge, with violence, at its holes, so Bertha often would conjecture what might be at the heart of Tarr. Laughter was the most apparently central substance which, to her knowledge, had uncontrollably appeared. (*T2* p. 56)

We are not far from music hall and 'The Laughing Policeman' (1922) here. To which it could be added that Bertha's conjecture is of a kind with the words of the showman, which introduce this essay. 'Primitive', 'central', associable with ideas of pre-rational science/alchemy, and insusceptible to repression or sublimation, laughter has to Lewis an importance analogous to that understanding of the Dionysian which Nietzsche's *The Gay Science* (1887) develops into a primary means of determining value.[20] We may also note an anticipation of Mikhail Bakhtin's theory of laughter and 'carnival'. The showman's reference to his 'grotesque realism', which was the phrase used by Bakhtin of the body's central place in folk laughter, suggests that Lewis's conception of laughter aspires to the universality that, according to Bakhtin, disappears with the Renaissance.[21] Hence the declaration: '*everyone* should be laughed at or else *no one* should be laughed at. It seems that ultimately that is the alternative' (*MWA* p. 89).

Tarr is indeed laughed at. Beneath the broad joke of an anti-humourist who cannot stop laughing, we may discern in Tarr's progress a reflection of Lewis's own reputation. Certain hidden values come to light, as the novel questions the authority of its noisiest ideas. The relationship between Tarr and Anastasya Vasek (a notable representation of a 'free spirit') is of great interest in this respect. Lewis criticism has traditionally interpreted the conversation between the couple in which Tarr announces the principle, 'deadness is the first condition of art' (*T2* p. 265), as aesthetically definitive for Lewis. The habit is to associate what Tarr tells Vasek with Lewis's instructions on 'the method of *external* approach' (*MWA* p. 103). A recent critic has referred to what Tarr says here as 'a theory of art' and 'typically Lewisian in its . . . philosophical ambition'.[22] This overestimates the authority of doctrinal conversation in modernist fiction and ignores the complex ways in which one writer tends to respond to another.

Tarr's principle of deadness is conceivably a variation on the theme of Stephen Dedalus's lecture to Cranly, in which the emphasis is on 'stasis' and 'arrest' as conditions of aesthetic appreciation, and sculpture (here, the paradigm), is deprecated.[23] Cranly's sarcastic response, which empties Stephen 'of theory and courage', is taken up in Vasek's description of Tarr's theory as 'drivel' (*T2* p. 271).[24] The theory is an opportunistic response to the death of Kreisler (a disordered German artist with whom both have been involved); but it is also a reaction (and, arguably, a barren one) to the manner in which Vasek has in an earlier scene (in Tarr's studio) persuaded Tarr's conception of art towards the beginning of life, as the development of a child's activity. It is worth examining in some detail how this comes about. When she asks Tarr, '[H]ow would you like to be a show-girl[?]' (*T2* p. 258), Vasek's taunt effects a disturbance of gender, resonating with a remark made by Tarr to Bertha: 'Like a woman luxuriously fingering a merchant's goods . . . I philandered with the idea of marriage' (*T2* p. 54). (The etymology of 'philander' is suggestive.) But masculinity is doubly disturbed, since the manner in which he is eyeing her reduces Tarr to a 'small boobie' (*T2* p. 258), an insult from which recovery is a challenge. What we witness here may remind us of Lewis's attachment to Dostoyevsky, to whom Bakhtin attributed that competition of novelistic voices over value and authority that he called the 'dialogic'.[25] The development of Bakhtin's theory into a 'feminist dialogics' has been undertaken in criticism of *Women in Love*, in which the modification of Birkin's sermonising by the voice of Ursula Brangwen calls to mind the Tarr–Vasek conversations.[26] The phenomenological interest of *Tarr*, however, is that the female voice effects its modification because its subject is the body.

Vasek turns Tarr's home scene into a vaudeville in which he, as 'audience', is pulled on stage. Quavering that he is 'hallucinated', the booby quotes Dryden's translation of Chaucer: 'The Man dreams but what the Boy believed' (*T2* p. 258). The *Nun's Priest's Tale* (from which the line originates) is much concerned with the presentation of dreams and their meaning.[27] Thus the conception of art as dream to which we are attending in this essay is presented as a matter of recapitulated naivety. As the child's game of make-believe is a version of primitive attachment to illusion, so the man's dream preserves the perspectives of childhood and primitiveness.[28] Vasek's suggestion that a man may look as attractive in stockings as a woman produces a 'breathless' reversion of that emphasis upon the ocular that is supposedly doctrinal in Lewis's art:

> I meant only that everything we *see* – you understand, this universe of distinct images – must be reinterpreted to tally with all the senses and beyond that with our minds: so that was my meaning, the eye alone sees nothing at all but conventional phantoms. (*T2* p. 262)

This suggests that we may be something more than 'surface-creatures' (*TWM* p. 377) after all.

The Apes of God (1930) is an extended tour of the 'bourgeois Bohemia' that appears in *Tarr*, but with the action transplanted from Paris to London. Among its concerns is a question that has its eye on the Renaissance business of artist and patron (or client) relationships, namely: who pays for modernism? The answer Lewis gives is 'no one', since those who could afford to pay for it prefer to spend their money being coterie artists themselves. These artists and their hangers-on are put on show in *The Apes*, for the inspection of a booby called Dan Boleyn, conducted by another of Lewis's showmen, Horace Zagreus, in a series of visits modelled on the salon culture of Proust's *In Search of Lost Time*.

Probably no major work of modernism has more suffered from its author's doctrinal noise. This, issuing in works such as *Satire & Fiction* (1930) and *Men without Art* (1934), stipulates externality and ocularity, the so-called 'philosophy of the EYE' (*MWA* p. 97), as principles of satire – which term Lewis had begun to use commutatively for 'art' itself. Criticism, having largely observed such stipulation and exaggeration, and desisted from enquiring why Lewis should introduce the 'philosophy of the eye' by means of a pretty explicit analogy with sadism (*TWM* pp. 133–4), has found the novel 'virtually unreadable' (*JFA* p. 5). Yet careful scholars of Lewis have noted that even if *The Apes* is putting 'Tarr's *externalist theory* into *literary practice*', it is marked by a quality of stylistic excess that can 'offer an opening out of satire's possibilities, in the same way that the "wild" body's existence contains much more than the observer can fathom'.[29]

Such an opening out has been recognised by Ian Patterson, who has seen how far the satiric portrayals of the Apes abut on the phenomenological theme of the body-subject. Patterson draws attention to those elements of discomfort, repetition, and accretion in Lewis's descriptions that cause the reader to experience him-/herself through bodily representation, as if 'trying on' the various characters: 'The figures paraded before us are denied the possibility of being mere mechanisms or surfaces by the demands Lewis's prose makes on the phenomenology of our reading.'[30] The body, thus presented, becomes the way to the self.

This may be observed in the extended portrayal at the Lenten Party of Knut, a poetic Finn: 'in a very tight and shabby suit of clothes of a dark green check, [he] sat bolt upright throughout the banquet – his staring eyes of intense polar green appearing to light up his rigid, long-lipped grin-from-ear-to-ear' (*AG* p. 356). Superficially, Knut is a bore and a stooge, as well as being a dubious poet (though one who warns against satire) (*AG* p. 396). Yet Lewis's description presents the character as uncannily as, say, a person disclosed in a dark room by a table-lamp – regarding whom, the question 'what is he/she doing?' spontaneously follows. The repetition of 'green' is strangely effective here, as is the adjectival flux: 'this strange painted shamanised northern wanderer – who possessed no home' (*AG* p. 356). Enraptured in spite of its designs, the narrative pursues what it cannot fully know. Such instances explain the limit to satire as surface-knowledge that is intimated by Zagreus: 'No man can guarantee to circumscribe, with cast-iron cartesian [sic] definition, all that they [the Apes] do' (*AG* p. 385).

We may also be taken beyond this limit by the description of Knut's voice and his designation as the 'recognised Soggetto', an allusion to a sixteenth-century mode of composition in which a text to be sung is 'carved' to fit the elements of the solmisation scale.[31] It is little noticed how far sound and voice form a theme of this novel. The regular comparison of characters to musical instruments is obviously related to the theme of reification; but music is also the expressive art closest to the primary form of embodied consciousness, the voice. Certainly, *The Apes* abounds in representation of mannered and silly speech, but its concern with voice also produces passages of music-hall banter, and of baroque and humorous pseudo-learning, in which satiric definition of the Apes pauses at their sound (see, for example, *AG* pp. 377–8 and pp. 382–5).

The ambivalence of this novel is particularly rich in its relationship with Proust. Paul Edwards has remarked of *The Apes* that 'subtly encoded' modernisms are 'subjected to formal, substantive or allusive critique' (*EWL* p. 344), the work of Proust being among them. If the matter of 'subtle encoding' were to be given priority over that of 'critique', a new theme of collaborative assimilation might be fruitfully explored in Anglo-French modernism. Given that salon life is an object of mockery, but also a source of fascination, in Proust and Lewis, the rough treatment of the Proust connoisseur, Lionel Kein, might be taken in a collegiate rather than doctrinal spirit. We would then begin to recognise that the principal task for Lewis was creative rather than critical, namely, the invention of a style suited to a world resembling that which Proust's narrator enters and passes beyond in the act of describing. To this style, which is more richly comic than Proust's, and more impressive in its power of presentation, though intellectually narrower, Paul Edwards has attributed an 'electric vitality' (see *EWL* p. 347).

The sense that Lewis is responding to Proust is caught in the scene where Zagreus (a variation on Proust's Baron de Charlus) is arrested by a vision at the Keins' door: 'He saw the horse, black and primitive "like a pompeian fresco," that drew the mortuary chariot from which Proust peeped. That processionary fresco extended from Pompeii to Kein's door' (*AG* p. 237). The vision, responding to the cab ride of Proust's narrator and dying grandmother in which their shadow is conceived as a fresco, red and black, is an acknowledgement of the uncanniness of Proust, and functions here as a doorway to the latter's split world.[32] The conception of Proust's narrator that life is everywhere supernatural because its ordinary instances seem to have a necromantic relation to the world of images (as if people were paintings come to life), is at Lewis's shoulder.[33] From beginning to end, *The Apes* entertains the supernatural in a generic language of ghostliness and occult agency; such language decorates a basic sense of uncanniness in Lewis (see *AG* pp. 7, 256, 305, 310, 327–45, 357–65, 370, and 478–9). In the novel's climactic scene, Zagreus removes a door from its frame, and Dan and two others dance upon it, to the sound of a flute (*AG* pp. 603–4). The image is no less haunting than Proust's presentation of a living frieze.[34]

III

Professing to explain everything by laughter entailed general consideration of that phenomenon, notably in two essays of 1927: 'The Meaning of the Wild Body' and 'Inferior Religions'. The former has been described by Bernard Lafoucarde as 'a landmark in the history of the theory of the comic' (*CWB* p. 156). It is supposed that here 'Lewis establishes the fundamental principles for his own comic art.'[35] Criticism seems to have been impressed by the logical terminology: 'First, to assume the dichotomy of mind and body is necessary here, without arguing it; for it is upon that essential separation that the theory of laughter here proposed is based' (*CWB* p. 157). This dichotomy accepted, all being appears 'absurd'. Some ontological musing follows, before the dichotomy fades out as Lewis tries a redaction of Bergson's theory of laughter:

> The root of the Comic is to be sought in the sensations resulting from the observations of a *thing* behaving like a person. But from that point of view all men are necessarily comic: for they are all *things*, or physical bodies, behaving as *persons*. (*CWB* p. 158)

The temptation is to interpret this as evidence of Lewis's 'inherently *inhuman* perspective'.[36] But we have only to insert an implied 'nowadays' as the final word, for the statement to function as a parody of behaviourism – a critical issue in Lewis's thought in this period.

In fact, neither the dualist nor the positivist 'theory' is particularly explanatory. It is when the essay turns to surreal examples of the 'anomaly' (*CWB* p. 159) that human existence is simultaneously objective and subjective, that it evokes Lewis's practice in the 'Wild Body' stories. We should note the association of the comic with 'wonder' and the 'miraculous'.

A fair impression of Lewis's rhetorical affinity with the Renaissance is offered by a baroque sermon that T. S. Eliot called 'indubitable evidence of genius' (*CWB* p. 148). 'Inferior Religions' is a challenge to interpretation (to this reader at least). With regard to meaning, the essay vacillates between scepticism and faith, 'inferior' functioning ambiguously. But there is difficulty, and splendour, in the detail.

The opening sections contain remarks upon freedom and individuality, comparing Lewis's practice with that of Dostoyevsky, Shakespeare, Dickens, and Cervantes. The concern is that as pattern, comic character amounts to a 'standardizing of self', an inertial or repetitive phenomenon. With one eye on *The Apes*, the thinking seems also to have in view modern ideas of the 'death instinct', 'bad faith', and 'pseudo-individuality'.[37] An accommodation with tradition supervenes. Character is now associated with God-formation, in a manner that suggests Nietzsche's thinking on naivety and illusion in the Apolline phase of Greek culture (Apollo being also a reassuring agent of individuation).[38] The designation of Boswell's Johnson and Falstaff as 'minute and rich religions' and 'little grotesque fetishes' attributes a religious power to 'english [sic] humour, and its delightful dreams' (*CWB* p. 151). The Absolute need not be immense, Lewis writes elsewhere (*TWM* pp. 374–6). Section IV offers aphoristic evaluations of laughter and tragedy, formulating the concern expressed in *Tarr* to elevate comedy above an art of death – a concern still pursued late in Lewis's career. It is backed by primordial definition: 'The Wild Body is this supreme survival that is us, the stark apparatus with its set of mysterious spasms: the most profound of which is laughter' (*CWB* p. 152).

Doubt follows. The *danse macabre* presented here, influenced perhaps by Renaissance woodcuts, we may interpret as a dream-condensation of those visions of death-at-the-party in Proust and Joyce:

the King of Play is not a phantom corresponding to the sovereign force beneath the surface. The latter must always be reckoned on: it is the Skeleton at the Feast, potentially, with us. That soul or dominant corruption is so real that he cannot rise up and take part in man's festival as a Falstaff of unwieldy spume. If he comes at all it must be as he is, the skeleton or bogey of veritable life, stuck over with corruptions and vices. (*CWB* p. 153)[39]

Yet this *memento mori* with its sombre zest is not without a note of *hilaritas*.[40]

Hilaritas may be the best word for the spirit of *Time and Western Man* (1927). This has the reputation of being 'the doctrine according to Lewis', though attempts to explain its thesis may be exercised by both its form and object – as well as Lewis's own practice. 'The merit of a book is not solely dependent on its organization' (*TWM* p. 456), notes Paul Edwards, commenting that Lewis's object could be construed as the 'result of a hobby-horsical eccentricity' (*TWM* p. 455).[41] The possibility is worth pursuing. Edwards's monograph begins with a comparison between Lewis and Toby Shandy, calls Lewis's *Enemy of the Stars* the most 'self-reflexive text . . . in English since *Tristram Shandy*' (*EWL* p. 165), and compares *Snooty Baronet* to that novel (*EWL* p. 439). We may note as well that Lewis singled out Sterne's characterisation as more '*real*' than life itself (*TWM* p. 188) and that the alchemy professed by the showman gave Walter Shandy a name for his son.[42] There is in all this a persuasion, unscholarly perhaps, to appreciate *Time and Western Man* for its Shandean persistence and humour. Dietrich Bonhoeffer described *hilaritas* as 'defiance of the world and popular opinion', 'a high-spirited self-confidence'.[43] 'Explaining everything by laughter' may as well be an attitude as a solution.

On the side of scholarship, *Time and Western Man* could be interpreted as a defence of the life-world (or God's 'picture gallery') against the dissolving and abstracting effects of modern science and its associated 'philosophy'. The confusion is that Lewis seems to take the side of the rational against the intuitive. Since it has been demonstrated here that in Lewis's fiction, showing life as dream, phantasmagoria, embodied consciousness, and subjectivised space, is indeed 'art's business', this contradiction is not easily understood. So, has *Time and Western Man* something decisive to tell us about Lewis's way of seeing, by which the contradiction may be explained?

In what Edwards describes as an instance of '"genuine" mysticism' (*EWL* p. 312), Lewis declares:

If you say that creative art is a spell, a talisman, an incantation – that it is *magic*, in short, there, too, I believe you would be correctly describing it. That the artist uses and manipulates a supernatural power seems very likely. (*TWM* p. 187)

Here and in *The Apes*, there is a persuasive case for Lewis's inclusion in the growing scholarship on modernism and magic.[44] Certainly, Lewis's *Human Age* trilogy engages with the supernatural on a scale unparalleled by any other modernist. Yet the declaration has a basis in direct experience:

> To make things *endure* . . . is of course, as well, a sort of magic, and a more difficult one, than to make things *vanish*, change and disintegrate (though that is very remarkable too). Of these opposite functions of magic we daily perform one, in our sense-perception activity, better than magic could. This function we justly call 'creativeness': and, we have just said, it is a much more difficult type than that of destruction. (*TWM* p. 350)

Behind this statement one may discern Kant's 'principle of the ideality of all sensible intuitions'.[45] But the notion is phenomenologically transfigured by the particularity of Lewis's own experience. Here, perception itself is magic because the manner in which mind entertains the object of sense experience is characterised by a quality of 'twiceness', a spark of *déjà vu* (see *JFA* pp. 75–6). It is for this reason that Lewis thinks of the objects of perception as in general 'uncanny' (*TWM* p. 350). Let these objects include persons, and we understand why the showman witnesses Bestre *twice* at once. So, pattern contains anomaly as its incongruous (and therefore comic) essence. Of this truth, Lewis conceived his style as constituting the authority.

'The wonder is not that things should be; it is that there should be such things.'[46]

Notes

1. See Charles Taylor, *Sources of the Self: The Making of the Modern Identity* (Cambridge: Cambridge University Press, 1989), Chapters 1, 11, and 24; and Gabriel Josipovici, *What Ever Happened to Modernism?* (New Haven, CT, and London: Yale University Press, 2010), Chapters 2–5. A classic expression of modernity's lost horizon occurs in Friedrich Nietzsche, *The Gay Science*, trans. Walter Kaufmann (New York: Vintage, 1974), Sections 108–53. The theme of groundlessness is expounded in Martin Heidegger, 'What is Metaphysics?', in David Farrell Krell (ed.), *Martin Heidegger: Basic Writings* (San Francisco: Harper, 1977), pp. 91–112. A systematic criticism of rationalism occurs in Edmund Husserl, *The Crisis of European Sciences and Transcendental Phenomenology: An Introduction to Phenomenological Philosophy*, trans. David Carr (Evanston: Northwestern University Press, 1970). See, for example, 'The Vienna Lecture', pp. 269–99.
2. This theme is developed by Peter L. Caracciolo in 'From Signorelli to Caligari: Allusions to Painting and Film in *The Human Age* and its Visual

Precursors', in Carmelo Cunchillos Jaime (ed.), *Wyndham Lewis the Radical: Essays on Literature and Modernity* (Bern: Peter Lang, 2007), pp. 137–57.

3. Philip Head, 'Ideology, Utopia, Myth: Lewis's "Politics of the Intellect"', *Wyndham Lewis Annual*, 4, 1997, pp. 20–32. See also Michael Baxandall, *Painting and Experience in Fifteenth-Century Italy* [1972] (Oxford: Oxford University Press, 1990), pp. 94–103.

4. See also T. S. Eliot, *T. S. Eliot: Selected Prose* (Harmondsworth: Penguin, 1958), p. 117 and p. 68.

5. For discussion, see Michael Nath, '"By Curious Sovereignty of Art": Wyndham Lewis and Nihilism', *The Journal of Wyndham Lewis Studies*, 2, 2011, pp. 1–22: pp. 8–10.

6 Maurice Merleau-Ponty, *Phenomenology of Perception*, trans. Colin Smith (London: Routledge, 2008), pp. xxiii–xxiv.

7. Ibid., pp. 60–74.

8. See Husserl, *The Crisis of European Sciences*, pp. 5–7, and 46–53.

9. Ibid., pp. 155–7.

10. See, for example, James Mansell, 'Sound and the Cultural Politics of Time in the Avant-garde', in *WLC* pp. 111–25.

11. See Paul Valéry, 'On Mallarmé', trans. Anthony Bower, in *Selected Writings of Paul Valéry* [1950] (New York: New Directions, 1964), pp. 213–17.

12. María Jesús Hernáez Lerena, 'Are Lewis's Short Stories Pathological?', in Cunchillos Jaime (ed.), *Wyndham Lewis the Radical*, pp. 39–68. The entire essay is of interest.

13. Merleau-Ponty, *Phenomenology of Perception*, p. 71.

14. James Joyce, 'An Encounter', in Harry Levin (ed.), *The Essential James Joyce* [1914] (London: Jonathan Cape, 1950), pp. 30–8: pp. 32–3.

15. See Baxandall, *Painting and Experience*, pp. 60–1 and Merleau-Ponty, *Phenomenology of Perception*, p. 108.

16. Merleau-Ponty, *Phenomenology of Perception*, pp. 411–12. My attention was first drawn to this passage by Ian Patterson, in the essay cited below.

17. See David A. Wragg, *Wyndham Lewis and the Philosophy of Art in Early Modernist Britain: Creating a Political Aesthetic* (Lampeter: Edwin Mellen Press, 2005), pp. 33–47.

18. In general, see Charles Taylor, *Sources of the Self*, pp. 143–58 and pp. 185–92. For Lewis, see Emmett Stinson, 'The Vortex as Ontology in *The Apes of God*: Self-Reflexive Satire and Apophaticism', *The Journal of Wyndham Lewis Studies*, 3, 2012, pp. 123–42: p. 132.

19. See, for example, D. H. Lawrence, *Women in Love* [1920] (Harmondsworth: Penguin, 1960), pp. 160–72 and pp. 208–10.

20. See Friedrich Nietzsche, *The Gay Science*, trans. Walter Kaufmann (New York: Vintage Books, 1974), pp. 327–31.

21. See Pam Morris (ed.), *The Bakhtin Reader: Selected Writings of Bakhtin, Medvedev, Voloshinov* (London: Arnold, 1996), pp. 204–9. See also M. M. Bakhtin, *Rabelais and His World*, trans H. Iswolsky (Bloomington: Indiana University Press, 1984).

22. See Rebecca Beasley, 'Wyndham Lewis and Modernist Satire', in Morag Shiach (ed.), *The Cambridge Companion to the Modernist Novel* (Cambridge: Cambridge University Press, 2007), pp. 126–36: p. 129.

23. See Joyce, *A Portrait of the Artist as a Young Man* (1916), in *The Essential James Joyce*, pp. 203–432: pp. 378–98.
24. Ibid., p. 337.
25. See Morris, *The Bakhtin Reader*, pp. 89–112. From M. M. Bakhtin, *Problems of Dostoevsky's Poetics*, trans. C. Emerson (Minneapolis: University of Minnesota Press, 1984).
26. As expounded in Carol Siegel, *Lawrence Among the Women: Wavering Boundaries in Women's Literary Traditions* (Charlottesville: University Press of Virginia, 1991). See *D. H. Lawrence: The Rainbow / Women in Love*, ed. Richard Beynon (Cambridge: Icon, 1997), pp. 129–33.
27. Geoffrey Chaucer, *The Canterbury Tales* (London: Chancellor Press, 1985), pp. 247–64. Lewis's interest in this tale is also hinted at in his unpublished poem 'The Liquid Brown Detestable Earth' (see *CPP* p. 205).
28. The idea of art as a game of make-believe is expounded in detail by Kendall Walton, *Mimesis as Make-Believe: On the Foundations of the Representational Arts* (Cambridge, MA: Harvard University Press, 1990). My references to illusion and naivety derive from Friedrich Nietzsche, *The Birth of Tragedy*, trans. Shaun Whiteside (London: Penguin, 1993), pp. 7–8 and 21–6.
29. See Wragg, *Wyndham Lewis*, pp. 287–8 and p. 297.
30. See Ian Patterson, 'Beneath the Surface: Apes, Bodies and Readers', in Paul Edwards (ed.), *Volcanic Heaven: Essays on Wyndham Lewis's Painting and Writing* (Santa Rosa: Black Sparrow Press, 1996), pp. 123–34: p. 133. The essay is of the first importance for understanding Lewisian characterisation.
31. See Lewis Lockwood, 'Soggetto cavato', in Stanley Sadie (ed.), *The New Grove Dictionary of Music and Musicians*, Vol. 23 (London: Macmillan, 2001), pp. 620–1.
32. See Marcel Proust, *In Search of Lost Time – Volume 3: The Guermantes Way*, trans. Mark Treaharne (London: Penguin, 2003), p. 316.
33. Ibid., pp. 187–8.
34. Proust, *The Guermantes Way*, pp. 412–13.
35. See Shane Weller, 'Nietzsche among the Modernists: The Case of Wyndham Lewis', *Modernism/modernity*, 14.4, 2007, pp. 625–43: p. 639.
36. See Stinson, 'The Vortex as Ontology', p. 123.
37. See, for example, Sigmund Freud, *Beyond the Pleasure Principle*, trans. James Strachey (London: Norton, 1989), pp. 23–4 and pp. 44–7; Jean-Paul Sartre, *Being and Nothingness*, trans. Hazel Barnes (London: Routledge, 1991), pp. 47–70; and Theodor Adorno and Max Horkheimer, *Dialectic of Enlightenment*, trans. John Cumming (London: Verso, 1992), pp. 154–6.
38. See Nietzsche, *The Birth of Tragedy*, pp. 21–6.
39. See, for example, Roland Mushat Frye's discussion of the *memento mori* and funerary art in *The Renaissance Hamlet: Issues and Responses in 1600* (Princeton: Princeton University Press, 1984), Chapter 6. See Marcel Proust, *In Search of Lost Time – Volume 6: Time Regained*, trans. Andreas Mayor and Terence Kilmartin (London: Vintage, 2000), pp. 215–451; Joyce, 'The Dead' (1914), in *The Essential James Joyce*, pp. 160–202: pp. 173–4.
40. I have in mind the thoughts on *hilaritas* in Dietrich Bonhoeffer, *Letters and Papers from Prison* (London: SCM Press, 2002), pp. 73–6.

41. Edwards's 'Afterword' (*TWM* pp. 455–508) does much to elucidate the principles and complications of Lewis's argument against 'time-philosophy', as do remarks in *EWL* pp. 305–16.

42. Laurence Sterne, *The Life and Opinions of Tristram Shandy* (1759–67), ed. Graham Petrie, introd. Christopher Ricks (Harmondsworth: Penguin, 1987), p. 281.

43. Bonhoeffer, *Letters and Papers from Prison*, p. 73.

44 See, for example, Leigh Wilson, *Modernism and Magic: Experiments with Spiritualism, Theosophy and the Occult* (Edinburgh: Edinburgh University Press, 2013). Valuable work on sources has been undertaken in Peter L. Caracciolo, 'Wyndham Lewis, M. R. James and Intertextuality: Part 1, Ghosts', *Wyndham Lewis Annual*, 6, 1999, pp. 21–8.

45. See Lewis White Beck (ed.), *Kant: Selections* (New York: Macmillan, 1988), p. 109.

46. Valéry, *Selected Writings*, p. 90.

Chapter 13

The Human Age

Scott W. Klein

In *A Portrait of the Artist as a Young Man* (1916), James Joyce says of his young protagonist Stephen Dedalus, 'It pained him that he did not know well what politics meant and that he did not know where the universe ended.'[1] Wyndham Lewis's *The Human Age* – the novels *The Childermass* (1928), *Monstre Gai* (1955), and *Malign Fiesta* (1955), three instalments towards an unfinished four-novel project about the afterlife – is modernism's largest attempt to rectify this incomprehension by proposing that politics and cosmology are one and the same. Its constituent novels reflect Lewis's shifting ideas about politics and novelistic form. Taken as a whole, *The Human Age* represents Lewis's most sustained attempt to imagine alternative versions of the Universe as embodiments of his consistent yet constantly revised sense of the relation between individuality and political power.

The work consists, depending on one's perspective, of one, two, three, or even potentially four works. *The Human Age* emerged at roughly the same time as a massive treatise planned by Lewis after the First World War, and was once thought to be part of it. *The Man of the World* contained half a million words and was composed of sections that Lewis later broke into the separate volumes *The Art of Being Ruled* (1926), *The Lion and the Fox* (1927), and *Time and Western Man* (1927), all meditations on politics, ontology, and social organisation.[2] *The Childermass* first emerged alongside these non-fictional works, all intended by Lewis to demonstrate in philosophic terms his sense of the struggles and traumas of the human subject after the First World War. Once it stood on its own, however, Lewis intended *The Childermass* to be the beginning of a fictional trilogy about the afterlife. He was contracted to write the subsequent volumes as early as 1928 by Chatto and Windus, but subsequent projects prevented him from moving beyond the original volumes for many years. Only a radio adaptation of *The Childermass* by the BBC in 1951 and subsequent commissions from the

BBC to finish the work for further adaptations in 1955 led to the creation of *Monstre Gai* and *Malign Fiesta*, first as radio dramas and later as fully fledged novels. These were issued as a single volume by Methuen in 1955, with the new aggregate title *The Human Age*. A fourth volume that would have completed the series, with the working title *The Trial of Man*, was left unfinished at Lewis's death.[3]

The Human Age is both one work and multiple works. There is a temporal and stylistic fissure between *The Childermass* and the later books, despite the fact that the 'plot' of the whole appears to follow on consistently between volumes. It is a challenge, then, to think of the whole as simultaneously pursuing a single fictional and philosophical trajectory. In addition, it is the product of two distinct periods in Lewis's work: the periods after the two world wars, and their respective intellectual, cultural, and political concerns. *The Childermass* emerges from debates during the 1920s about the relation between style, form, and social cohesion. Lewis's dystopian fantasia dramatises ideas about art and individuality that were also expounded in his then-contemporary polemical works, while also engaging with the philosophic critique of avant-garde literary style (for example in the works of his contemporaries James Joyce and Gertrude Stein) waged in such critical texts as *Time and Western Man* (1927). Understanding its unusual thematic focus and style – its fantastical subject matter, obscurity, and break into dramatic form for most of its second half – requires the context both of Lewis's own contemporary cultural thought and his earlier experiments with fictional and dialogic form.

Monstre Gai and *Malign Fiesta*, both written after the Second World War, manifest more straightforwardly Lewis's ideas about the relationship between the exceptional man and political power – exemplified by his intellectual protagonist Pullman, who 'collaborates' first with the Bailiff and later with the devil in Hell, and is finally kidnapped by angels of God. In these books, Lewis's version of the afterlife – routinised and bureaucratised, not notably different in its concerns with the shape of society and the uses and abuses of power from the Earth below – takes more conventional novelistic shape. Where *The Childermass* takes place in an amorphous world of constant transformation and satiric political theatre, *Monstre Gai* recasts the welfare state of post-war Britain as cosmological farce, and *Malign Fiesta* presents an afterworld all too similar to both literary and real political horrors: where the tortures of Dis are modelled on the work of Dante, and technologies of torture invoke the horrors of the Nazi concentration camps.

The Childermass has been called 'by far the most difficult of Wyndham Lewis's fictions to explain'.[4] Its obscurity, indeed, lies in both its subject matter and its corresponding narrative techniques. I. A. Richards said of this first volume: 'We don't know – to an agonizing degree we are not allowed to know – what it is all about.'[5] Part of this is programmatic, as the reader shares the confusion of the main characters, Pullman and Satterthwaite – who are also called Pulley and Satters, nicknames from their shared schoolboy days – who find themselves after death in a vast plain of the afterlife. They are surrounded by mountains, part of a refugee camp of souls waiting to be admitted as petitioners to the Magnetic City, which may or may not be a version of the conventional Heaven. The first half of *The Childermass* establishes the vexed relationship between Pullman and Satters. They are old school friends, yet they also represent antagonistic aspects of the human intellect in a dystopian landscape where human identity after death is frozen in time into one of the individual's most representative modes on Earth. Thus Pullman, an intellectual, appears as a dapper young man in his late twenties, while Satters is frozen in time as a schoolboy.

Yet 'frozen', let alone 'time', are misnomers, because the two characters, as well as both time and space, are constantly shifting and transforming. Pullman and Satters change in various ways: in perceived gender (as when Pullman, in the role of nursemaid to Satters, is called 'Miss Pullman') and in size. Nor is the landscape stable. As Pullman and Satters wander the environs of the city, the contours of the world shift strangely around them, as in Robert Browning's poem *Childe Roland to the Dark Tower Came* (1855). Unlike Browning's protagonist, however, neither character knows why he is on this particular quest, or what to expect if he is ever allowed admission to the city.

This malleability – as well as the range of literary allusion – is part of the point. The world of the afterlife is inexplicable and absurd. It is riddled with the husks of literary culture, from Milton to Joyce (most notably the drafts of *Finnegans Wake* (1939), then appearing in print), and of the shells of various kinds of human types. When Satters, the newcomer, asks Pullman towards the beginning of the book, 'Is it too preposterous?' he receives the answer 'No more preposterous than everything else here' (*C* p. 4). And the book's baroque level of ornamental detail underlines the point. One of the decorations of the exterior of the city is 'pigs made of inflated skins, in flight' (*C* p. 7). This is, indeed, a kind of satiric utopia – a literal 'no place' that could only exist, in the slang term, when pigs fly.

It is difficult by definition to find a stable point of entry into this world. As Satters says, 'How *fearfully weird* all this is!' (*C* p. 20). One point, however, is suggested by a notable and extended passage two-thirds of the way through the characters' travels through the landscape. They wander into an area known as the 'Time-Flats' in which the eighteenth century has been frozen into a kind of semi-living panorama. Here they approach the Old Red Lion Inn, where, as Pullman explains, Thomas Paine wrote his book *Rights of Man* (1791). Satters, having regressed to an enormous infancy, is more interested in the apparently tiny eighteenth-century men as toys than as thinkers. He reaches for the Lilliputian Paine with a giant Gulliverian hand, and when Paine bites him, he stamps him to oblivion with Swiftian finality (C p. 103).

This passage suggests a preliminary locus for Lewis's satire. Human rights, and their redefinition through history, will be at stake throughout *The Human Age*. So will the tendency of human nature to regress to its most infantile common denominator. For as Lewis had argued in his polemical works of the 1920s, human identity (and therefore political identity) depended strongly on both intellect and the ability to think of oneself as an individual, not as a part of a group defined from outside. To do so is to lose both one's political autonomy and one's sense of identity as fixed, given early twentieth-century philosophy's desire to sublimate ideas of 'reality' to the regime of time and of Bergsonian flux. *The Childermass*, and *The Human Age* as a whole, questions whether the received Enlightenment idea of man is sufficient to explain social organisation in the age of world wars. Indeed, the very end of *The Art of Being Ruled* suggests a way into *The Childermass*:

> Our minds are all still haunted by that Abstract Man, that enlightened abstraction of a common humanity, which had its greatest advertisement in the eighteenth century. That No Man in a No Man's Land, that phantom of democratic 'enlightenment,' is what has to be disposed for good in order to make way for higher human classifications, which, owing to scientific method, men could now attempt. (*ABR* p. 375)

The phantom of democratic 'enlightenment' wandering in a No Man's Land – the contested zone between claims of opposing rights, and a phrase popularised in English to refer to the forbidden area between trenches during the First World War – is a fair enough description of *The Childermass*. For the novel also takes its name from another locus of slaughter, the Massacre of Innocents in the New Testament, or 'Childermas', when King Herod ordered the execution of all young male children near Bethlehem when he learned of the birth of Jesus. While the remainder of *The Human Age* will ultimately try to make good on Lewis's turn towards the idea of 'higher human classifications', *The Childermass* is first and foremost a satiric lament for the debasement of human potentiality. Implicitly the 'emigrant mass' (C p. 1) of the book is largely composed of men who were killed during the First World War.

Satters, who moves with a 'shell-shock waggle' (C p. 12) and wears a medal from Mons, died from gas. Yet the dead's status as 'children' cuts in two opposed directions. To be sure, they are also murdered innocents, killed on Earth, like the contemporaries of Jesus, by political leaders who sought to consolidate their temporal control. Yet they have also been less sympathetically constituted by twentieth-century culture as an anti-intellectual mob incapable of mature reflection or social organisation, automata who wander a No Man's Land (which is, ironically, composed solely of men) between unclear eschatological alternatives. Satters's infantile crushing of Thomas Paine is the book's figure for a generation too confirmed in its infantilism to learn the lessons of history or Enlightenment thought – where it is easier to destroy than to think.

Lewis's Pullman stands both within and against this mass. Somewhat older than the others – supposedly on Earth only eighteen months longer than Satters, but appearing to be in his late twenties in this changeable world – he is a figure of the modern intellectual. He holds liberal beliefs, and is described at one point as something of a demiurge, an 'absent-minded creator' himself, holding Satters's head as though he were creating man from clay (C p. 58). Apparently Pullman survived the war – explaining 'I was a schoolmaster before the war. Afterwards I chucked it' (C p. 69) – and he shares, satirically, some of the biographical features of James Joyce and his creation Stephen Dedalus. He taught English at Berlitz in either Spandau or Trieste, and once, he explains, broke his glasses (C p. 94). Pullman is the largely detached observer of the world around him – a portrait of the artist as a phantasmal man – and for the first half of The Childermass he acts as Satters's best guide to both the populace of the afterlife and to its politics.

These politics are largely embodied by the other main character of The Childermass, the Bailiff, whose appearance midway through the narrative changes both the tenor of The Childermass and its narrative form. A grotesque figure, the Bailiff and his elaborate entourage – a bizarre admixture of Western courtroom and oriental caliphate – are the visible embodiments of power in this afterlife, the gatekeepers for the appellants who wish to enter the presumably paradisal city. His oratorical techniques threaten to overwhelm the second half of the narrative and are a combination of populist crowd-pleasing – 'I am a plain man like yourselves', he claims, while noting 'my pacifism is a byword' (C p. 145) – music hall antics, and political demagoguery. Upon his entrance Pullman and Satters shift from the centre of the narrative to its periphery. They become little more than occasional choral commentators on the obscure political rituals they witness for the second half of the narration.

As a figure of satire, the Bailiff has drawn a great deal of praise and attention from commentators – yet from two apparently paradoxical points of view. He has been seen as in part a conduit for Lewis's own social and political ideas of the 1920s, but also as a grotesque manifestation of the confluence of twentieth-century authoritarian politics, manipulation of the public by media and popular culture, and the abuse of language for political ends.[6] Part of the Bailiff's absurdity is his ability simultaneously to present an at-times defensible if abstract philosophy of the human (and extra-human) condition, while also embodying a variety of kinds of rhetoric for rhetoric's sake. His pandering to the crowd, his crocodile tears when members of his court commit acts of violence against political 'opponents' among the appellants, even his spouting at one point parodic approximations of the language of Joyce's *Finnegans Wake*: all suggest the various modes of quasi-empathetic rhetoric, manipulations of mass culture, and linguistic abuses by which early twentieth-century political figures were learning both to control large populaces and to occlude the sources of their power in brute force.

While the Bailiff's title suggests that he has only a secondary level of power – as one empowered to maintain order in a court – he has, at least in *The Childermass*, absolute power over the appellants. His criteria for letting petitioners into the city beyond are both relatively well demarcated and uninterpretively enigmatic. In theory the Bailiff rewards individuals who are able to maintain a stable sense of unique self in this land of transformation (as long as that personal identity is not politically threatening). In practice, as in the comparable bureaucracies of Franz Kafka, what constitutes a successful plea for entrance is obscure. The individual petitioners the Bailiff confronts in the course of the book are treated alternately with contempt, with feigned philosophical dignity, and with arrant violence – as when the Bailiff's heiduks attack and dismember Macrob after a particularly contested disagreement. From the Bailiff's point of view, and to some degree the book's, membership in larger groups (regional and linguistic, as in the Carnegies or Macrob) or in the assumed groupings of political parties (as in the Hyperideans) obscures human identity even as it claims to define it. Yet not to be a member of a larger group is to risk, at the risk of a pun, dismemberment – dissolution as a singular self, let alone a singular body.

And from these enigmatic questions – what constitutes human personality and organisation? How might one meet the approval of the powerful in the afterlife? – arise the book's political theatrics. The Bailiff's self-presentation is expressly a performance, part puppet-show, part Greek tragedy, performed for the mob. It presents both philosophical dialogue and bread-and-circuses, complete with visual effects out of silent films and an interval that features an orchestra that, in the most 'modern' style, mixes Mozart with jazz. Pullman has earlier thought of the appellants literally as 'the audience' (*C* p. 56), and at the book's halfway point it assumes the form of a play – or perhaps more accurately, an extended Platonic dialogue. In *The Art of Being Ruled* Lewis had lamented the erasure of the line between spectator and performer in contemporary Russian theatre, seeing in that conflation an incursion of group-ideology into the realm of aesthetics (*ABR* pp. 157–8). By turning stylistically into a piece of political theatre, *The Childermass* asks how aesthetics can in turn reflect issues in contemporary ideology. To what degree is power, and rule, a matter of show rather than substance? What political role is played by the observer – such as Pullman – who stands on the sidelines, as chorus, but never involves himself in the 'show' itself?

What makes these questions even more difficult to interpret is the ambiguity of the various parties involved in the 'performance'. Lewis's afterlife reflects the contemporary parties and symbols of Europe in the 1920s, the metaphorical theatres that postdate the more literal Theatres of War. The Bailiff appears, alternately, to present a philosophy of mock-democratic humanism mixed with crypto-royalism – at one point he proclaims '*[l]e mob c'est moi*' (*C* p. 266) – and a mocking proto-communism. His chief ideological opponents among the appellants are the Hyperideans, 'a heretical faction' (*C* p. 255) who boast the signs of emergent European fascism. Followers of Hyperides, who dress in mock-Greek attire and take on Classical-sounding names, call him the 'last Aryan hero', and in one case wears a swastika (*C* p. 253).[7] Yet the main emblem of the Communists – the hammer and sickle – appears in *The Childermass* only in relation to the subhuman peons (*C* p. 15), and despite his proclamations to the contrary, the Bailiff stands for a form of authoritarianism scarcely different from the claims of the Hyperideans. The political theatre of *The Childermass* seems less devoted, then, to parsing worldly politics than to revealing that all politics are nothing but pure performativity and rhetoric scaffolded only by the power that helps them hold sway. As such the 'parties' of the afterlife embody Lewis's observation in *The Art of Being Ruled* that 'all varieties of political belief, the more outwardly they seem violently to differ, inwardly grow alike. They agree to differ in order to resemble each other, so that the more they ostensibly change, the more they are the same thing' (*ABR* p. 17).

The details of the political and philosophical debates of *The Childermass*, then, are in a sense less important than is their complexity and paradoxicality, as pointers to the kinds of ideological distortions that led to such an event as the First World War in the first place and the ways in which such arguments would lay the groundwork for further European strife. At one point a passing character identified only as 'the Cassandra of the Circus' calls out 'Delenda est Europa!' (*C* p. 254). *The Childermass* suggests that it does not matter what confluence of political forces combine to destroy Europe. Surely Europe will be destroyed, inevitably witnessed from the sidelines by the like of Pullman and Satters, types respectively of the detached intellectual and the soldier–victim. Taken as a solitary volume, *The Childermass* is both a manifestation of the literary avant-garde and a warning about the uses and abuses of obscurity in political, and therefore cultural, movements. The Bailiff's 'muddy fountain of images' (*C* p. 180) suggests a satire that interrogates the intractable rift between the ruled and the ruler, individuality and the 'state', and the internal paradoxes of the political theatre of the 1920s.

Monstre Gai takes us into a different world, literally, figuratively, and stylistically. Because a quarter of a century had elapsed between composition of the parts, the world satirised in the later books is no longer the vexed landscape of the 1920s, and Lewis's style has changed to become something closer to received novelistic style. Pullman and Satters enter the gates of the city only to discover that they are still not in Heaven, but in the rather familiar European-style metropolis called Third City. And, much as the novel leaves behind the highly allusive high modernist experimentation of *The Childermass*, so are the characters transformed from 'metaphysical' to 'physical' characters – embodied both literally (in their sudden needs to eat, say, and to evacuate), and in their consolidation as recognisable literary 'characters'.

The world has changed from a place of political philosophy to a world of *realpolitik*, in which the ideological conditions of the afterlife are more than ever nearly indistinguishable from the politics of Earth. Third City is a model of the post-World War Two welfare state: all of its inhabitants are given money by a central office according to their status before death; few inhabitants work; and the masses of inhabitants are nearly indistinguishable morons, bludgeoned into passivity by the two unnamed wars: 'a hatless generation . . . impoverished by two cataclysms' (*HA* p. 17). In *The Childermass*, the Bailiff claimed 'the Kingdom of God is composed as far as possible of *children*' (*C* p. 317), and in that volume these children were, implicitly, the generation massacred by the First World War. Now the entire populace of Third City is frozen in time as middle-aged children. As one inhabitant explains: 'Provided with money by the State, we exist in suspended animation, sexless, vegetarian, and dry, permanently about forty-six' (*HA* p. 25).

Monstre Gai offers an afterlife with little in the way of religious or spiritual elevation. Its world is material. Neither Heaven nor Hell, Third City is implicitly a cheerless version of post-war London in the age of the Cold War, relegated in political power to the likes of Washington and Moscow. Nominally ruled by an angelic Governor, the Padishah, the real power in Third City belongs to the Bailiff. It is, however, vulnerable to the same kinds of political manoeuvring that take place between the great 'foreign powers' on Earth. Major set-pieces in the novel recount an attack on the city waged by the devil in Hell, including what seems like a version of an atomic blast and its aftermath; a description of a flying dragon that has crashed during this 'Blitz' unmistakably invokes Londoners' experiences of the Second World War (*HA* p. 82). A diplomatic mission from Hell that escalates into an airborne battle between angel and devil suggests that Lewis has in mind that when Blake said that Milton was 'of the Devils [sic] party without knowing it' he spoke more than he knew.[8] In this world, at least, being with the Padishah or with the devil is as much a matter of political and 'national' allegiance as it is a matter of the spirit.

It is in this spirit that the Bailiff explains the true nature of Heaven and Hell to Pullman – 'The *Good* and the *Bad* are blurred, are they not, in the modern age?' (*HA* p. 131) – and it is Pullman's increasing engagement with what he sees that is the main subject of *The Human Age*. In *The Childermass*, despite his scepticism and Satters's clear disapproval, Pullman was a bystander who seemed to believe that overall the Bailiff was actually on the side of the people. In *Monstre Gai*, the Bailiff singles him out for political and material favour, largely because of what we learn was his eminence on Earth, and he becomes closely involved – for better and worse – in the political process. In *The Childermass*, Pullman is no longer simply described as a former school-teacher and aloof intellectual who 'never looks at the object of his solicitude but busies himself in the abstract' (*C* p. 19). Now (like James Joyce) he is revealed to have the first name of James, to have been brought up by Jesuits in Ireland, and to be 'a writer of his experimental sort' (*HA* p. 173) who reads Homer's *Odyssey* (*HA* p. 175). The Bailiff calls him 'the greatest writer of your time' (*HA* p. 136), whose books were iconoclastic enough to have been on the Catholic Church's index of banned books on Earth, and were 'understood only by the intellectuals' (*HA* p. 235).

Monstre Gai shows Pullman as a representative of the highest aesthetic and literary sophistication being drawn slowly but firmly into the Bailiff's dubious moral ambit. On one hand, Pullman flatters himself on never having taken political sides in the past: 'On the earth', he explains to the Bailiff, 'I never was a partisan' (*HA* p. 250). On the other hand, he becomes increasingly aware of the material advantages of political patronage, such as his lodgings at the Phanuel Hotel, and he is flattered that the Bailiff would turn to him for advice on political strategy – a strategy that leads, however obliquely and by association, to the brutal assassination of Hyperides. Pullman becomes self-aware of his dilemma, becoming gradually conscious that he has fallen into a moral trap set, in a sense, by himself. As a political animal, he becomes 'ashamed of himself' as being manoeuvred politically into the Bailiff's party, despite finding him to be a 'loathsome individual' (*HA* p. 234).

Only at this point does the full significance of Pullman's name become clear. He carries the name of a luxury railroad sleeping car – or of its inventor.[9] Like a railroad carriage, he has been set in hurtling motion as part of a larger mechanism – in his case the structures of social and intellectual activity – through the afterlife. But how conscious or intentional are his actions? A character in a piece in Lewis's journal *The Tyro* in the early 1920s states: 'I am a machine that is constructed to provide you with answers. I am alive, however. But I am beholden for life to machines that are asleep.'[10] Pullman's status as author and his name suggest that he, too, is one of these kinds of superior machines. But are his decisions intentional, or is he, too, prone to a kind of automated motion, an ethical sleepwalking? Or, more pointedly: does a writer's aesthetic ability necessarily lead to political perspicuity?

This subject had deep personal ramifications for Lewis, given his short-lived and recanted enthusiasm for Hitler in the early 1930s, and the support for Italian fascism of his long-time friend Ezra Pound.[11] Indeed, as Pullman becomes more and more opportunistically involved with the Bailiff's increasingly obviously illegal political activities, the book itself begins to refer to him as its 'hero-rat' (*HA* p. 254). For Pullman appears to base his political decisions less on their ethical or even spiritual relevance than on whether he finds them purely intellectually interesting. As Jeffrey Meyers has pointed out, the novel's title comes from a supposed quotation from Voltaire that appears twice in Nietzsche's *The Will to Power*: '*un monstre gai vaut mieux qu'un sentimental ennuyeux*', which translates into English as 'a gay monster is worth more than a sentimental bore'.[12] The Bailiff, for all of his posturing and outrageous behaviour is, to Pullman at least, a far more engaging character than the bored and boring Padishah. Pullman's politics or lack of politics at this point in his moral development suggest to him that whoever supports him is 'a good man' (*HA* p. 173).

In *Malign Fiesta*, the dangers of Pullman's political collaboration become acute on a cosmic scale, as he and Satters are forced to flee Third City to Matapolis, a city in Hell. There the Bailiff is revealed to be strictly a minor power, and Pullman falls under the direct patronage of the devil himself.[13] Even here, the afterlife is devoid of an elaborated theology beyond the simple structure of Heaven versus Hell. Matapolis has its own modernist urban architecture, which Pullman admires, its own ethnic subcommunities of men and angels, and its own suburbias. Heaven and Hell are simply related structures of power, in which the devil – known here as Lord Sammael – is beginning to chafe under what he sees as his political assignment under God's rule and the received structure of sin and punishment. Earthly sinners are punished in a grotesque facility known as Dis, a kind of highly technological version of a Nazi concentration camp.[14] But Sammael takes no pleasure in his executive role over the damned. It is merely the remnant of a long cosmological arrangement that is, Sammael believes, due for renegotiation.

Only at this point in the series of novels does the reason for the overall title *The Human Age* emerge. Sammael wishes to challenge the status quo in Heaven by breaking free of his age-old and commanded role as punisher. He finds angelic culture stultifying, and angels – as Pullman had found the Padishah in Third City – to be stupid, incapable of understanding, for instance, the complexities of human literature. Yet, as Sammael puts it: 'Man is developing. It seems to me that Man is on the eve of modifying his existence' (*HA* p. 431), and he hopes, with Pullman's help, both to establish a new University in Hell for the angels' education and to cross-breed the angels with humans (as in the early days of the Old Testament) to create a new hybrid race more human than angelic: to create a new Human Age.

To this degree, *Malign Fiesta* finally clarifies a consideration of the nature of 'the human' implicit in the earlier volumes. Early in *The Childermass*, a description of Pullman's metaphysical figure suggests: 'It has taken the measure of its universe: man is the measure' (*C* p. 3). And while the Padishah in Third City has no interest in man – 'Clearly everything to do with Man filled him with an immense fatigue, a passionate lack of interest' (*HA* p. 154) – others in Third City certainly do. As one of the characters, Platon, asks Pullman: 'We would like to know what part the human plays in this comedy' (*HA* p. 158). Late in *The Childermass*, the Bailiff flatters Hyperides by calling him half-mockingly 'a man of the world' (*C* p. 284). But one might well ask: what does it in fact mean to be a man of the world? Is it merely a matter of polite intellectual sophistication? Or do the world – or the cosmos – and the nature of man in some way reflect one another?

Lewis does not provide a straightforward answer to the question. In *The Art of Being Ruled*, Lewis states that to be a true ruler one needs to have made a 'pact with the Devil' (*ABR* p. 93). That is literally

Pullman's position in *Malign Fiesta*. In helping Sammael lay the ground for a proposed 'Human Age' that will go against the will of God, Pullman becomes a political advisor, Machiavellian organiser of a secret police (with the Bailiff as its head), and events planner. The 'Fiesta' that gives the volume its title is a huge fair of the performing arts intended in part to reinvigorate the sexuality of the angels – a parody of post-war nationalist events such as the Festival of Britain held by Clement Attlee's government in 1951. Only in this final volume does Lewis identify Pullman specifically as a 'satirist' (*HA* p. 343), finally a figure perhaps less like Joyce and more like his author. For the Festival, and Sammael's plans, collapse under the weight of their own absurdity, and Pullman comes more and more to understand that he has thrown in his lot with power at the expense of his own better instincts. At the novel's end, when Pullman is carried away by two of God's angelic soldiers, he has come to realise what no previous character in a Lewis novel has ever considered, let alone articulated: that man – and therefore the Universe – has value: 'God *values* man: that is the important thing to remember. It is this valuing that is so extraordinary' (*HA* p. 528). Pullman comes to see that pure yearning for power is a delusion, because 'power destroys value'; Sammael, despite his surface charms, is 'a valueless vacuum' (*HA* p. 528). Even the foot of an angel of God come to fetch Pullman is an implement of pure and destructive power. It crushes a peony that Satters was growing in a glass box, leaving behind only 'a crushed handful of glass and a meaningless mash of vegetation' (*HA* p. 562).

By the end of the completed sections of *The Human Age*, Pullman has risked becoming mashed and meaningless himself: a portrait of the satirist satirised, and to some degree of the author's own past intellectual mistakes.[15] In this respect he comes from the same source as the character of René Harding in Lewis's contemporaneous novel *Self Condemned* (1954). Pullman, however, is not technically condemned. In the unwritten fourth volume, Lewis may have primed him, indeed, for a kind of salvation, whatever that would mean in Lewis's peculiar cosmology. Pullman becomes aware that he has been an opportunist, has overvalued intellectual patterns and pride over humane and spiritual matters. He has not been duped by the likes of the Bailiff and Sammael so much as seduced by their vitality and power; he has been flattered by his ability to join a game of cosmological brinkmanship. While he may avoid the triviality of Satters's experience of the afterlife in Third City and Matapolis – becoming a member of a youth gang, for instance, and having tickle-fights with angels – he has nonetheless forgotten the limits of his own cosmological and political importance. If he is a man of the world, he has realised the nature both of man and of the universe too late.

Lewis did not live long enough to complete *The Human Age*, and indeed he might have had difficulty in doing so. As reported by D. G. Bridson, who commissioned the work for the BBC, Lewis wrote to him about the difficulties of imagining Heaven: 'God is a big problem.'[16] What Lewis did complete, however, is his single largest novelistic canvas and his most ambitious imaginative attempt to deal in fiction with his ever-developing ideas about human value, power, and politics. *The Childermass*, by far the most stylistically experimental section of *The Human Age,* bears comparison to other fantastical experiments between the wars to imagine alternative worlds and cosmologies by such other major modernists as James Joyce in *Finnegans Wake*, Virginia Woolf in *Orlando* (1928), and William Butler Yeats in *A Vision* (1925; 1937). The more materially fantastical *Monstre Gai* and *Malign Fiesta*, on the other hand, may be read in their own literary moment as the missing link between the dystopian fictions of Aldous Huxley and George Orwell and the later dystopias – technocratic and urbanised – found in speculative fiction by such writers as J. G. Ballard and Alasdair Gray, whose novel *Lanark* (1981) owes an acknowledged debt to *The Childermass* and to *Monstre Gai*. In tracking Pullman and Satters through the afterlife, Lewis provides his readers with a tour of twentieth-century politics, and the pitfalls of privilege and individuality. Pullman eventually discovers, as do we, that even if God does ultimately value man, there is no escape for man from social organisations. Whether divine, diabolic, or something ambiguously in between, they inevitably, and eternally, begin and end with the ineradicable fact of power.

Notes

1. James Joyce, *A Portrait of the Artist as a Young Man*, ed. John Paul Riquelme [1916] (New York and London: W. W. Norton & Company, 2007), p. 14.
2. See *TWM* pp. 481–93.
3. A rejected first chapter of *The Trial of Man* – inaccurately described as a 'synopsis' – appeared as an appendix to the paperback edition of *Malign Fiesta* (London: Calder and Boyars, Jupiter Books, 1966), pp. 213–28 and pp. 231–40.
4. Alan Munton, 'A Reading of *The Childermass*', in *MWL* pp. 120–32: p. 120.
5. I. A. Richards, 'A Talk on *The Childermass*' (1952), printed in *Agenda*, Wyndham Lewis Special Number, 7.3–8.1, Autumn–Winter 1969–1970, pp. 16–21: p. 16.
6. Hugh Kenner calls the Bailiff 'mass-psychology personified . . . the greatest satiric creation of the 20th century imagination' (afterword to *Malign*

Fiesta, as per note 3, above, p. 234). Fredric Jameson notes: 'The figure of the Bailiff indeed includes and recapitulates within itself every conceivable feature and variation of Lewis' political and social polemics ... As one might suspect, he thereby becomes Lewis' most lively character' (*JFA* pp. 148–9). However, Paul Edwards equally accurately finds in the Bailiff 'the only fully convincing representation of the modern totalitarian demagogue in fiction' (*EWL* p. 324).

7. The Hyperideans represent German and French far-right movements, such as the *Action Française*. The Bailiff asks Alectryon at one point whether he was one of those students of *French-Action* type' and met in Austria 'students of *Steel-helmet* type' (*C* pp. 295–6). See also *EWL* p. 529.

8. William Blake, *The Marriage of Heaven and Hell* (1790) in David V. Erdman (ed.), *The Complete Poetry & Prose of William Blake* (Berkeley and Los Angeles, University of California Press, 2008), pp. 33–44: p. 35. Blake here refers to Milton's apparent sympathy for the character of Satan in his epic poem *Paradise Lost* (1667).

9. The Pullman Sleeping Car, invented by George Pullman in 1857, was intended for overnight passenger travel.

10. Wyndham Lewis, 'Tyronic Dialogues – X. and F.', *The Tyro*, 2, 1922, pp. 46–9: p. 49.

11. See Lewis's volumes *Hitler* (London: Chatto and Windus, 1931) and *The Hitler Cult* (London: Dent, 1939). Pound's support for Mussolini is a well-known part of his later cultural notoriety, and led to his detention by American forces in Pisa after the Second World War.

12. See Jeffrey Meyers, '*Monstre Gai* in Wyndham Lewis and Saul Bellow', *Notes on Contemporary Literature*, 40.3, May 2010, pp. 6–8. The quotation appears in Friedrich Nietzsche, *The Will to Power*, trans. and ed. Walter Kaufmann (New York: Vintage, 1968), p. 23 and p. 56.

13. Lewis may have been ironically aware that he was writing a fiction of the dangers of political patronage while he was himself under the 'patronage' of the BBC. See Alexander Ruch, '"The Best in the Worst of All Possible Worlds": Corporate Patronage in Wyndham Lewis's Late Work', in *WLC* pp. 145–61.

14. J. G. Ballard noted this explicitly in his review of *The Human Age* for the magazine *New Worlds* in 1966: 'The institutional hells of the present century are reached with one-way tickets, marked Nagasaki and Buchenwald, worlds of terminal horror even more final than the grave.' See J. G. Ballard, 'Visions of Hell', in *A User's Guide to the Millennium: Essays and Reviews* (New York: Picador USA, 1996), pp. 140–4: p. 140.

15. Indeed, in the radio version, and the original conception for the novel, the angel appears to crush Pullman himself rather than the flower. See D. G. Bridson, '*The Human Age* in Retrospect', in *MWL* pp. 238–51: p. 240.

16. Ibid., p. 250.

Chapter 14

Self Condemned:
Casualties of the Vortex

Miranda Hickman

Lewis's late novel *Self Condemned*, published in 1954, three years before his death, draws much of its material from the six years Lewis and his spouse, Gladys Anne ('Froanna'), spent in North America during the Second World War. The couple left their native England on the brink of the war (they sailed a day before conflict broke out, nearly booking on a ship that was torpedoed) in hopes of Lewis finding work painting commissioned portraits in North America, which he initially thought would be a more favourable context for his work than England. Lewis also planned to explore familial linkages to Canada: born on his father's yacht off the coast of Nova Scotia, he held a Canadian passport; and his father's family was American with French-Canadian branches. Unexpectedly, the Lewises found themselves obliged to remain in North America for the duration of the war, without sufficient funds for return tickets – in Lewis's reiterated word, 'marooned' (*SC* p. 176; *L* p. 311).[1]

After a brief sojourn in the United States marked by a disappointing reception (Lewis was only able to secure a few commissions), by 1940, Lewis and Froanna had established themselves at the Tudor Hotel on Sherbourne Street in Toronto, in what Lewis disparaged as the 'sanctimonious ice-box' of Canada (*L* p. 309), eking out a life in a cultural climate generally inhospitable to Lewis's work. Accordingly, *Self Condemned* takes place in Momaco, a city based on small-scale mid-twentieth-century Toronto, which Lewis's protagonist René Harding derides as dominated by puritanical Methodism and parochial narrowness of spirit. Through René and his wife Hester, Lewis unleashes on 'Momaco' (named after a Torontonian suburb, Mimico) much typically biting satire, using a vitriolic vocabulary Lewis honed in letters of what he called his 'Tudor period' (*L* p. 311). Ultimately, however, this novel is only in the scantest ways about Toronto and Canada, despite its excursuses on bone-chilling Canadian winters and the demographics of a Canadian city of this time.[2] Narrative attention falls instead on the

Hardings' dire situation and their embittered and distorted readings of Momaco as a bleak Siberia.

Above all, Lewis uses Momaco as a locus for an existential *agon* following from René Harding's drastic decision to leave the life he has known – the choice which catalyses the novel's events. A professor of history, Harding resigns from his Chair at a major British university out of principled refusal of the approaches to interpreting and teaching history which his academic career has required. Quitting England as part of this gesture of repudiation, he lands in Canada an exile, cut off from former friends, family, and culture not only by geography and circumstance, but more importantly by philosophical dissidence. Harding is initially 'self-condemned' in that he is self-exiled in an unfamiliar land unwelcoming of his talents – he has imposed this on himself. As the novel unfolds, the narrative increasingly implies another reading of 'self-condemnation', one perhaps inspired by the Catholic thought with which the late Lewis became familiar – penitent condemnation of an action or element of the self as part of an inner transformation towards renewal.

Lewis was still in Canada when he began writing the novel, which became his most commercially successful book (see *MTE* p. 312).[3] He completed it during the years after his return to England, some of them after the onset of blindness in 1951. Fittingly, the novel's focus is a grave blind spot generated by a mode of thought that had become a mainstay of Lewis's imagination and work. To invoke the language of Byron's closet drama *Manfred* (1817), from which Lewis takes the novel's title, *Self Condemned* suggests an effort to perform an 'exorcism' of a pivotal dimension of Lewis's own thought that, by the end of his life, he could no longer accept.[4]

As many commentators caution, it is well not to read the novel as strictly autobiographical. Lewis transforms his North American years into a fictional construct whose details differ significantly (if sometimes only subtly) from those of the biographical record – and whose bursts of typically Lewisian expressionism often disrupt a predominantly realist narrative. But through this novel, in a project of what Andrzej Gąsiorek persuasively identifies as 'coded auto-critique' (*GWL* p. 104), Lewis relentlessly probes one of his own central habits of thought. Harding, the historian-philosopher, refuses to continue a career whose fundamental premises and dominant practices he can no longer countenance. In a Joycean *non serviam* gesture, he chooses a principled exilic condition deeply familiar within the culture of modernism. Through René, Lewis thus revisits a type that appears frequently in his writing – one representing a philosophical position that Lewis himself often maintained:

that of the artist whose defiant commitment to his *métier* sets him at a cold distance from, and often in conflict with, the stuff, sensuality, and mediocrity of ordinary life – invoked in *Self Condemned* as 'the compromise of normal living' (*SC* p. 163). This figure is not quite the strategically contrarian 'Enemy' of Lewis's polemical work, but it is a close relative. This type, and the philosophical stance of detachment from 'normal living' it represents, Lewis often presented as pivotal to the creation of vital art. Lewis began to explore such a type in his first novel *Tarr* (1918). Frederick Tarr is an artist scornful of the life of 'appetite' to which, as a human animal, he must succumb, but which, as an artist, he feels he must surmount.[5] As John Russell and Gąsiorek (*GWL* p. 7) suggest, *Self Condemned* reads as a deliberate look back at and revision of *Tarr*.[6] The two novels are read productively as a pair; the latter revisits and advances thought on the constellation of problems they share. Much as female characters in *Tarr* like Tarr's girlfriend Bertha – and the sexual life such women in the Lewisian imagination both represent and incite – stand for the realm of 'life' opposed to that of 'art' (the typical Lewisian dichotomy of life versus art is foregrounded in *Tarr*), so René's wife Hester represents the realm of 'life' that René must sometimes reluctantly accommodate but which he often satirises mercilessly and strives to overcome.[7] The type suggested by Tarr and René, if often caricatured in Lewis's fiction, also indicates a philosophical attitude to which Lewis often committed as necessary to art – that of passionately rational, satirical detachment from the flux of life.[8] As I have suggested elsewhere, I read this characteristic detachment, at the core of Lewis's work and thought, as a kind of Wildean artist's principled aloofness from 'Life', permuted by Lewis's deliberately anti-Wildean aggressive severity of tone (the latter marking Lewis's anxious dissociation from what he read as the unwelcome effeminacy suggested by *fin-de-siècle* aestheticism).[9] This detached stance Lewis initially theorises during his early career as integral to Vorticism; his continued attention to it carries a Vorticist concern into his post-Vorticist work.

Such Vorticist detachment is again on display in *Self Condemned* – this time within a framework of painful self-reckoning. Towards the end of his life, Lewis again wrestles with his convictions about what is necessary for the production of great art and significant creative activity more broadly, and, this time, he considers with unprecedented seriousness the moral problem of what an individual's principled adherence to a stance of critical detachment might cost in human terms. As he often does in his fiction, he makes of *Self Condemned* a kind of laboratory (see *JFA* p. 56). In this case, for the experiment of what happens to a man like René who maintains an extreme Lewisian critical detachment, one that fuels both his professional disenchantment and his acerbic perspective on ordinary life.[10] Lewis plays out a similar experiment in the early *Tarr*, but in *Self Condemned*, rather than feature an artist figure, he highlights a professional historian. In constructing René Harding as a disillusioned philosophical historian, Lewis not only considers the plight of the artist/writer from a constructive remove, but also registers how his own thought was always fundamentally concerned with philosophy and theories of history. Even Lewis's early manifestic writing of *BLAST* intimates what later comes to the fore in his work of the 1920s and 1930s: that he concerns himself as deeply with theorising artistic practice as with creating art, and the philosophical views informing his theories engage the domains of both art and contemporary history. Lewis's commitment to 'detached thinking' (*TWM* p. xi) was consistently pivotal to such views. In keeping with the early Vorticist cultural project of *BLAST* and the views explored through *Tarr*, the mid-career Lewis continued to advocate a philosophical position of critical detachment with respect to 'Life'. This position underwrote his excoriating critique in *Time and Western Man* (1927) of the 'Time-philosophy' or 'Time-Cult' that Lewis read as pervading his era and that was epitomised by 'Bergsonism' – that is, work influenced by early twentieth-century philosopher Henri Bergson, which plunged into life rather than remaining at a cool remove from it.

From early in his career, Lewis registers awareness that such Vorticist detachment, essential to his favoured satirical mode, can carry terrible effects in human terms. But in *Self Condemned*, Lewis judges such consequences far more harshly than he does in earlier work. In this late novel, as John Russell suggests by way of Northrop Frye, the satire seems to round on the satirist, or, more precisely, on a particular satirical *modus operandi*, exhibited through René, which has formed a main vector of Lewis's career.[11] *Self Condemned*, however, does not feature Lewis's satirical machine spun out of control, like the kind of vortex gone berserk he sometimes displays, turning on everything including itself (such as Kreisler's mad whirling dance at Frau Lipmann's in *Tarr*); nor the wild 'non-moral' satire-for-satire's sake that Lewis theorises and celebrates in *Men without Art* (1934). Instead, especially in view of Lewis's choice to situate some of the last moving scenes of *Self Condemned* in a Catholic college (and to offer a markedly respectful portrayal of the faith of the Catholic priests there), here Lewis engages in a deliberate, ethical critique of the philosophical underpinnings of his signature satirical mode and its potentially dangerous consequences. Late in *Self Condemned*, when René is at last offered and accepts an academic position in Canada, Hester, stranded in a land she detests and now harrowingly certain that her husband will never return to England, throws herself under a truck. The grisly '*graffito*' (*SC* p. 371) of Hester's body in the morgue, together with René's ensuing decline into a glacial 'shell of a man' – who ultimately cannot even grieve for Hester's death but in a narcissistic rage blames her for a form of 'insane coercion' (*SC* p. 391) – starkly presents what we are invited to understand as the terrifying fruit of René's defining philosophical vision and selfish exile.

Again, Lewis has insisted on probing such cruel consequences from early in his career. In *Tarr*, he makes the abstractionist artist Tarr (a figure for the Lewisian Vorticist of the *avant-guerre*) obviously callous and self-absorbed, and he displays the human price of Tarr's idealistically severe position through violence inflicted on the hapless Bertha. Like many women in Lewis's Otto Weininger-influenced fictional vision, Bertha stands for a 'lower form of life' (*T2* p. 278), below the superior level of art.[12] She is raped by Otto Kreisler, a character placed as Tarr's double, so that we are cued to read Kreisler's violence to Bertha as a narrative casualty of Tarr's artistic aloofness and concomitant 'scorn for women' and life.[13] Again exploring the casualties of the detachment associated with the vortex in *Self Condemned*, Lewis reaches a new stage in thinking about them. This time around, if Lewis's protagonist René decides to scorn life, he does so in ways that initially elicit readers' sympathy rather than (as in *Tarr*) chiefly incredulity and ridicule. As *Self Condemned* opens, René embarks on what reads as a principled idealistic course, all the more admirable for his refusal to read it as such when his brother-in-law praises him. But as is not the case in *Tarr*, the logic of *Self Condemned* suggests that, in a kind of Lewisian physics, life lashes back to avenge itself on the man who refuses the compromises it demands – and the novel's tone suggests that it does so rightfully.

From here, the chief categories through which I will aim to deepen this account of different facets of the project of *Self Condemned* are 'History as Vortex', 'the room', 'the woman', and 'the shell'. Also valuable for capturing the work of *Self Condemned*, I would suggest, is the concept of *metanoia* – an idea derived from classical rhetoric and art, later associated with Christian thought, that suggests both the evolving state of mind Lewis traces through René and a dominant structuring principle of the novel. In Greek, *metanoia* means 'change of mind and heart' and 'after-thought' (*OED*), suggesting a return to what has been thought before with a new perspective born of reflection and inner transformation; in Catholic theological contexts, it suggests a spiritual turn to repentance.[14] Although I do not have sufficient evidence to credit Lewis with deliberate engagement with *metanoia* per se, it is striking that he closes one of *Self Condemned*'s late chapters with René's admitting an interest in Catholicism at the College of the Sacred Heart, together with a phrase keenly reminiscent of *metanoia*: 'And it was not long after this that he began to experience a change of heart or a change of mind' (*SC* p. 388). I would also suggest that the idea of *metanoia* might shed light on ways in which *Self Condemned* reprises and revises many central problematics of *Tarr*. Several signature cues from Lewis's earlier work (such as 'vortex' and 'shell') recur conspicuously in ways that show Lewis revisiting from a new angle not only *Tarr* but also several conceptual loci from the Vorticist years more generally.

History as Vortex

At the outset of *Self Condemned*, Lewis's detailed attention to the substance of René's critique of 'History' suggests his desire to explore this radically quixotic position to see where its logic leads. Notably, this position does not capitulate to the passive approach to 'History' that Lewis excoriates in *Time and Western Man*, where it is associated with Oswald Spengler. After René's mazy attempts to explain to his family the reasons for his departure for Canada (he meets with much bewildered incomprehension), Lewis presents the meticulous explication of René's colleague Parkinson, who has followed René's work with a disciple's admiration. In a notably extensive scene, Parkinson reads aloud to René the draft of an article he has written to explain his friend's new position, as articulated in René's recent book, *The Secret History of WWII* (already published in 1939, and presciently about a war that has not yet occurred). Parkinson notes:

> I can hardly hope to give more than a caricatural idea of the views of Professor Harding ... Our author does not suggest, for instance, that all history should be abolished, only that it should be approached in a different way with radically changed accents. The story of ideas, theory of the state, evolution of law, scientific discoveries, literature, art, philosophy, the theatre and so on, these are the proper subjects of history. (*SC* p. 83)

For Harding, the 'proper subjects of history' are the 'creative happenings' of a culture. But unfortunately, for him, what instead 'provides the basis for the story of mankind we encounter in history books' are the 'proceedings of the uncreative mass', represented and 'climaxed by the outrageous blackguardism of hereditary or elective government' (*SC* p. 83). Thus, rather than dignifying by registration and emphasis the 'wars' and 'civil massacres' associated with the 'uncreative life stream', Harding's new critical historian should accord admiration and weight to 'the inventive and creative few' (*SC* p. 84), 'those heroic creators who attempt to build something' (*SC* p. 86). Harding will not accept that the 'genuine' historian simply records, without prejudice, ethical standards, or the 'good and the evil, the rational and irrational, indeed whatever . . . can be proved to have *happened*' (*SC* p. 93). Instead, Harding's new historian 'should reject entirely anything . . . which is unworthy of any man's attention, or some action which is so revolting that it *should not* have happened, and must not be encouraged to happen again' (*SC* p. 93).

Inter alia, this notably lavish account (Parkinson's hyperbolic language is typical of Lewisian satiric gusto, but here generates a chiefly sympathetic portrait) suggests how Lewis imagines the importation of his own signature critical/polemical mode into historiography. Also signalling an affinity between René's approach to history and Lewis's creative vision is the quasi-Vorticist imagery through which Parkinson captures René's preferred way of charting history, presented somewhat tongue-in-cheek:

> The history of our century would not be one mainly of personalities . . . What we should see would be big, ideologic currents, gaudily coloured, converging, dissolving, combining or contending. It would look like a chart of the ocean rather than a Madame Tussaud's Waxworks; though there would be faces (one with a toothbrush moustache), like labels of one or other of the big currents of ideas. (*SC* p. 90)

However, the novel's attention at this point to unfurling a new 'theory of history' is then eclipsed by another project of *Self Condemned*: an exposé of the attitudes at the wellspring of René's *avant-garde* theory of history – attitudes notably like those underwriting the position on art Lewis had long championed.

Metanoia

When, very late in the novel, Lewis's narrator considers what he calls 'the process of radical revaluation' (*SC* p. 401) in which René has engaged throughout the narrative, he addresses not only the re-evaluative philosophical work that René's theory of history emerges from and fuels, but also the attitude sponsoring this theory – that is, the radical critical detachment that the novel spotlights. Using the novel to engage in his own process of 'radical revaluation' (a phrase suggesting *metanoia*), Lewis takes up this *topos* of detachment in order to reflect, with a hitherto uncharacteristic sense of conscience, on its human costs.

Again, the novel's title suggests a metanoiac process involving self-examination and contrition – one that is relevant both to the states of mind evoked by the novel and its structural arc. In Byron's *Manfred*, to which the novel's title alludes, the agonised Manfred struggles to come to terms with the consequences of having lived as a defiantly aloof Byronic hero. The parallels between Manfred's state of mind and René's are many: Lewis invites us to construe René's Lewisian detachment (however rational and neoclassical it may initially appear, since René seems to be named after Descartes) as that of a Romantic figure estranged from ordinary human intercourse. As Manfred observes of his nature:

> . . . from my youth upwards
> My spirit walk'd not with the souls of men,
> Nor look'd upon the earth with human eyes;
> . . .
> My joys, my griefs, my passions, and my powers,
> Made me a stranger; though I wore the form,
> I had no sympathy with breathing flesh[.][15]

The phrase 'self-condemned' then appears in the context of a repentance *manqué*, in which Manfred turns away from a Christian Abbot's efforts to encourage him towards penitence:

> Old man! there is no power in holy men,
> Nor charm in prayer, nor purifying form
> Of penitence, nor outward look, nor fast,
> Nor agony, nor, greater than all these,
> The innate tortures of that deep despair
> Which is remorse without the fear of hell
> But all in all sufficient to itself
> Would make a hell of heaven, – can exorcise
> From out the unbounded spirit, the quick sense
> Of its own sins, wrongs, sufferance, and revenge
> Upon itself; there is no future pang
> Can deal that justice on the self-condemn'd
> He deals on his own soul.[16]

The *Manfred* allusion thus invites us to credit *Self Condemned* with a conceptual vector involving self-critique, recognition of wrongdoing, and attempted exorcism of 'wrongs', and to read the novel as featuring a kind of 'justice' dealt to those who cannot 'tame' their 'nature' (in this case, René, whose 'nature' involves an inhuman Lewisian detachment from life).[17] Through René, Lewis suggests a Manfredian repentance unachieved. Although at first René is deeply self-reproachful after his wife's death in the refuge of the Catholic college, ultimately he shows himself incapable of a completed repentant gesture involving self-knowledge and self-condemnation. As he has not in previous work, here Lewis provides readers with resources for feeling cathartic terror and pity in response to a tragically flawed figure, presented here fated to a mode of life that abjures 'human eyes'.

'The Room'

Throughout the novel, Lewis frequently externalises René's increasing psychic imprisonment (his inner 'hell') in various confining dwellings. Fredric Jameson observes that 'his whole life long', Lewis was 'haunted' by 'rooms and houses' (*JFA* p. 42). Evidence of such 'haunting' is especially pronounced in *Self Condemned*. For instance, in broad, almost caricatural strokes, Lewis's narrative repeatedly focuses on the 'Room' (in *Self Condemned*, the word is often eccentrically capitalised, sometimes rendered entirely in majuscules) that the Hardings inhabit in Momaco's Hotel Blundell. Certainly 'the Room', 'twenty-five feet by twelve' (*SC* p. 169), is initially featured to highlight the extremes of the couple's poverty, confinement, and exile:

> They never left this Room, these two people, except to shop at the corner of the block. They were as isolated as are the men of the police-posts on Coronation Gulf or Baffin Bay. . . . They had practically no social contacts whatever. (*SC* p. 170)

But the intensity with which 'the Room' is repeatedly invoked in the novel suggests that it serves a role in this project in excess of that which it plays overtly. Beyond exteriorising René's self-entrapment, I would suggest that Lewis's marked emphasis on 'rooms', here and elsewhere, is also partially shaped by his consistent, not always deliberate, concern with the problem of the artist–intellectual's conditions of production (which also fuels his career's sustained attention to the mode of critical detachment he reads as crucial to great art). As Valerie Parker suggests: 'From the beginning Lewis was obsessed by art and the conditions necessary for creation.'[18]

Signalling this in *Self Condemned* is how the *topos* of the 'Room' operates in conjunction with an adjacent idea: 'The House that Jack Built'. Even before the Hardings' departure for Canada, the narrative details their living space, marked as eccentric, cramped, and showing the precarity suggested by 'The House that Jack Built' (a phrase Lewis uses idiomatically to suggest 'a badly constructed building'). When Harding visits Parkinson, the phrase recurs, now as part of an explanation of why, in contrast to his friend, Harding favours such teetering domestic spaces. Parkinson is nostalgically described as enjoying amenities suited to a bachelor intellectual of an older type, now threatened with extinction on the verge of war:

> This was 1939, the last year, or as good as, in which such a life as this one was to be lived. Parkinson was the last of a species. Here he was in a large room, which was a private, a functional library. Such a literary workshop belonged to the ages of individualism . . . It was really a fragment of paradise where one of our species lived embedded in his books, decently fed, moderately taxed, snug and unmolested. (*SC* p. 76)

René admires his friend's 'spacious room' and 'well-arranged shelves'. In some sentences, Harding and Parkinson are placed as kindred members of this 'dying breed' of intellectual man:

> Both of them knew that this was the last year of an epoch, and that such men as themselves would never exist on earth again . . . They knew that as far as that quiet, intelligent, unmolested elect life was concerned, they were both condemned to death. (*SC* p. 78)

But elsewhere, Lewis is at pains to underscore the differences between a Harding and a Parkinson: 'Parkinson was a man of method, and René was not' (*SC* p. 77). This difference accounts for Harding's 'preferring' to 'stop where he was' – rather than in the 'large' rooms of a Parkinson: '[M]en like himself were always to be found in Houses that Jack Built, working in a book-lined area the size of a bathroom' (*SC* p. 78). This, I would suggest, inscribes Lewis's effort to decipher the significance of the difference between his own kind of dissident intellectual and the intellectual of more legible legitimacy – revealingly, Parkinson has the 'accents' of an 'educated don' (*SC* p. 76). Curiously recurrent in these passages is the word 'unmolested', which appears three times in three pages of description of Harding and Parkinson. The repetition suggests that Lewis's mind is caught by the problem of the conditions intellectuals need in order to work unimpeded, and is typically concerned with how easily forces of the outside world can jeopardise (in the Lewisian imagination, even assault) such work requiring retreat.

Lewis thus strikes close to a problem that Virginia Woolf – famously marked by Lewis as one of his cultural enemies in such texts as *The Apes of God* (1930) and *Men without Art* (1934) – addresses from a feminist perspective in *A Room of One's Own* (1929), a text that Lewis knew. Accordingly, I would accent this as yet another important dimension of the cultural work of *Self Condemned*. Here Lewis works out his own theory of 'a room of one's own' for the artist, emphasising the particular needs and problems of the male artist of his time and type, in a kind of spiky reply and counterpart to Woolf's project. If Woolf critiques from a feminist perspective the taken-for-granted loci of young male intellectual aspiration of her time, Lewis criticises such sites from another perspective, which is also dissident with respect to normative patriarchal discourse. Accordingly, the abundance of narrative energy dedicated to the 'ROOM' – continued in the later Hotel Blundell episodes – suggests Lewis's interest in domiciles of precarity as markers of and conditions of possibility for the outlaw intellectual position in which he invests.

Then, however, it is these very conditions of possibility Lewis decides to destroy in the massive fire that ravages the Hotel Blundell three-quarters of the way through the novel. Within the novel's *diegesis*, crazy ill-management of the hotel and wartime circumstances are to blame, but on a symbolic level, the violent conflagration suggests both the unsustainability of René's incendiary mode of intellectual practice and the damage it can do.

'The Woman'

In the hotel fire, the manager Mrs. McAffie, the Hardings' friend, is brutally killed, though notably not by fire – instead by a murder committed in the pandemonium of the fire's circumstances, suggesting that violence is feeding on violence in a weird associational chain. Her death anticipates Hester's gruesome suicide. Both deaths, in turn, form part of a ghoulish parade of episodes in the novel in which women are injured, die, or are killed in larger-than-life ways: the charlady Mrs. Harradson inexplicably falls down stairs during the war; René's sister nearly falls under a train after parting ways with him (in significant proximity to his explanation of the decision to leave England); René's mother dies, her death hastened by wartime tensions; then Affie and Hester perish. If the hotel fire provides a symbolic outlet for the chthonic violence we feel lurking beneath the surface of Lewis's constructed world, suggesting the inflammatory consequences of René's mode of life, this conspicuous excess of female casualties likewise suggests such symbolic significance, implying an uncanny force at work. Again, Lewis has used this *topos* of damage to women before. In *Tarr*, for instance, Bertha is raped, while pregnant April Mallow in *The Vulgar Streak* (1941) haemorrhages and dies together with the foetus inside her. In Lewis's work, women, associated in the Lewisian perspective with 'the herd' and ordinary life, are consistently in harm's way when in the vicinity of the typical Lewisian artistic mode with its characteristic cold eye. But in *Self Condemned*, this pattern is intensified to a startling degree. At the same time, in *Self Condemned* Lewis also treats René's wife Hester, and the relationship between René and Hester, with atypical care and tenderness. He likewise endows with notable tenderness René's conversations with his sisters (three of them – another site of excess, especially for Lewis, who had no siblings). The many sympathetic portraits of women in this narrative extend the possibility of forms of love between men and women that are valuable and even redemptive. What might Lewis be suggesting through all this?

I would suggest that here as elsewhere, with his strategic excess of damage to women, Lewis generates a display, involving what feels like a line of self-recognition, of the misogynistic logic built into the mode of critical detachment he has featured and placed under scrutiny. Much as does Bertha's rape in *Tarr*, in *Self Condemned* with more unequivocally damning judgement, the deaths or near-deaths of women expose the cost to those culturally positioned as 'women' of the stance of the detached Lewisian artist–intellectual–critic. And in *Self Condemned,* the notably moving relationships between René and many women in the narrative sharpen readers' dismay at such logic considerably beyond what we are invited to feel in Lewis's earlier work. Given the special respect accorded in *Self Condemned* to the comradeship that grows, then fades, between René and Hester, we bleed especially for the extinction of both Hester and this bond. In view of the Woolfian filaments in play here, Lewis might also be said to offer his own turn on 'angels in the house' (or in the 'room') who must die so that the creator-figure may survive. Lewis's suggestion, as I read it, is that the creator who lives at the expense of such deaths reaps only a bitter fruit.

'The Shell'

Whereas Lewis ultimately leaves ambiguous *Tarr*'s attitude towards the novel's eponymous hero, at the close of *Self Condemned*, he clearly features René's degeneration into a 'glacial *shell* of a man' (*SC* p. 407, emphasis added), and the narrative judges René partially culpable for this decline. Hester's suicide is of course the immediate cause thereof, but René's final callousness about Hester's death suggests that his consistent callousness towards her throughout the narrative (and towards the ordinary life and human needs she represents) has significantly contributed both to her self-destruction and his own downward spiral. As one of the novel's last pages notes:

If the personality is emptied of mother-love, emptied of wife-love, emptied of the illusions upon which sex-in-society depends, then the personality becomes a shell. In René's case that daring and defiant act, the resignation of his professorship in 1939, had made imperative the acquisition of something massive to counterbalance the loss, else disequilibrium could not but ensue. But, reacting with bitterness to criticism, he began hurling overboard the conventional ballast, mother-love going first. (*SC* p. 400)

This paragraph wryly answers the question posed by the title of an earlier chapter, when the Hardings are shipboard: 'How Much Can We Jettison?' There is a twinge of the old Lewisian Enemy's disdain in the narratorial phrase 'conventional ballast' (suggesting a perspective which construes love as merely a counterweight), but the novel's main line of commentary judges that René's errors have left him sadly wrecked. Just after this, the narrative moves directly to explicit discussion of the 'process of radical revaluation', suggesting that such unfortunate jettisoning of human love, at dear cost, is necessarily part of such 'revaluation', which in turn has been closely linked to Lewis's featured mode of critical-satiric detachment.

As many commentators have recognised, Lewis creates a conspicuous rhyme between René's 'glacial shell of a man' and the Hotel Blundell, which after the fire becomes a massive 'hollow iceberg': 'It was now an enormous cave, full of mighty icicles as much as thirty feet long . . . This hollow berg was an unearthly creation, dangerous to enter because so unstable' (*SC* p. 296).[19] (René, after Hester's suicide, is also said to have a 'fire in his brain'; *SC* p. 397.) This unforgettable image of the scorched hotel not only invests the novel's final assessment of René with greater significance but also recalls the weird, blazingly icy imagery of Lewis's early Vorticist play from *BLAST* – *Enemy of the Stars* – and, more generally, the wintry northern climes featured in *BLAST* as conditions of possibility for Vorticist art. Here again, Lewis summons a prominent image from earlier in his *oeuvre* and reframes it, endowing it with a markedly different significance. In this new context, such a 'cave of ice' signifies not a Coleridgean sublime, an artist-genius hurling defiance at the stars, but a felt disaster. Lewis performs another such metanoiac juxtaposition through the word 'shell', used with conspicuous frequency in the latter part of *Self Condemned*. This word clearly harks back to the aesthetic theories of Frederick Tarr, which, with Wildean irony, suggest Lewis's own early philosophical-artistic explorations. In a famous passage, Lewis has Tarr observe:

deadness is the first condition of art. The armoured hide of the hippopotamus, the shell of the tortoise, feathers and machinery, you may put in one camp; naked pulsing and moving of the soft inside of life . . . goes in the opposite camp. Deadness is the first condition for art: the second is absence of soul. (*T2* p. 265)

The phrase 'the shell of the tortoise' is repeated in Tarr's explanation. Tarr's claim suggests Lewis's early justification for what became a central commitment to focusing on the *external* in his art – what he called the 'ossature' (*SF* p. 47) of life – and for accordingly refusing the emphasis of much fiction by his contemporaries on interiors, psychic or otherwise (here was Lewis's chief quarrel with high modernists such as Woolf and Joyce). In *Men without Art*, Lewis registers this commitment to an artistic-intellectual approach focused on externals by commenting on his book *The Apes of God* (1930). As he notes with proud hyperbole: '[N]o book has ever been written that has paid more attention to the *outside* of people. In it their shells or pelts, or the language of their bodily movements, come first, not last' (*MWA* p. 97). He opposes his own 'externalist art' of satire, which he privileges, to the '*inside* method' (*MWA* p. 120) of fiction such as that deployed by Henry James, James Joyce, and Virginia Woolf.

By returning, pointedly and repeatedly, to the concept of the 'shell' at the close of *Self Condemned* (in the last brief chapter, 'The Cemetery of Shells', the word 'shell' appears five times), Lewis metanoiacally rereads a crucial element of his own lexicon. No longer a shorthand for his principal artistic commitments, 'the shell' now only signifies emptiness. The novel's last sentence (again featuring the word 'shell') offers Lewis's turn on T. S. Eliot's 'hollow men' who are 'filled with straw': 'The Faculty had no idea that it was a glacial shell of a man who had come to live among them, mainly because they were themselves unfilled with anything more than a little academic stuffing' (*SC* p. 407). If Lewis's long-time comrade Ezra Pound ends up exiled in 1946 in a room at St Elizabeths that seems a figure for where his course of intellectual practice eventually led, in the late 1940s and early 1950s, Lewis invites readers to recognise a kindred dead-end state (a kind of narrow 'Room') to which René's philosophical path brings him. At the end of the novel, no longer a dissident's site of creation, this is instead the sterile room of a shell-like mind and being. Commenting on an upsurge of mental instability that René inadvertently reveals to his friend McKenzie at the end of the novel, Lewis's narrator notes carefully that 'The outburst at McKenzie's had not been a confession, but was something like it' (*SC* p. 406). Like Manfred, René stops short of confession and repentance, but through the metanoiac work and world of *Self Condemned* Lewis places the idea of repentance notably in the offing. That René never attains complete repentance points to the failings that prevent his doing so; by presenting a chillingly critical view of René in the novel's final episodes, Lewis reaches further than René does into a zone of contrition.

Matthew Arnold once noted that 'metanoia' denoted a 'change of the inner man'.[20] René never achieves such a thoroughgoing internal change, but through René the 'externalist' Lewis now points towards the desirability, even necessity, of an effort to revise and redeem what lies within. If, in his disquisition on art, Tarr expostulates that '[d]eadness is the first condition for art; the second is absence of soul', it is 'absence of soul' that Lewis again summons through the 'glacial shell' featured at the end of Self Condemned – this time with unironised regret.

Notes

1. For biographical information on Lewis, see MTE and SSG.
2. See Hugh Kenner's 'Introduction' to Self Condemned (Chicago: Henry Regnery Company, 1965) on how Lewis's 'expressionist fiction' transforms material drawn from life. For Lewis's distortion of Toronto, see Northrop Frye, 'Neo-classical Agony', Hudson Review 10.4, 1957, pp. 592–8: p. 598.
3. On the novel's composition, see Rowland Smith, 'Afterword' (SC pp. 411–21).
4. The language of exorcism, quoted later in this article, appears in III.i. Quotations are drawn from Lord Byron, Manfred: A Dramatic Poem (London: John Murray, 1817).
5. See T2 pp. 12–14 for Tarr's comments on 'appetite'.
6. John Russell, Style in Modern British Fiction (Baltimore: Johns Hopkins University Press, 1978), pp. 123–57.
7. As Tarr notes to Anastasya: 'Life is art's rival in all particulars. They are de puntos forever and ever.' When Anastasya notes her status as 'the woman', Tarr pontificates: 'As such . . . you are the arch-enemy of any picture' (T2 pp. 263–4).
8. See Andrzej Gąsiorek, 'Wyndham Lewis on Art, Culture and Politics in the 1930s', in WLC pp. 201–22: p. 217.
9. See Miranda Hickman, The Geometry of Modernism (Austin: University of Texas Press, 2006), Chapter 1.
10. As Gąsiorek suggests, Harding's 'rejection of history' is shown to 'derive from an ascesis that cannot tolerate the impurities of life' (GWL p. 110).
11. Russell, Style in Modern British Fiction, pp. 152–3.
12. Lewis's early letters suggest his interest in (though not necessarily entire agreement with) the thought of Weininger, author of the influential treatise Sex and Character (1903). In critical response to the feminism of his time, Weininger posits 'male' and 'female' principles, possessed to varying degrees by individual men and women, suggesting that the 'male' principle (clearly privileged in his account) permits an 'ego', 'soul', and 'rational thought', whereas the 'female' involves interest only in sexuality. As women can be no more than half 'male' in Weininger's reading, he suggests that

women lack both a soul and the rational capacities of their male counter-parts.

13. 'Scorn for woman' ('*disprezzo della donna*') appears in the first manifesto of Futurism by F. T. Marinetti. Although Lewis famously distanced Vorticism from Marinetti's Italian Futurism, Marinetti's work clearly bore affinities to Lewis's and catalysed many of his artistic decisions of the *avant-guerre*. The view of women Lewis's work often features, with varying degrees of irony, bears significant resemblance to this 'scorn'.

14. See Kelly Myers, 'Metanoia and the Transformation of Opportunity', *Rhetoric Society Quarterly*, 41.1, 2011, pp. 1–18: p. 8, for this definition from Liddell and Scott, *A Greek-English Lexicon* (1948).

15. Byron, *Manfred*, p. 33.

16. Ibid., pp. 57–8.

17. Ibid., p. 60.

18. Valerie Parker, 'Enemies of the Absolute: Lewis, Art, and Women', in *MWL* pp. 211–25: p. 211.

19. For instance, Allan Pero, 'Introduction', *Self Condemned* [1954] (Toronto: Dundurn Press, 2010), pp. 7–22: p. 20; and Hugh Kenner, 'Introduction', *Self Condemned*.

20. Matthew Arnold, *The Works of Matthew Arnold – Vol. 7: Literature and Dogma: An Essay Towards a Better Apprehension of the Bible* (New York: AMS Press, 1970), p. 196.

Chapter 15

Legacy
Paul Edwards

The sheer quantity and formal variety of Lewis's literary *oeuvre*, coupled with the fact that it is doubled by an equally various visual *oeuvre*, mean that posterity so far has found it hard to make sense of, let alone to love. The present essay will attempt to make sense of the long critical process of understanding its significance. Each age has its own priorities and reads in different ways, reshaping its objects of study as new critical approaches reveal qualities previously ignored. If Lewis's work has a higher profile now than previously, it is partly because its current appreciation is associated with such a critical paradigm shift.

It has long been agreed that Lewis's work is best understood in relation to modernism, but because the idea of modernism itself has been transformed Lewis's relationship to it remains fluid. According to Morag Shiach's introduction to *The Cambridge Companion to the Modernist Novel*, from about 1990 'a new consensus began to emerge that understood modernism less as the age of Pound, Eliot and Lewis and more as the age of Woolf, Richardson and Mansfield'.[1] Yet in fact Lewis had never achieved secure canonical status under this consensus, and it is unlikely that his novels would have been given a chapter in a *Companion* produced before 1990, as they do in Shiach's.[2] Rebecca Beasley, in the *Companion*'s chapter on 'Wyndham Lewis and Modernist Satire', points out that Lewis's presence there 'reflects a significant shift in our conception of the modernist novel over the past fifteen years', but one that has produced a 'more congenial climate' for his work; this can hardly be the same shift as the one Shiach mentions.[3] The grounds of Lewis's importance shift, even within a single volume. In truth, Lewis's work has always had to battle against some prevailing current, and its significance to many critics has always lain in that fact – either to its benefit, or more usually to its detriment – and intermittent prophecies that it was about to be canonised as an achievement in its own right alongside the work of better-liked authors such as Woolf or

Joyce have remained wishful thinking. Lewis's politics have understandably meant that he has not seemed the kind of writer that people would want to like.

But this seemingly isolated figure (the 'lonely old volcano of the right', in Auden's much-quoted phrase), actually engages more directly with more aspects of his culture than any of his canonised fellow-modernists, even to the extent of constantly resituating himself in relation to their work, which is everywhere present in his own. This is why his work is, in Alan Munton's word, profoundly 'relational'.[4] His presence as an influence on other writers' work is correspondingly diffuse and occasionally unexpected. The links with fellow 'Men of 1914' have been well studied, but Lewis was clearly also a resource for Samuel Beckett.[5] In the Lewis–Joyce disputation following Lewis's hostile critique of Joyce in the first issue of *The Enemy*, Beckett critically supported Joyce. But Lewis's 'Inferior Religions' can be read almost as a recipe for Beckett's *Endgame* (1958) – minus the play's sense of apocalypse – just as *Enemy of the Stars* (1914) and *The Childermass* (1928) are precursors of aspects of *Waiting for Godot* (1953). A very different author, Saul Bellow, frequently admitted his fascination with Lewis's ideas; while David Storey (more often compared with D. H. Lawrence – a kinship he repudiated) also acknowledged Lewis's great influence. Finally, Lewis is also present in the post-modernist poetry of J. H. Prynne.[6] None of these writers is 'Lewisian', and it is perhaps fatal to imitate his writing too closely. It is the critical legacy rather than his influence that is the subject of this chapter, however.

It is difficult now to realise the domination of English studies by F. R. Leavis in England, and by the New Criticism in the United States, from the 1940s to the 1960s. Leavisite critical valuations were premised on a recoil from the socially dissolvent effects of modernity: its perceived transformation of 'community' into the 'mass-public' and of the clerisy into an uprooted metropolitan elite. Literary criticism was conceived as a *sui generis* activity opposed in its very nature to the reductivism of modernity's abstract rationality. The word 'Life' stood as shorthand for desired cultural values, and both this and the anti-rationalism (or anti-reductivism) of Leavisite practice form a tacit link to the vitalist philosophy of Henri Bergson, which was so influential on the formation of modernism. Lewis's whole work could be described as a hostile dialogue with Bergson's philosophy, however. As early as 1914 he derided reliance on 'Life' as a self-evident and self-sufficient value in '"Life is the Important Thing!"' (*B1* pp. 129–31). In 1926 he asserted the 'not necessarily inhuman proposition that life itself is not important. Our values make it so: but they are mostly, the important ones, non-human values'

(*ABR* p. 59). So Leavisite criticism had no need to go very deeply into Lewis's writings, and exploration was blocked by his implicit judgement that Lewis was one of those who, in D. H. Lawrence's words, 'do dirt' on life.[7] He also seemed the epitome of the metropolitan urban intellectual, as *America and Cosmic Man* (1948) later confirmed, with its 'Case against Roots' and its enthusiasm for American popular culture, from jazz to Elsie the Cow (*ACM* pp. 163–74, 186, and 50). None of the other 'Men of 1914' fared so badly as Lewis under this dispensation, and although the Leavisite heritage was transformed in the work of Raymond Williams and Terry Eagleton, the distaste for Wyndham Lewis remained.

'Unity' in a work of literature – that is, an organic co-ordination of parts – was essential in this tradition, and it was valued implicitly as an analogue of a coherent society. Literature should be integrated and integrative, and this combined quality and function went all the way down: from the range of social and moral reference of narrative and subject (content) to the medium of composition (form). Since form and content are actually inseparable, not only does it go all the way down, but if unity is present in the work's language, its presence all the way up is virtually guaranteed. Metaphor served to radically unify experience; object and subject would cohere in a seamless expression that silently 'placed' experience within a desiderated vision of 'life'. Irony was valued for its dependence on shared communal values and on the flexible discriminations that maintaining them requires; and satire, while an inherently inferior mode, came in for some of the benefits of irony, but only for the positive values its negations implied.

There were not many tests of value in this critical manifold that Lewis's work could satisfy. His was a metropolitan (indeed cosmopolitan) world – that of modernity – and he showed little interest in the rural 'organic' society that modernity had replaced, or in the values it had supposedly infused into the language and life-world of Englishmen. It was sceptical, too, of the possibility of the creation of any unalienated society in the future. Lewis's prose feels alienated from its object, whether subjective or objective. When it projects a fictional character's consciousness, it often depicts a subjectivity similarly alienated. A random paragraph from the 1928 edition of *Tarr*, not assigned to any consciousness (though within the magnetic field of Kreisler's):

> The late spring sunshine flooded, like a bursted tepid star, the pink boulevard: beneath, the black suited burgesses of Paris crawled like wounded insects hither and thither. A low corner-house terminating the Boulevard Kreutzberg blotted out the lower part of the Café Berne. (*T2* p. 64)

The image blazes briefly into one of Ludwig Meidner's apocalyptic street scenes; its intensity is in excess of its occasion, and there is no time to measure its significance. Leavisite criticism could accept such an effect were it clearly diagnostic, but it is not: there is actually no language of authenticity conveying a continuous and integrated personality at one with its world in Lewis's writing, so there is nothing to measure such moments against. Consciousness instead acts by seizure, the exterior world rips into subjectivity, or subjectivity overblots the world for a moment with its tangential and disproportionate images: not organic metaphors but haphazard analogies.

Critics working within this paradigm who nevertheless admired Lewis's writing had to make a case almost in spite of its most 'Lewisian' characteristics, judging major works such as *The Childermass* or *The Apes of God* (1930) as failures. W. H. Pritchard in 1968 found them at best necessary stepping stones to later 'triumphs' (the novels of the late 1930s and 1950s), at worst 'a general vulgarization of Lewis's ideas' (*The Childermass*) or 'a monumentally dead book' (*The Apes*).[8] Timothy Materer virtually ignored *The Childermass* in his 1976 *Wyndham Lewis the Novelist*, and complained that 'Lewis's cold, "objective" approach in *The Apes*, as in *Tarr*, freezes over the source of fictional vitality.'[9] The precedent for such judgements was Hugh Kenner's 1954 statement in his short study, *Wyndham Lewis*, that 'this decade saw the squandering of an unprecedented talent' (*KWL* p. 93), a decade that in his next chapter becomes a 'twenty-year parenthesis' (*KWL* p. 119).

Kenner's study is a tour de force and certainly the most important book written on Lewis up to that point – and for a long time afterwards. Taking salient features of Lewis's writing, it extrapolates a narrative that makes sense of his imaginative world, and still, sixty years later, has the power to impose itself on Lewis's admirers, despite its disapproval of the quasi-solipsism and nihilism it attributes to Lewis. What is particularly compelling is how Kenner grapples with those aspects of Lewis's style that are alien to the Leavisite critical paradigm. He, too, disapproves, but is fascinated: 'What is happening is that Lewis is elevating his vices into a style. He has always been prone to the fear that his people would slip away unless battered against the wall occasionally by a stream of vocables' (*KWL* p. 92). Artfully, Kenner adapts phrases from Lewis's own satirical denigration of Ernst Volker in *Tarr* (*T1* p. 83) and his denunciation of the '*internal* method' of psychological fiction (*MWA* p. 104). This is homage of a kind, but also a strategic repudiation to enhance what Kenner dramatises as the 'incalculable' (*KWL* p. 117) arrival in Lewis's *oeuvre* of *The Revenge for Love* in 1937: 'on the far side of utter nihilism [Lewis] produced his greatest works of painting and of fiction' (*KWL* p. 118).

Kenner sees Lewis's later, more 'human' writing, from *The Revenge* onwards, as his greatest. This is a judgement fully in accord with the values of the critical hegemony of the period but supported by what now seem unbalanced judgements: the well-intentioned but thin *The Vulgar Streak* (1941) is 'a superb novel' (*KWL* p. 139) while *Snooty Baronet* (1932) is a 'failure' (*KWL* p. 112): 'a peppy and pointless novel' (*KWL* p. 109) about 'a fragmented nullity' (*KWL* p. 93). The idea that the 'break' Kenner locates in Lewis's writing should be attributed to a quasi-miraculous access of 'humanity' is still scarcely questioned. The message of Kenner's first 120 pages is that Lewis's errors resulted in twenty years of nihilistic over-writing; of the final thirty-five that he suddenly began to produce the humane masterpieces for which he should be remembered. But the implicit message carried by this page ratio is that Lewis's inhuman 'failure' is more compelling than his humane success.

Lewis's was a career still in progress as Kenner wrote, and Kenner's sense of him as still speaking directly to his time is shared by John Holloway's essay, 'Wyndham Lewis: The Massacre and the Innocents', written just before Lewis's death. Holloway subordinates Leavisite 'moral discriminations' to the capacity of the novel to offer 'fresh knowledge in the sense of massive or violent insight into a reality which is normally the reality of [the novelist's] time'.[10] Lewis supplied this insight into the post-1945 world in a way that his contemporaries could not, Holloway maintains. Only Lewis's work 'was crowned by a decisive achievement, and settled into a crystallising comprehensiveness . . . late in his life'.[11] Holloway identifies three main dimensions in Lewis's work, anchoring it to mid-twentieth-century modernity: '*violence*, the *machine*, the *megalopolis*'. Surprisingly, he makes no comments on Lewis's style, beyond some remarks about prolixity and 'wooden patches'.[12]

Holloway set an agenda for Lewis studies that was not taken up. Instead, academia suddenly noticed that the great modernists were anti-democrats hankering after authoritarian politics, including fascism. John R. Harrison's book, *The Reactionaries* (London: Gollancz, 1966) looks at Yeats, Pound, Lawrence, and Eliot, besides Lewis. He presents a narrow selection of Lewis's observations and ideas as a broadly coherent authoritarian and elitist system. Harrison's Lewis is contemptuous of the masses, wishes to breed an elite (with himself and his kind as rulers), and favours classical art. It is a simplistic reading, but important as the earliest study to contend that modernist aesthetic achievements should not simply be insulated from politics. More than anything else, Lewis's sometimes repellent political views (in the widest and narrowest senses) are what now deter new readers. However, Harrison's assumption that opinions could simply be fished out of the sea of Lewis's *oeuvre* now seems naive.[13] Lewis's treatises and polemics are themselves 'modernist', and allow a free play of point of view that makes for a high degree of relativity. Not all his views are by any means compatible with each other (and it is possible to assemble a different selection of them into a system that is not especially 'offensive'). Books such as *The Art of Being Ruled* demand an open-minded response to the differing propositions they put forward, and thereby reveal both the boundaries and the possibilities of their readers' own political worlds. Such boundaries and possibilities change with history. It therefore requires sensitivity to history to produce a reliable account or critique of Lewis's political views. An early attempt to set them in historical context was D. G. Bridson's *The Filibuster: A Study of the Political Ideas of Wyndham Lewis* (London: Cassell, 1972), a usefully unsophisticated but detailed account of the context of Lewis's political interventions, particularly in the 1930s.

Bridson's study coincided with the new hegemony of 'modernism' as a critical concept (few books with the word in their title appeared before the 1970s). Kenner's immensely influential, but highly disputed, account of the movement, the 1972 *The Pound Era*, took off from Lewis's identification of the 'Men of 1914' and presented an interwoven narrative, both of ideas and individuals. Study of the group, premised on Kenner's idea of interaction, took off. Books by Timothy Materer, Dennis Brown, Erik Svarny, Reed Way Dasenbrock, and Scott W. Klein all contributed to understanding Lewis through his relations with allies and 'enemies'.[14] Julian Symons characterised his *Makers of the New* (1987) as a kind of 'anti-*Pound Era*'.[15] Symons, along with Geoffrey Grigson and E. W. F. Tomlin, was an associate of Lewis's from the 1930s, and like them championed his work throughout the Leavisite period of occultation (he and Tomlin both compiled anthologies of Lewis's writing).[16] Symons disagreed with Kenner's elevation of Pound and wished to demonstrate Lewis' importance, which he felt had been 'understated or even almost ignored, especially by American writers'.[17] His chapter, 'Lewis and Eliot Separate themselves from Modernism', indicates a fissure that would be addressed in later criticism. This 'separation' (effected through Lewis's critiques of high modernism in *The Enemy* (1927–9) and *Time and Western Man* (1927) and through his later fiction) has now been seen as providing a foundation for the 'late modernism' of the 1930s and beyond. Tyrus Miller's *Late Modernism* places Lewis among Djuna Barnes, Samuel Beckett, and Mina Loy, while Rod Rosenquist's *Modernism, the Market and the Institution of the New* sees his critiques as foundations for the late modernism of Laura Riding, Henry Miller, and Louis Zukofsky.[18]

In the meantime a larger critical revolution had begun in the 1970s, changing the methods and objectives of literary studies and thereby changing 'modernism'. Lewis's concern with cultural history and its intermeshing with material history and politics now made books like *Time and Western Man* look quite different to the bizarre *olla podridas* they seemed to Leavisite critics: that he discusses Anita Loos and Charlie Chaplin alongside Gertrude Stein no longer seems odd. In the 'Introduction' to *Men without Art* (1934) he makes the case for the study of the ideological dimension of culture (whether 'high' or merely 'popular') concisely but fully. Under this new paradigm, elitist validations of high cultural forms (in which modernists – including Lewis as a practitioner before 1930 – were heavily invested) were set aside, and a new view of culture as a field of historical and ideological process also affected the delimitation of the object of study. The self-contained 'work' or 'novel' no longer took priority over the merely quantitative material 'text'; 'unity' was no longer desiderated, and evaluation took second place to (or became implicit in) exposition of the ways in which text engaged in and revealed historical process (interpreted, admittedly, in progressivist terms).

Leavisite 'weaknesses' under this paradigm become critical strengths, since they are conditioned by, and reveal, the processes of history (see *JFA* p. 32). So the fragmentation of character and subjectivity that had 'marred' Lewis's novels was revalued. Fredric Jameson was at the cusp of this critical paradigm shift, and his work directly reshaped Lewis studies. He introduced 'theory' to them, but, just as important, his accounts of Lewis's writing show a gusto in its stylistic excess that transcends theory. Jameson points to the methodological difficulty of bridging the critical gap between close stylistic analysis and analysis of larger narrative structure (what he calls the 'molecular' and the 'molar' respectively), and it must be said that it is on the molecular level that he is most spectacularly successful. Analysis of Lewis's style had up to this point mainly consisted of comments on its 'energy', its visual and 'objective' bias, or its careless vulgarity.[19] Lewis repudiated modernist canons of prose according to which the uniqueness and intensity of experience should (impossibly) be re-created in linguistic formulations that bypass the ready-made and extensive, apparently without mediation. The inevitable compromise is registered as self-consciousness, self-reflexivity, or self-regard (the 'traces of Paterian unction' Jameson finds in Joyce; *JFA* p. 72). Lewis's prose, by contrast, alienates experience but then makes its analogues available to the reader by referring it to disparate ready-made categories, drawn from what Jameson calls 'the warehouse of cultural and mass cultural cliché . . . the junk materials of industrial capitalism, with its degraded commodity art, its mechanical reproduceability, its serial alienation of language' (*JFA* p. 73). He thus produces a Flaubertian *sottisier* and also performs another (dismal sounding) aesthetic function more successfully than other modernists: his style 'can be said to "produce" the ideological as an object for our aesthetic contemplation and political judgement' (*JFA* p. 22).

Jameson is methodologically eclectic, prolifically generating readings as he adopts and adapts theories almost at whim. His own Marxist presuppositions function structurally to provide a destination for his prolific dialectical energy, which might otherwise, it seems, lead almost anywhere, since Lewis's work itself hardly offers a brake. According to Jameson the repressed structural centre of Lewis's work is really its opposition to Marxism, and his conscious intentions or arguments can only be inadequate projections that conceal – but reveal to the Marxist-Freudian critic (who finds even the unconscious political) – realities Lewis cannot allow to become conscious.[20] This is a self-validating position, since both Freudianism and Marxism claim Archimedean leverage over all other theories. In practice, the consequence is that Jameson is often too casual a reader of what he calls the 'official' meanings developed in Lewis's works – their 'molar' dimension.

Most important, however, is the fact that Jameson is really the first critic to look at Lewis from within a 'theory'-based critical paradigm. The service he performed simply by reading from within a European tradition is immense. Lewis's intellectual formation was almost entirely due to his immersion in the Parisian art scene of the early years of the twentieth century.[21] The central points of reference were such figures as Henri Bergson, Georges Sorel, Friedrich Nietzsche, Fyodor Dostoyevsky, Charles Péguy, and Pierre-Joseph Proudhon. Before the mid-1970s it should not have been difficult to see this, but under the prevailing critical paradigm it could only have provided evidence against him.[22]

The European tradition that Lewis engaged with – in a captious, polemical, but nonetheless serious way – is that out of which thinkers such as Lyotard, Deleuze, Barthes, and Derrida later emerged. One of its presuppositions is that both fiction and philosophy need to be consciously critical of their own foundations, and that both are modes of thought through which modernity must be understood.[23] In this context Lewis becomes a far less cranky figure than when he is viewed in a predominantly Anglo-American perspective. The door was opened to a new generation of critics who saw Lewis as a thinker whose ambitions to speak on equal terms with Nietzsche or Bergson should at least be taken seriously enough to be tested by close analysis.

Fables of Aggression, however, owed its academic importance more to its theoretical elaborations than to its celebration of Lewis, and Jameson has recently regretted that he has 'never been able to convert anyone to genuine admiration for Lewis and his extraordinary achievement'.[24] One consequence of his work, then, was the spread of a vulgarised version of Lewis as, in the words of Alan Munton, the 'person about whom anything can be said'. A great deal of subsequent commentary based on a loose reading of Jameson and relative ignorance of Lewis's texts is tendentious and unreliable.[25]

Perhaps in emulation of Jameson's identification of a central explanatory fact of Lewis's writing, other critics have identified central preoccupations and oppositions. For David Ayers, it is Lewis's cryptic anti-Semitism; for Vincent Sherry, the ocularcentric aesthetics of French neoclassical aesthetics; for David Wragg, the Kantian aporia between aesthetics and Enlightenment rationality; and I have myself suggested above that Lewis's hostile dialogue with Bergson could also be regarded as key.[26] For Toby Foshay the key is Lewis's formation 'by the Nietzschean critique of metaphysics'.[27] A persuasive and comprehensive account that takes Lewis's complex and conflicted attitudes to women, gender, and sexuality as central has yet (at least to my knowledge) to be written; given that the feminist revolution in literary studies is probably the most transformational since the 1970s, this is surprising. So far no literary critic has followed the feminist art historian Lisa Tickner in her exemplary art-historical and cultural study of Lewis's 1912 painting, *Kermesse*.[28]

Evaluations – or at least tastes – theorised or not, remain stubbornly unaffected by critical revolutions. Foshay returns to a quasi-Leavisite version of Lewis insufficiently committed to 'life', now seen in directly Nietzschean terms as the superabundant vitality from which the 'new sort of man' – the artist or 'overman' – is able to create. Foshay takes as a premise of his critique the death of God and the transcendent posited by Nietzsche, and nowhere does he recognise that Lewis continued to believe in God.[29] Certainly, Lewis claimed that for pragmatic reasons it is best to *say* that there is no God (so concerned was he with the danger that our individuality might be swallowed up by an all-engulfing Absolute), but as a metaphysician he insisted on the need for a transcendent God (*TWM* pp. 377–8). As he grew older, this God, originally posited for strictly limited philosophical ends, began to acquire more of the character of the God of Christian myth. Foshay virtually ignores those works that have a clear theological dimension (notably

The Human Age), so that it is only within limits that his subtle critical exposition – or any other that seeks a single key to Lewis's work – can apply.

Other writers take a position virtually the reverse of Foshay's. The most 'religious' Lewis is Marshall McLuhan's gnostic version.[30] For him all personality and all matter are dead and unreal; only the Plotinian One is real, and the artist partakes in it through a 'divine spark'. Lewis's achievement is to have created a huge negation, through satire and polemic, that reveals the deadness and unreality that modernity has created in imitation of a Plotinian world-soul.[31] From a Catholic point of view, Lewis's work is acceptable as 'a revelation of the hollowness of merely human hopes' (but presumably unacceptable as a positive doctrine).[32]

In his preface to *The Reactionaries*, William Empson presented an equally absolutist Lewis whose insistence on a transcendent deity licenses the vilest inhumanities. '"Because all men are infinitely below God, some men ought to be free to bully others – the ones who are on God's side, like I am"', Empson's 'Lewis' (conflated with T. E. Hulme) says. Postulating a transcendent God leads, in Empson's view, to the justification of, for example, the assassination of President Kennedy (which he virtually equates morally with Lewis's invention of the fictional Punishment Centre in *Malign Fiesta*).[33] After the Second World War only a lowest-common-denominator Benthamite humanism is safe for mankind, Empson thinks.[34] For him, Lewis's transcendentalism involves, as it does for McLuhan, 'unnaturalism', and a denial of incarnation. Neither as a theist nor as an atheist, it would seem, was Lewis sufficiently committed to 'life'.

Empson is surely right to identify theological issues as central to Lewis's work, and to *The Human Age* in particular. Unwittingly, however, his criticism echoes Lewis's own criticism of religious absolutes: 'the true religionist is such a scourge that his God is always an engine of destruction' and 'All-Fathers have always been Battle-Fathers, used by us to exterminate our "enemies"' (*TWM* p. 379). For Lewis, a transcendent God is necessary, but we need to turn our backs on him; and the divine should not be dissolved into the human. But divine punishment of sinners was morally deficient by human standards, even though our values are 'mostly, the important ones, non-human'. How could these positions be reconciled? In the projected 'The Trial of Man', Pullman, the wayward hero of *The Human Age*, would be forgiven, the gates to a transcendent Heaven would be opened to receive him, and he would be assimilated to the divine (instead of the divine being assimilated to the human, which is Sammael's – Satan's – project). To accomplish this narrative, Lewis would at last have had to become a dialectical writer, resolving and sublating contradictions or antinomies in a higher synthesis, with Pullman retaining his free individuality at the same time as he became one with the Whole.

This was not going to happen. Without antinomies there would be no progression, no space for Lewis to operate as an artist. In *Rude Assignment* (1950) he mocks Edouard Berth's indifference to inconsistencies, tracing it to Proudhon's 'attitude to antinomies' (that 'consistency was made for slaves'; *RA* p. 40). Yet Lewis himself manifests a 'good' version of such indifference, as António Feijó and Daniel Schenker both point out. Feijó sees it as a 'deliberately evasive procedure', however – which it sometimes is. Lewis mounts one case with overwhelming rhetorical force but reserves the right to take credit for also holding the opposite views.[35] But there is usually something more fundamental than evasion going on. Schenker quotes Proudhon's rejection of the Hegelian system of sublating thesis and antithesis in a synthesis: 'FOR THERE IS NO RESOLUTION OF THE ANTINOMY. This is the fundamental flaw in Hegel's philosophy. The terms are in a state of BALANCE either with each other or with the antinomic terms.'[36] Lewis's explanation of the 'Hegelian' method of *The Art of Being Ruled* fits this Proudhonian tolerance of antinomies better than it does the Hegelian dialectic he says he was 'inspired by'. He intended 'opposites to struggle in the reader's mind' (*RA* p. 183) and did not supply his own syntheses, though he is often taken as doing so. Totalitarianism, the desire that the state should be the unified expression of a single purpose, was alien to Lewis (though anti-democratic authoritarianism was not) and in his work the simultaneous deployment of opposites goes back at least as far as *BLAST*.

Anne Quéma, in her 1999 study of Lewis, *The Agon of Modernism: Wyndham Lewis's Allegories, Aesthetics, and Politics*, conducts a comprehensive harvest of the irreconcilable antinomies in Lewis's output. Her Lewis is torn between the nihilism of the avant-garde and a metaphysical nostalgia for tradition, which is evidenced on every level (stylistic, generic, thematic, sexual, and political) of his work. The contradictions, she claims, 'create an agon at the level of meaning', and this *agon* is actually the defining characteristic of modernism itself.[37] No longer an incoherent outsider, Lewis becomes an incoherent *insider*, revealing more clearly the nature of modernism than anyone else.[38]

The tragic *agon* does not have much of a place in Lewis's work before *The Revenge for Love*, however (*Enemy of the Stars* being the main exception). There is more laughter than tears in his work and there have correspondingly been many expositions of his theory of laughter. Laughter has an important generic function: 'Laughter is the representative of tragedy, when tragedy is away' (*CWB* p. 151). It comes always at a moment of recognition (by the reader) of the incompatibility of opposites, somewhat like tragic *anagnorosis*: suddenly realised in consciousness but realised as unresolvable. It is the physical sign of the recognition that 'although helpless in the face of the material world, we are in some way superior and independent of it' (*WLA* p. 204). Through it Lewis not only accomplishes Holloway's 'massive or violent insight into . . . reality' but also attains a metaphysical reach beyond this, going right back to the irreconcilability of being and non-being that is momentarily dissolved in the laughter of 'tragic delight' (*CWB* p. 157 and p. 151). Laughter is Lewis's substitute for the impossible moment of sublation and synthesis of antinomies that would take place in the Hegelian dialectic.[39]

Partly because of changes in academic priorities, monographs (which have been the chief focus of this survey) are now less common than collections of essays such as the present one. The multiplicity and variety of the Lewisian 'field'– kept open by his refusal ever to let antinomies be more than provisionally decided – make him the ideal subject for such treatment. But there is a danger that this multiplicity, and the corresponding critical choice of quantitative 'text' rather than individual works as the field of study, can lead to criticism in which an eclectic selection of points are arranged into new constellations that effectively misrepresent this 'enemy of all the constellations and universes' (*CPP* p. 198). Curiously, such criticism, which usually aims for historical understanding, often takes a synchronic approach to Lewis; but truthtelling involves careful analysis both of the moment and of its place in a changing series. My own main critical book on Lewis is capacious enough to at least attempt this, covering all sides of his work (including his painting) and its chronological development, while devoting detailed discussion to individual works. If it is any kind of landmark, it is so in the first place simply for impertinently treating Lewis as a truly major figure whose work in all its forms would repay the kind of close and extended attention considered normal for a Joyce or a Picasso – or even a David Hume (see *EWL*).[40] Its attention to Lewis's painting imports a more metaphysical perspective than had been common in discussions of the writing. On a more concentrated scale, Andrzej Gąsiorek's *Wyndham Lewis and Modernism* provides a version of Lewis as a writer with a coherent though far from straightforward development (see *GWL*). After such a study Jameson's idea that Lewis is not truly dialectical because he was not sufficiently self-reflexive (*JFA* p. 126) looks very odd indeed.

It is a very rare work of criticism that *changes* minds – the most that can be expected is that it might help *form* minds and tastes; Jameson has probably been too pessimistic in assessing the effect of his own writing on Lewis. Criticism usually wears the blinkers of its time, but it also assimilates and builds on earlier critical 'discoveries', so that we can truthfully say that we now understand Lewis's achievement more fully than readers did in the 1960s. But critical paradigms will shift again, and it remains for the future to tell whether Lewis's work has the capacity to take on new meaning and significance. As a first step, the projected Oxford University Press edition of Lewis's writing will provide much new evidence for critical exploration of the genesis and development of his texts.[41] But, irrespective of criticism, the continuing life of his work will always depend on its finding new readers who, fascinated and excited by such passages as 'In thin clockwork cadence the exhausted splash of the waves is a sound that is a cold ribbon just existing in the massive heat. The delicate surf falls with the abrupt crash of glass, section by section' (*C* p. 34), want to find out more.

Notes

1. Morag Shiach, 'Reading the Modernist Novel: An Introduction', in Morag Shiach (ed.), *The Cambridge Companion to the Modernist Novel* (Cambridge: Cambridge University Press, 2007), pp. 1–14: p. 5.
2. Nor a standard history of literary criticism. See Vincent Sherry, 'Wyndham Lewis', in A. Walton Litz et al. (eds), *The Cambridge History of Literary Criticism – Vol. 7: Modernism and the New Criticism* (Cambridge: Cambridge University Press, 2006), pp. 138–50.
3. Rebecca Beasley, 'Wyndham Lewis and Modernist Satire', in Shiach (ed.), *Cambridge Companion to the Modernist Novel*, pp. 126–36: p. 126.
4. Alan Munton, '"Quotation"', in *WLC* pp. 17–35: p. 30.
5. See Dennis Brown, *Intertextual Dynamics within the Literary Group – Joyce, Lewis, Pound and Eliot: The Men of 1914* (Basingstoke: Macmillan, 1990), p. 118.
6. See the preface to Saul Bellow, *It All Adds up: From the Dim Past to the Uncertain Future* (New York: Viking, 1994); William Hutchins, *The Plays of David Storey: A Thematic Study* (Carbondale: Southern Illinois University Press, 1988), pp. 16–17; and J. H. Prynne, 'The Ideal Star-Fighter', *Brass* (London: Ferry Press, 1971), pp. 27–8.
7. See F. R. Leavis, 'The Wild, Untutored Phoenix', *The Common Pursuit* (Harmondsworth: Penguin, 1966), pp. 233–9, where Lewis is presented as the negation of Lawrence's 'health and sanity'.
8. W. H. Pritchard, *Wyndham Lewis* (New York: Twayne, 1968), pp. 71, 74, and 78.
9. Timothy Materer, *Wyndham Lewis the Novelist* (Detroit: Wayne State University Press, 1976), p. 96.
10. John Holloway, 'Wyndham Lewis: The Massacre and the Innocents', *The*

Charted Mirror: Literary and Critical Essays (London: Routledge and Kegan Paul, 1960), pp. 118–36: p. 119.

11. Ibid., p. 119.

12. Ibid., p. 130.

13. John Carey's *The Intellectuals and the Masses: Pride and Prejudice among the Literary Intelligentsia, 1880–1939* (London: Faber, 1994) is the *reductio ad absurdum* of this Little Jack Horner strategy.

14. Timothy Materer, *Vortex: Pound, Eliot and Lewis* (Ithaca: Cornell University Press, 1979), includes a chapter on Joyce; Erik Svarny, *The Men of 1914: T. S. Eliot and Early Modernism* (Milton Keynes: Open University Press, 1988); Reed Way Dasenbrock, *The Literary Vorticism of Ezra Pound and Wyndham Lewis: Towards the Condition of Painting* (Baltimore: Johns Hopkins University Press, 1985); Brown, *Intertextual Dynamics*; and Scott W. Klein, *The Fictions of James Joyce and Wyndham Lewis: Monsters of Nature and Design* (Cambridge: Cambridge University Press, 1994).

15. Julian Symons, *Makers of the New: The Revolution in Literature, 1912–1939* (London: André Deutsch, 1987).

16. Julian Symons (ed.), *The Essential Wyndham Lewis: An Introduction to his Work* (London: André Deutsch, 1989); E. W. F. Tomlin (ed.), *Wyndham Lewis: An Anthology of his Prose* (London: Methuen, 1969); Geoffrey Grigson, *A Master of our Time: A Study of Wyndham Lewis* (London: Methuen, 1951). See also Stan Smith, 'Re-Righting Lefty: Wyndham and Wystan in the Thirties', *Wyndham Lewis Annual*, 9–10, 2002–3, pp. 34–45.

17. Symons, *The Essential Wyndham Lewis*, p. 10.

18. Tyrus Miller, *Late Modernism: Politics, Fiction, and the Arts between the World Wars* (Berkeley: University of California Press, 1999); Rod Rosenquist, *Modernism, the Market and the Institution of the New* (Cambridge: Cambridge University Press, 2009).

19. An exception is John Russell, *Style in Modern Fiction* (Baltimore: Johns Hopkins University Press, 1978).

20. For Jameson, Lewis's insistence on visual detachment (the painter's eye) 'allows him to repress the structural center of his work . . . his lifelong opposition to Marxism itself' (*JFA* p. 18).

21. An invaluable account of that world is Mark Antliff's *Inventing Bergson: Cultural Politics and the Parisian Avant-Garde* (Princeton: Princeton University Press, 1993).

22. Geoffrey Wagner presents Lewis as primarily under the influence of 'classicist' right-wing thinkers such as Charles Maurras and Henri Massis – a strange misreading. See Geoffrey Wagner, *Wyndham Lewis: A Portrait of the Artist as the Enemy* (London: Routledge and Kegan Paul, 1957).

23. See M. Stuart Hughes, *Consciousness and Society: The Reorientation of European Social Thought, 1890–1930* (London: McGibbon and Kee, 1959).

24. Fredric Jameson, 'Wyndham Lewis's *Timon*: The War of Forms', in *VNP* pp. 15–30: p. 16.

25. Alan Munton, '"Imputing Noxiousness": Aggression and Mutilation in Recent Lewis Criticism', *Wyndham Lewis Annual*, 4, 1997, pp. 5–20;

and 'Fantasies of Violence: The Consequences of Not Reading Wyndham Lewis', *Wyndham Lewis Annual*, 5, 1998, pp. 31–49. Munton's various essays make a persuasive case that Lewis's work is open, radical, and liberatory.

26. See Vincent Sherry, *Ezra Pound, Wyndham Lewis, and Radical Modernism* (Oxford: Oxford: Oxford University Press, 1993); David Ayers, *Wyndham Lewis and Western Man* (Basingstoke: Macmillan, 1992); and David A. Wragg, *Wyndham Lewis and the Philosophy of Art in Early Modernist Britain: Creating a Political Aesthetic* (Lewiston: Edwin Mellen, 2005).

27. Toby Avard Foshay, *Wyndham Lewis and the Avant-Garde: The Politics of the Intellect* (Montreal: McGill-Queen's University Press, 1992), p. 5.

28. Lisa Tickner, 'Wyndham Lewis: Dance and the Popular Culture of *Kermesse*', *Modern Life and Modern Subjects: British Art in the Early Twentieth Century* (New Haven, CT: Yale University Press, 2000), pp. 79–115.

29. See Foshay, *Wyndham Lewis*, Chapter 3, especially pp. 64–8.

30. H. Marshall McLuhan, 'Nihilism Exposed', *Renascence*, 8.2, 1955, pp. 97–9.

31. This 'world soul' is thus a nightmare version of McLuhan's Global Village about which McLuhan concealed his true feelings. Daniel Schenker's excellent *Wyndham Lewis: Religion and Modernism* (Tuscaloosa: University of Alabama Press, 1992) makes no mention of Gnosticism or Plotinus (but does discuss Manichaeism).

32. McLuhan, 'Nihilism Exposed', p. 99.

33. William Empson, 'Preface' to John R. Harrison, *The Reactionaries* (London: Gollancz, 1966), pp. 9–12: p. 10.

34. In contrast, Empson finds Joyce's Hell in *A Portrait* acceptable because it 'made the young Joyce [sic] vomit' (ibid., p. 11). For Lewis's satire as the work of an uneasily justified executioner, see Michael Nath, 'Wyndham Lewis: A Review of the Thersitean Mode', *Wyndham Lewis Annual*, 1, 1994, pp. 10–14.

35. António Feijó, *Near Miss: A Study of Wyndham Lewis (1909–1930)* (New York: Peter Lang, 1998), p. 4.

36. Pierre-Joseph Proudhon, *Justice in the Revolution and the Church*, quoted in Schenker, *Wyndham Lewis*, p. 105.

37. Anne Quéma, *The Agon of Modernism: Wyndham Lewis's Allegories, Aesthetics, and Politics* (Lewisburg: Bucknell University Press, 1999), p. 28.

38. For Wragg, on the other hand, Lewis's endorsement of Hitler in 1931 represents an abandonment of the *agon* of sustaining antinomies.

39. For Ayers it is anti-Semitism that performs this function.

40. George Steiner, who finds most of Lewis's work 'illegible [sic]', in a review of my book complained of its discussion of the arguments of *Time and Western Man*, 'as if it were Aquinas or Hume' ('The Wyndhams of our Mind', *The Observer*, 27 August 2000 – available at http://www.theguardian.com/books/2000/aug/27/biography.art (accessed 24 November 2014).

41. A process begun in the series of editions of Lewis published by John Martin's Black Sparrow Press in the 1980s and 1990s.

Index